P.O.
Lansing, MI 48908

MOODY WITHOUT SANKEY

By the same author

The Cambridge Seven
Hudson Taylor and Maria
Billy Graham
George Whitefield and the Great Awakening
Wilberforce
The Siberian Seven
The Apostle: A Life of Paul
The Master: A Life of Jesus
Amazing Grace: John Newton's Story
John Wesley
Fear No Foe: A Brother's Story
Gordon : The Man Behind the Legend
and other books

MOODY
WITHOUT
SANKEY

JOHN POLLOCK

CHRISTIAN FOCUS PUBLICATIONS

© J. C. Pollock
ISBN 1-85792-167-4

Published in 1995
by
Christian Focus Publications Ltd.
Geanies House, Fearn, Ross-shire,
IV20 1TW, Scotland, Great Britain.
First printed in 1963

Cover design by Donna Macleod

Printed and bound in Great Britain by
The Guernsey Press Co. Ltd., Guernsey, Channel Islands

Contents

CHIEF DATES IN MOODY'S LIFE

1837: 5 February, Birth at Northfield, Massachusetts
1854: Goes to Boston
1855: 21 April, Conversion
1856: Goes to Chicago
1858: Founds a Sunday School
1860: Gives up business. Works for YMCA
1861-5: Lay chaplain in Civil War
1862: Marries Emma Revell
1866: President, Chicago YMCA
1867: First visit to Britain
1870: Meets Sankey
1871: Chicago Fire; spiritual crisis; his 'Pentecost'.
1873-5: First British Campaign
1875: Settles at Northfield
1876: Builds Chicago Avenue church
1876-7: Campaigns in Chicago, New York, Boston etc.
1880: Founds Northfield Seminary for Girls
       Founds Northfield Conference
1881: Founds Mount Hermon School for Boys
1882: Cambridge University Mission
1883-4: Second London Campaign
1885: Helps found Student Volunteers
1889: Founds Moody Bible Institute
1891-2: Further Missions in Britain; visits Palestine
1899: His last campaign, and breakdown at Kansas City
       22 December, Death at Northfield

FOREWORD

Nearly a century after his death D L Moody remains a towering figure. The influence of his evangelism is still felt; the institutions he founded in America continue to flourish; his place in history is secure. But it is his personality that commands attention: rugged, delightful, compassionate, a man of total integrity, with a supreme gift for bringing Christianity before the whole range of contemporary hearers, and putting them to work for God.

When I began to delve into D L Moody's original letters in the archives at Chicago and at Northfield, Massachusetts, I had little knowledge of his story or character beyond an awareness of a massive and unusual American who crossed and recrossed the story of British religion in the nineteenth century and strongly marked his own country. As I read through letter after letter in his unpunctuated, misspelt scrawl, and waded through the great bulk of printed material, I could not fail to be impressed by the astonishing events of his swift rise to fame and power: in 1873 he landed at Liverpool utterly obscure, in 1875 he sailed away with Scotland, Ireland and England at his feet. And the more I read, the more I enjoyed this warm-hearted, strong-willed, genial heavyweight.

I did not get, as it were, on Christian-name terms with him at all easily. Dwight Lyman Moody never liked his first name and would not let his wife use it. Most of the family called him 'D L'. In public he was never Dwight L Moody – it was always 'D L Moody and Ira D Sankey'. Perhaps this should have warned a biographer! There were so many sides to him. He was extraordinarily difficult to capture within the covers of a book.

Moreover, a life crammed with action, documented by piles of manuscript and millions of words of print demanded discrimination if this book was to stay within reasonable compass. I sought to focus on Moody's development, a most intriguing quality being his capacity for growth right until the end; to get under the skin, understand his motives in the context of their day; and to convey the contagion of personality and the impact of actions as nearly as they were felt by his contemporaries.

When this book was first published, more than thirty years ago, the *New York Times* was kind enough to say: 'By the time a reader has finished this book he has the impression that he knows Moody, has heard him and even shaken hands with him'. This was certainly my aim, to bring to life a unique figure who 'put one hand on Britain and the other on America and lifted them both nearer to God'.

John Pollock
Rose Ash
Devonshire
August 1995

INTRODUCTION

Every Christian should read *Moody Without Sankey*. I have read it at least a half dozen times! No one can read this book without getting tremendously excited, motivated and deeply moved by God. It is one of the few books that I say is 'must' reading for every Christian.

This book records the life story of one of the greatest heroes of the Christian faith. Such books thrill me because they reveal how God can and does use ordinary men like D L Moody to accomplish great tasks. Ordinary people whose lives shared these particular characteristics: personal holiness, sensitivity to God, much prayer and in-depth study of God's Word, humility, a consuming passion for the salvation of the lost, and a definite indication of the power of God in their lives.

The influence upon society of men like D L Moody is still felt today through their converts, their writings, their courageous stand for the authority of the Word of God, and their personal relationship to Jesus Christ.

Unfortunately, we do not study church history and the heroes of the faith wrapped up in that history as we should, do we?

I remember in school wondering how certain teachers could make something so exciting as history so boring! Especially church history. Church history is people, ordinary people used mightily by God – people like D L Moody. It is the stimulating and far-reaching events that impacted the lives of these people.

In *Moody Without Sankey*, author John Pollock gives us one of the most accurate and detailed studies of Moody's life ever made. Here is the story of a man who rose from poverty with only a minimum of education to bring two continents to repentance. Here's the story of a warm-hearted, unpretentious heavyweight who rose from obscurity to work with as much ease among ragamuffins as he did among millionaires, royalty, and the ecclesiastical and political leaders of the world.

Dwight L Moody was an evangelist to the masses. He was the pacesetter in methodology. It has been said that Moody travelled over a million miles in his lifetime and preached the gospel to over 100 million people.

In John Pollock's electrifying book we see some of the secrets to why God was able to use Moody with such incredible power: he was 100 per cent committed to reaching as many people as possible for Jesus Christ in his lifetime; he was in the deepest sense a man of prayer and student of the Bible; he did not question the authority of God's Word; he was incredibly humble; though he could have been financially a very successful businessman, he was free from the lust of money; he fully understood the meaning of Galatians 2:20 – 'no longer I, but Christ in me'.

God desires to use you and me with 'power from on high' just the way he used D L Moody. I believe that if you read this book with clear eyes and an open heart you will realise your accountability before God to help our generation hear the gospel and the voice of God.

Moody may have lived 100 years ago, but his life's story speaks to this generation with the same power that it did in the 19th century. The great city masses that Moody loved so much are with us on even a greater scale today, three generations later.

The consuming passion that Moody had for the salvation of the lost should inspire us today. His strategy – 'reach the big cities and you reach a nation' – is even more valid today because the centres of influence (such as the media) are housed in our metropolitan areas.

As you can see, I have a natural interest in this man, D L Moody, because I feel our evangelistic team has profited immensely from his example. We are trying to follow in his footsteps by preaching the gospel to the masses in our generation.

Everywhere Moody went he delighted audiences, whether it was a mass rally or a personal interview with some head of state. University students were held spellbound by this man who only went to school from age 5 to 13. Corporate executives were touched by the authority and power that they saw in him. Street toughs were literally disarmed by this man's compassion for all people.

Moody was more than a humble Bible teacher. He had the genius of a military strategist. As Christians we are in a spiritual war and this book, I believe, can move the most educated Christian and the humblest believer to move out into the warfare with greater confidence, boldness and faith as we are directed to do in Ephesians chapter six.

As I have studied the life of D L Moody, I have been impressed by three events that seem to have prepared him for his famous international campaigns.

First, in February 1868, Harry Moorhouse was invited to the pulpit at Moody's church. For seven nights he preached from the text, John 3:16, 'For God so loved the world, that He gave His only begotten Son, that whoever believes in Him should not perish, but have eternal life.' Night after night, Moorhouse gave proof from the Bible that God loves sinners. In private counselling, he told Moody, 'Teach what the Bible says, not your own words, and show people how much God loves them.'

This teaching shattered Moody's belief that God hates the sinner, as well as the sin. 'I never knew up to that time that God loved us so much,' said Moody. 'This heart of mine began to thaw out: I could not keep back the tears.'

A second incident occurred at the 1870 annual convention of the YMCA, an organisation Moody was president of from 1866-69. During the 1870 meeting, Moody, while directing a prayer meeting that lacked enthusiasm, asked for a volunteer song. A 29-year-old delegate from Pennsylvania named Ira David Sankey stood up and sang, 'There is a Fountain Filled with Blood'. Moody was so impressed by Sankey's voice that he asked him to come to Chicago and help in the work of campaign evangelism. Sankey left his post office job in Pennsylvania and joined Moody in early 1871. They became an evangelistic team to God's glory.

The third incident took place on October 8th, 1871. While preaching at Farwell Hall, Moody asked the congregation to evaluate their relationship to the Lord and return the following week to make their decision for Christ. That crowd never regathered for within minutes the great Chicago fire erupted, destroying the entire city. This incident so devastated Moody that he vowed never again to close a meeting without inviting people to receive Christ as Saviour.

Among the thousands of anecdotes written about Moody, one that has remained with me over the years is the now famous account of a meeting between young Moody and an evangelist named Henry Varley, who Moody met during his visit to the British Isles in 1872.

The story I remember was how Moody and Varley were sitting on a park bench in Dublin, I believe, and Varley remarked, 'Moody, the world has yet to see what God will do with a man fully consecrated to Him.'

The remark was made casually, and Moody did not comment, but for days the words burned inside him. 'The world has yet to see what God can do with and for and through a man who is fully consecrated to Him,' Moody kept repeating to himself. 'Varley was referring to any man. He didn't say he had to be educated or scholarly. Just a man. Well, by the Holy Spirit in me I'll be that man.'

'The eyes of the Lord are toward the righteous, and His ears are open to their cry' (Psalm 34:15).

Moody later commented that Varley's remark and Charles H Spurgeon's preaching (which he also heard whilst in Britain) focused on something he had never realised before – 'It was not Spurgeon who was doing that work; it was God. And if God could use Spurgeon, why should He not use me?'

After reading this book I believe you will realise how God can use you as well. God is not looking for established saints, scholars and super-heroes necessarily. He simply wants to use ordinary people like you and me.

The requirement? Full consecration. Let the resurrected indwelling Lord Jesus use you by the Holy Spirit, to the glory of God the Father.

'And whatever you do, whether in word or deed, do it all in the name of the Lord Jesus, giving thanks to God the Father through him' (Colossians 3:17).

Has the world yet seen what God can do through you?

Luis Palau
Evangelist

Part One

CRAZY MOODY
1837-71

1: The Boy with the Crooked Finger

From the round-topped hill a muscular youth took a last look at the majestic curve of the Connecticut River. Although he was seventeen, his eyes filled with tears.

It was a wrench to leave the Valley, perhaps never again to climb the little hill (he called it 'a mountain') and watch the sunset, and the colours reflecting on the curve of the river, and the strong evening light on Brattleboro Mountain.

Dwight Lyman Moody turned, and gazed, and gazed again, at the fields and woods and houses of Northfield, where snow patches still lurked in dips and corners on this March day of 1854. He could see smoke curling from the white frame cottage where he had been born on February 5th, 1837.

Northfield in Massachusetts, on the New Hampshire and Vermont borders, once a last outpost in dread of Indian attacks, was now no primitive community but a typical New England rural township with about a thousand souls, a place of clapboard houses set roomily in their own gardens along a wide main street graced by a double avenue of elms and rock maples; and of farms scattered on both sides of the Great River and up into the pine-clad hills. Proud and cultured, its roots and concerns lay south and north along the Valley rather than eastward to distant Boston.

It was peopled with Moody's relations to the third and fourth generation. The Moodys and the Holtons, his mother's family, had been among the seventeenth-century pioneers of the Connecticut Valley. D L Moody was kin to a dozen New England worthies past, present and future, including Jonathan Edwards, Harriet Beecher Stowe, Oliver Wendell Holmes and President Cleveland; Franklin Delano Roosevelt, by his Lyman grandmother, was descended, like Moody, from William Holton, one of the first settlers of Northfield (Squakheag it was then called) in 1672.

Dwight Moody knew nothing about that. His boyhood, as he remembered it on the day when he was leaving all behind to make his fortune in Boston, had been dominated by the effects of his father's premature death.

Edwin Moody, a stonemason with a small farm in the northern area of the town, was a genial, shiftless, lazy fellow, adored by his wife Betsey and their numerous offspring, popular with the neighbours, but addicted to more whisky than was good for his heart. He died suddenly in May 1841 when Dwight was four; and died bankrupt. The creditor, Richard Colton, swept in and distrained everything he could, including most of the furniture, the horse and buggy, the cows except for one calf he did not discover. The older boys hid their father's tools, and the dower law of Massachusetts prevented Colton turning the widow out of her house.

Next month Betsey bore posthumous twins, Sam and Lizzie, making nine children of which Dwight was the fifth son; he now had six brothers and two sisters.

Four days after the twins' birth the mortgage on the farm fell due, and rich Ezra Purple from across the river came to collect. 'Betsey wasn't up since the birth of her twins,' recorded her brother Charles Holton, 'but she had him come to her bedroom, and told him that the money was not ready, but she would get it for him as soon as she could. Purple expressed his disappointment in unkind language, and soon left the house. Going down the hill the harness broke and he was thrown out on the ground – uninjured. Some of the townspeople, knowing the reason for his visit to Betsey, were so unkind as to say, "It was a pity he didn't break his neck." Hearing of the straits Betsey was in, Cyrus and I, the two brothers living near her, managed to raise the money that year'. D L Moody, forty years later on, took an apt revenge on the Purples.

Betsey's next sorrow was the disappearance of Isaiah, her eldest son and at fifteen her mainstay. He ran away, she knew neither why nor where.

Her hair had turned white, but she set herself to make what she could of the poor farm – 'a regular sand-heap' as her family thought – and of the trivial earnings of her sons. Dwight's boyish memories were of this tight-lipped yet cheerful mother in her grey homespun, who whipped them hard but held the ardent devotion of all her children. She could milk the cows, 'she made our clothes, and wove the cloth, and spun the yarn, and darned our stockings'. She bade her sons swear vengeance on whisky.

She sent them to school, but schooling was left erratic by the need to earn money in the fields, and by Dwight's own impatience at books. She sent them to Sunday school and church – the First Congregational Church which, as in most towns of New England in the early nineteenth century, had turned Unitarian. Everett, the minister was a pious, kindly man, a widow's friend, and his Unitarianism was moderate (he baptized the Moodys at one batch in 1842, in the name of the Trinity he denied).

A reaction from the bleak, systematized, high Calvinism of the Puritans, Unitarianism had not shed Puritan ethics. Betsey Moody's standards were of the strictest; she reared her brood to do their duty to God and their neighbour, and behave – or try to behave – as their Puritan ancestors had laid down: the Sabbath was kept from sundown on Saturday to sundown on Sunday, when 'we could run out and throw up our caps and let off our jubilant spirits'.

Dwight was taught that he must be good, could be good if he tried; a religion without warmth, irksome, thought about only on the long Sabbath. Farm work was irksome, too. Dwight loved to be free on the hills. He loved to run, 'and I could run like a deer'; to fight other boys; to swim, revelling in the cold water of the Great River; to be the leader in practical jokes such as stampeding a farmer's cattle with Indian war-whoops, or snowballing innocent riders.

By seventeen he was a broad, sloping-shouldered youth with plenty of muscle and stamina, of medium height, growing to five foot ten, though a tendency to let his head hang forward as if too heavy for his body made him look stocky. His eyes were darkish grey, his hair a rich dark brown, almost black. His lips had rather a pout. And the last joint of both little fingers had a crook inwards, so that the tips rested on the next.

With the boys able to earn, food cheap, firewood free, the crowded family made the little frame house echo with laughter. But Moody hated hoeing fields and husking corn barefoot. When carting, the slow gait of the old horse, Ring, maddened him. Chopping wood against the snowbound winter was a dreary chore, and he was 'sick

and tired' of doing it all for nothing. He did not grudge his mother
a penny, but wanted money to spend on himself too.

The railroad had come to Northfield when he was eleven. Soon
there were two lines, for the junction of the Vermont and Massachusetts and the River Road lay just across the Connecticut almost
opposite the Moody homestead, and the trains clanking across the
new bridge Boston-bound sang of a wider world until, from
Northfield as from all rural New England, boys and young men
drifted eastwards into the cities, or struck westwards to pioneer
lands. By the winter of 1853-4 D L Moody was decided. When the
snows cleared he put his few belongings in a carpet bag.

His mother grieved, his older brothers George, Edwin and Luther
reminded him brutally that his two previous absences, brief and
dismal, had ended abruptly. Young Dwight did not listen, hateful as
it was to leave home. He had no trace of doubt that one day he
would be famous.

Moody was Yankee to the core. His blood was pure Anglo-Saxon
like many of the local place-names, Warwick, Northampton,
Winchendon; but he was bred to that smouldering distrust of England left by the wars of Independence and of 1812. He would have
dismissed as a joke in poor taste any prophecy that fame should
first come in Great Britain, that Scotland and England would be
loved dearly.

Indeed, anyone who had told him exactly how it would happen
would have been answered by a choice Yankee oath.

2: Boston Sunrise

Samuel Socrates Holton, a prosperous shoe-craftsman aged thirty-
seven, was presiding over his shop in Court Street, Boston, just off
Scollay Square, when to his surprise and alarm nephew Dwight
swaggered in.

Dwight had broached the subject of taking a post in the Holton
shop at the previous Thanksgiving Day in Northfield. Holton had
made no reply. Later he questioned George, the eldest Moody

brother at home, and what he heard about Dwight was not to his taste. Therefore, on seeing his nephew six months later in the middle of the boots and shoes he invited him into his office, chatted pleasantly about the family and then, making plain that he had no more time, asked what Dwight proposed to do in Boston. Dwight, shaken, answered that he had come to find a position. Uncle Samuel Socrates said nothing. Uncle Lemuel, the younger partner who looked after the second shop farther up the street, suggested Dwight had better stay with him in his Winchester suburban house while looking for work.

Moody walked out of Holton and Co certain that he would soon gloat over his uncles' chagrin at missing a good assistant.

Up and down the hilly curving streets of Boston, still largely cooped up on its original peninsula, he called at shops and offices. Boston was filling fast; the Irish influx following the potato famine had not slackened, and if many immigrants went westward, or could not read or write, clerks enough were available to fill every vacancy twice.

Moody's confidence seeped. 'When they answered me roughly, their treatment would chill my soul. But when someone would say, "*I* feel for you. I would like to help you but I can't. But you'll be all right soon!" I went away happy and light-hearted.' At Winchester that evening he wore a brave, obstinate face for Uncle Lemuel and Aunt Maria.

By the afternoon of the second day Moody was miserable. 'The feeling ... that no one wanted you. I shall never forget those two dark days. Oh, the sadness, the loneliness.' He drifted to the docks and toyed with signing on as a sailor. He badgered the post office, although he knew the Northfield mail came only daily, until he got a letter – from little Lizzie, aged twelve, warning him against pickpockets; he shook his empty pockets ruefully, and as he trudged back to meet Uncle Lemuel made a boyish vow, quickly forgotten, promising God 'If He would give me some work I would serve and love Him'.

Moody greeted Lemuel defiantly. 'I am going to walk to New York!'

Lemuel judged that pride had nearly cracked. 'Ask your uncle for a job, direct,' he said.

Dwight refused. 'He knows perfectly well what I want.'

'Go on, ask him!'

Lemuel won. A chastened Dwight approached Uncle SS, as Samuel Socrates was known in the family, who gave him a look, long, silent, avuncular.

'Dwight,' he said at last, 'I'm afraid that if you come in here you will soon want to run the store yourself. Now my men here do the work as *I* want it done...' He read his nephew a homily, laid down certain conditions and offered him the week-end to think them over.

Dwight blurted out, 'I don't want till Monday. I promise now.'

Moody was genuinely grateful for the break. Twenty-four years later, when Samuel Socrates in 'great necessity' appealed to his newly famous nephew, Moody wrote, 'You gave me work & good advice & I look back to that hour as the turning point in my life & I feel as if I owe you a debt I can never pay so the money I send you is not a loan but a part payment of what I owe you...'

In the following week Dwight wrote home laboriously, 'I do not bord out to Uncle SS now I bord in the city Calvin and I are going to room together bimb bi that word is not spelt rite I guess...' He intended the good Yankee phrase 'by 'n by'. He wrote a hand that became, for a time, reasonably legible ('if you can read it you can do peter than I can'), but he spelt as he spoke, in the dialect and idiom of the Connecticut Valley; and he had inherited from his mother the peculiar habit of never inserting punctuation – the words tumbled on to paper as, when he talked, they tumbled from his mouth.

He slept over the shop. 'I have a room up in the third story and I can open my winder and there is 3 grat buildings full of girls the handsomest thare is in the city they will swar like parrets.' He had his meals at a hostel 'where there is about twenty-five clurcks and some girls we have a jolly time'.

He decided to join what he called 'the Christian saciation', the

Young Men's Christian Association of Boston, founded less than three years earlier, the first YMCA in the United States and only a week junior to the earliest in North America, that of Montreal. It gave him, at a dollar a year, a place where he could get away on his own 'and I can have all the books I want to read free of expense ... they have a smart room and the smart men of Boston lecter to them for nothing and they get up a question'.

Moody went to some of these lectures, having quickly discovered that to be a smart clerk he must not only read books but learn from the learned. Almost certainly he would have laughed with Oliver Wendell Holmes, who loved lecturing. He may have heard Longfellow declaim, John Lothrop Motley read turgid manuscript pages of the long book he was writing on the rise of the Dutch Republic. The Boston neighbourhood of 1854 teemed with intellectual life. Any day Moody might sell shoes to Emerson or Lowell, Dana or Whittier or Julia Ward Howe, or those cultured young Bostonians, Henry and William James and Phillips Brooks.

There were excitements: an accidental explosion on the Common, a dreadful fire at Sargent's Wharf; above all, the riots when Abolitionists attempted to prevent the extradition to the southern states of the fugitive slave, Burns. The final drama could be viewed from a precarious perch over the Holton store. 'I got up in to the secont story right over our shade and thare was all of 35 difrent compineys. Geo Beans and my self got up there a bout 10 aclock and thare we sat un till 3 in the afternoon thay tock him out a bout 2½ o such groaning and hising you never hird I was all burnt up in the son the polis came up to the store when he was clearing the street and told us to com down but we was up so he could not reach us and he told us to come down the secont time but we would not com so he at to let us be and so I see it all.'

In his scant leisure Moody loved the open, in summer running hard round Boston Common or penetrating the long passage-ways and gangplanks to Braman's Baths, the basin at the foot of Chestnut Street where he could swim in the salty waters of the Charles and gorge himself afterwards, so far as pocket allowed, on black mince slugs and apple doughbats. When winter came he joined the

great toboggan run or watched rich boys race their highly polished
sleds. He scrapped lustily too. 'I used to have a terrible habit of
swearing. Whenever I would get mad, out would come the oaths' –
and up came his fists.

Best of all was practical joking. 'I was full of animal life, and
shut up in the store through the day and sleeping there at night I
had to have some vent, and used to lie awake at nights to think of
some new joke to play upon somebody. My first victim was the
cobbler employed in the store. He was an Italian however, and although he liked me he had such an awful temper that my joking
him came near costing my life. One day I had fitted a lady with an
expensive pair of shoes and he was changing the buttons when
enraged by some trick I played upon him he took his knife and cut
the shoe he held into pieces. Another time, and this was the last
trick I played upon him – he seized the knife and sprang at me and
for a few minutes I had all I could do to keep out of his reach.'

Another amusement was Aunt Tryphena, Samuel Socrates' second wife. Uncle SS had married a Miss Elizabeth Clapp, and on
her death her younger sister Tryphena. The Clapps pleased him
well; when Tryphena died in 1857 he married the youngest sister,
Georgiana. Tryphena, a gay person, had a habit of sweeping into
the store. 'She wanted to have a talk and I guess she does for she
was in the store about two howers and she would talk all the time as
fast as she could make her tongue go so I could not git a word in
age ways.'

Moody had no regrets that he had left farming to be a salesman;
instead of mucking unresponsive weeds he was persuading people,
charming them and moulding their wills to buy more and costlier
shoes. He revelled in the battle to trade better than the other clerks.
And he had money, though little enough. He sent some to his mother,
but 'I would not go back a gain to liv for nothing,' he told her rather
unkindly in midsummer. 'I never enjoyed myself so well be for in
my life the time goes like a whirl wind.'

He would not admit it, but he was lonely. 'I wish the duse you
would some of you write to me,' he scolded his brother George.
'What in thunder the reason was I did not get a letter this morning

I could not make out ... I should like to go home this year if I could git away but it is all in vain cant wright any more so goodby resp. Yours Dwight L Moody HO GEO tells me what kind of a crop of corn this year and potatoes.'

'I go to meating at Mount Vernon St. Orthedx I don't know how it is spelt but you will know what I mean.' Betsey did indeed.

Samuel Socrates was not a Unitarian. And he had made Dwight promise, as one of the conditions, that he would attend the Mount Vernon Church and Sunday school, which was Trinitarian or orthodox Congregationalist. He did this in no partisan spirit but as a way of keeping his nephew out of mischief.

To Dwight church was church whatever its name, and he reported in a customary mood of dutiful boredom to the Sunday school superintendent. Superintendent Palmer has two claims to minor fame: he was a brother of Ray Palmer, who had written 'My faith looks up to Thee' at the age of twenty-one, and many hymns since; and because, after a few moments' interrogation following School Assembly that Sunday, he allotted D L Moody to the class of Edward Kimball. Had he chosen a tight-lipped, insensitive or even an older teacher, the story might have been different.

Moody followed Palmer to the class, already in session, and saw a strikingly tall man of thirty, a salesman in McGilvray's drygoods (drapery) store. Kimball smiled at the newcomer, handed him a Bible, told him to sit down and that they were on a lesson from the Gospel of John. Moody began thumbing hastily through Genesis. 'Out of the corner of their eyes the boys saw what he was doing,' Kimball records, 'and, detecting his ignorance, glanced slyly and knowingly at one another, but not rudely. I gave the boys just one hasty glance of reproof. I quietly handed Moody my own book open at the right place, and took his.' Moody said to himself he would 'stick by the fellow who had stood by him and done him a turn like that'.

Samuel Socrates hinted darkly among the deacons that it was Betsey's fault – no family prayers or reading of the Scriptures. He was wrong. The weighty family Bible had been 'about the only

book we had in the house when father died, and out of that book
she taught us'. But it was not to be handled by grubby little Moodys,
and Dwight had generally day-dreamed during the readings.

First attendance at Mount Vernon church service was
unpropitious too. Moody took a place at the back of the gallery.
Being tone-deaf he could not enjoy the excellent new organ. During the long sermon of Pastor Kirk, whom years afterwards he described as 'one of the most eloquent men I ever heard', he fell fast
asleep.

Dr Edward Norris Kirk was pastor of an unusual church 'gathered' only twelve years previously of Bostonians unsatisfied by
the rigid doctrinal exclusiveness of Park Street a few yards south-
west, but rejecting the free-thinking charms of King's Chapel a
few yards south-east. Kirk preached, with intellectual wealth and a
measure of fervour, not to make men orthodox but to move their
hearts. Here were no cold moral essays such as Everett had pro-
pounded from the Northfield pulpit with ethical exhortation. Kirk
spoke much of a sinful and undone race which could not attain its
ideal if it wanted. He spoke more of Jesus Christ who, he said, had
died for all mankind, had risen from the dead (Everett would have
winced) and lived to be the Friend of any who trusted Him. Kirk
uttered fearful warnings to those who refused this great salvation,
and verbally lashed young men who dared not or cared not to take
up the Cross and be Christ's disciples.

In the next eleven months Kimball's lessons and Kirk's preaching percolated the consciousness of Moody as he hustled his way
to the top of Holton's shoe-selling list ('I took as much as any one
last Saturday'... 'I am giting a long as fast as most of them'), or
swam, ran or tobogganed, or indulged in horseplay.

When first he began to grasp Kirk's drift he thrust the implica-
tions aside: 'I thought I would wait till I died, and then become a
Christian. I thought if I had the consumption or some lingering
disease, I would have plenty of time to become one, and in the
meantime I would enjoy the best of the pleasures of the world.' By
early 1855, with Boston under hard snow and the Charles River
frozen, Moody's colleagues saw the same jolly, wilful, quick-tem-

pered youth just eighteen; but, scarcely recognized by himself at
first, an inward struggle had developed.

Kirk stressed repeatedly that the spiritual issue was one of choice,
of deliberate submission of will to Another, of a moment of faith
leading to a life of service; sensing that Kirk was right, Moody
resisted. He could not mentally disentangle doctrines, but he recognized the issue and sought to avoid it. Forty years afterwards he
said: 'When I came to Jesus Christ, I had a terrible battle to surrender my will, and take God's will.'

In April the Mount Vernon Church held a revival, a term then
used synonymously with 'mission' as well as in the broader sense
of a spontaneous spiritual movement.

In the midst of the revival, on Saturday morning, April 21st,
1855, Edward Kimball walked out of his lodgings at America House,
having 'decided to speak to Moody about Christ and about his soul.
I started down town to Holton's shoe store. When I was nearly there
I began to wonder whether I ought to go just then during business
hours. And I thought maybe my mission might embarrass the boy,
that when I went away the other clerks might ask who I was, and
when they learned might taunt Moody and ask if I was trying to
make a good boy out of him. While I was pondering over it all I
passed the store without noticing it. Then, when I found I had gone
by the door I determined to make a dash for it and have it over at
once.'

He found Moody in the back part wrapping up shoes in paper
and stacking them on shelves. 'I went up to him and put my hand
on his shoulder, and as I leaned over I placed my foot upon a shoe
box.' Looking down into Moody's eyes he made what he thought
afterwards a very weak plea. Neither could ever recall the exact
words, but 'I asked him to come to Christ, who loved him and who
wanted his love and should have it.' There were tears in Kimball's
eyes.

'It seemed,' Kimball records, 'that the young man was just ready
for the light that broke upon him, for there, at once, in the back of
that shoe store in Boston,' Moody 'gave himself and his life to
Christ.'

Kimball slipped from the store a few minutes after he had entered.

Next morning, Sunday, as Moody came out of his room over the shut-up shop, 'I thought the old sun shone a good deal brighter than it ever had before – I thought that it was just smiling upon me; and as I walked out upon Boston Common and heard the birds singing in the trees, I thought they were all singing a song to me. Do you know, I fell in love with the birds. I had never cared for them before. It seemed to me that I was in love with all creation. I had not a bitter feeling against any man, and I was ready to take all men to my heart.'

Moody's first thought was for his family, his mother, brothers and sisters, and especially the young twin, Samuel, to whom he was devoted. 'Then and there I began to pray for them. I had never prayed for them before.'

He had sent home not only money but shoes, which he could buy at trade prices, and much unsolicited advice on everything; and now he wanted them to have this new, astonishing exhilaration and peace. 'I thought I could tell them what God had done for me. I thought I had only to explain it to have them all see the light.'

He was home for a few days quite soon (he helped in the potato and water-melon planting at the end of May) and attempted to tell what had happened. They looked at him blankly – could not understand what he was getting at. Betsey murmured that she would be a Unitarian till she died.

In Boston also he met rebuff. Mount Vernon as a Congregational Church did not admit to full membership except on oral examination by pastor and deacons to test spiritual sincerity. Unwisely, Kimball urged Moody to apply too soon, and he stood before them shaking with a nervousness which Kimball's presence could not calm. 'With utmost encouragement' they put their questions: 'Have you been awakened? Did you see yourself a sinner? Do you feel dependent on Christ for forgiveness?...'

Moody, who could outwag Aunt Tryphena, was tongue-tied. His sense of the Friendship that had invaded his life was helplessly inarticulate. He grunted and murmured 'Yes', or 'No', or 'Sure', which the clerk translated into doctrinally correct statements, until at length the chairman asked, 'Mr Moody, what has Christ done for us all – for you – which entitles Him to our love?'

'I don't know. I think Christ has done a good deal for us. But I don't think of anything particular as I know of.'

They deferred admission, and told off two kindly deacons to teach him. Moody wanted to be taught – he was upset when a fellow-clerk had worsted him with apparently watertight proofs that Christ had never risen from the dead; but he resolved to keep away from that committee: 'You might as well try to get a man to go before a Justice of the Peace.' It was not until the next year, in March 1856, that he appeared again and was accepted, although, in Kimball's words, 'little more light appeared'.

Afterwards the worthies of Mount Vernon were sheepish about their attitude. Kimball defended them: except that Moody no longer swore and that the Bible which had been 'the driest and darkest Book in the universe to me', was now his favourite reading, there had been nothing to hint that one day they would sit at his feet.

Moody at nineteen found Boston stifling. Its galaxy of talent, its old-established business houses, its set ways, stiff manners and rigid social levels combined to frustrate.

As early as October 1855 he had written inquiringly to his uncle Calvin Holton who had gone West to farm near Chicago. In the spring of 'fifty-six his cousin Frank had joined the jostling crowd of easterners and emigrants who answered the popular cry 'Go West, young man, and grow up with the country'.

In September Moody went.

3: Chicago Money-maker

He had not meant to go so soon.

Joined by his next older brother Luther, Moody now managed the newly opened Holton store farther up Court Street. Moreover, his mother wept when he talked of the west, and he wanted time to win her round. Then came the quarrel with uncle.

The cause is obscure. To his mother Moody merely wrote, 'Uncle SS objected to my goin', though adding in a second letter, 'I was fairly drove out of Boston'. To his younger brother Warren he was more frank. 'I hope you will never have anyone to cross your path as they have mine and blast your hopes.' Possibly Samuel Socrates had refused a rise. More probably he had demanded signed agreement that Moody would not go west, and on being refused had fired him; this would explain why Moody had money only for his fare to Chicago and for expenses until he should get a job, which was one reason against a farewell visit to Northfield. Whatever the cause, 'I thought the quicker I went and got out of [SS's] way the better ... I lov Boston and have got some warm friends there but as I was situated there it was not very pleasant.'

He bought a through ticket on an immigrant train, five dollars Boston to Chicago, and left from the Causeway Street depot of the Fitchburg Railroad at 4pm on Monday, September 15th, 1856.

He drew into Keene, twenty miles from Northfield, after dark, and felt slightly guilty at mother going to bed ignorant that her Dwight was disappearing west. The train rattled northwards, wood smoke from its enormous funnel swirling ash into the carriages to mix with the smelly whale oil of the swaying lamps, and crossed the Connecticut at Bellows Falls. At Rutland, Vermont, in the small hours of Tuesday, everyone turned out; Moody sat through the night on the station. A morning run beside Lake Champlain, then westwards all day to Ogdensburg on Erie, to take the lake steamer through the second night, and a slow Canadian train to Windsor opposite Detroit, where the ferry timing prevented his seeing his brother Isaiah, the prodigal who had returned after thirteen years, had been forgiven and now worked in Detroit.

The Michigan Central express ambled through the prairies until at length, during the night of Thursday, September 18th, behind schedule, it rumbled over the long trestle bridge above Lake Michigan mud into what Chicagoans asserted was 'the best depot in the country'. Thus came Moody, excited but apprehensive, to 'this far famed city of the west ... my western home', a thousand miles away.

Two ladies who had been kind to him travelled onward, 'and then I felt as if Christ was the only friend I had in Chicago'.

Jolly Uncle Calvin Holton of Des Plaines, a few miles out, promptly secured Moody a post at the Lake Street shoe store of *Charles and Augustus Wiswall*, Massachusetts men.

The following Wednesday a lawyer called King was introduced at the prayer meeting of 'Plymouth' Congregational Church to the newly arrived young man, 'one of the happiest looking I think I ever saw. His cheeks then were full, so red and rosy, and he possessed such a pleasant smile and look that he attracted much attention, and very soon became a general favorite, not withstanding his very limited education – if he did come from Boston'. Moody was delighted. 'As soon as I made myself known I had friends enough ... After meeting they com to me and seemed to be as glad to see me as if I were their earthly brother.'

He took to Chicago at once. 'It is a very lively city much more so than Boston.' Into this hub of the west poured, by sail, steamer and rail, immigrants and manufacturers from the East, iron and timber down the Great Lakes, stock and grain from the prairies. Slaughter-houses and tanneries made Chicago stink, foundries and factories filled it with smoke, Lake Michigan frequently coated it with mud. No one cared: the farther westwards the frontier pushed the more Chicago grew.

'The streets are all lade out strate and broad,' Moody wrote home. 'You can stand and look as far as the eye can reach and try to walk out of the city but it is almost impossible for you to get out of the limits of the city.' The land was not closely built over as at Boston, and this – most of the houses being timber – was fortunate, for Moody lost count of the fires he saw or heard.

The pace of life was much to his liking. He heard glowing tales of men who ten years back had arrived poor and now 'are worth from ten to fifty thousand dollars'. But his New England soul was shocked by Chicago Sundays: 'You dont know how anyone feels to be off in a city like this for it is so wicked the stores are open on the

sapath a grate many of them'. And he never became urbanized; his
heart stayed loyal to the countryside. 'You don't know how I like to
get letters from friends being off in this far far city all alone I think
of sweet home and of my younger days often.'

He was happy. He put on weight, had an enormous appetite,
was the same irrepressible joker in that oafish style which his generation thought funny. 'The cobbler in Wiswall's store was a queer
old character,' told Moody with huge delight at the age of forty-
six, 'as most of these cobblers are, and although he thought a good
deal of me and we were great friends I was always up to some trick
with him.' The naughtiest was to slit the leather seat of the cobbler's low stool, and place underneath a full pail of water. While
Moody watched out of the corner of his eye the cobbler returned,
and jumped up with a cry; he wiped the seat, sat down again, and
jumped, and so continued until he discovered the dirty trick.

Moody flung himself into the craft of selling shoes to those
who wanted or those who did not. 'His ambition made him anxious
to lay up money,' Charles Wiswall records, 'his personal habits
made him exact and economical.' He was a thruster and an enthusiast, and when Wiswalls started a jobbing department they let him
meet the immigrant trains and bludgeon newcomers by blunt speech
and boyish grins into buying boots. His aim, that of all Chicago,
was get rich quick: 'I used to pray God to give me one hundred
thousand dollars.' 'I can make money faster here thin I can in B,'
he wrote to his mother, adding, with Yankee hyperbole, 'I hav me
one of the best situations in the city ... I hav don the very best thing
in coming hear.'

Within a year he was showing the signs of a future millionaire,
putting his savings into land which he would sell at a profit, making loans at high rates, thinking up this scheme and that to increase
income and capital. He rejoiced especially in one excellent aid to
personal contentment and material progress: 'I tell you,' he wrote
to his brother George, 'hear is the place to make money... and that
is not all... I have enjoyed more Religion hear thean I have ever in
my life... I find the better I live the more enjoyment I have.'

Chicago already had a reputation for wildness, but religion lay

close beneath its thick skin. Because of the many from strict eastern homes who had drifted in spirit and morals, disaster or per-
plexity could touch off religious fervour; it was not all self-centred
or cynical.

On January 6th, 1857, Moody wrote: 'There is a great revival
of religion in this city. I go to meeting every night Ho how I do
enjoy it seems as if God was here himself.' This preceded by nearly
a year the similar and more lasting movement generated by the
Wall Street financial panic, which led to the establishment of prayer
meetings in many American cities and to the revival of 1859 in
Great Britain, and which caused Chicago's famous Democrat mayor,
'Long John' Wentworth, to comment, 'The effects of the present
religious movement are to be felt in every phase of Society'.

The revival of early 1857 tossed Moody out of his complacent
view of religion as primarily an aid to fortune.

He rented four pews at Plymouth Church and filled them with
young men from Wiswalls or near-by shops, or even passers-by at
service time. On Sunday afternoons he went slumming with a
slightly older architect named J B Stillson, who rated him 'a young
man of earnest purpose, plain habits and not very much education.
We became co-workers in scattering religious reading among sailors in saloons, boarding houses and hundreds of poor families living in shanties'.

Attempts to contribute to the life of Plymouth Church by opening
his mouth at prayer meeting made staid adults 'squirm their
shoulders when I got up'. They told Moody he did not know enough
grammar, and asked Uncle Calvin to silence him. Moody took the
hint. Meanwhile, he had grown an inveterate sermon-taster, Sunday
morning, noon and night. He had his pews at Plymouth, could be
found in the Methodist Episcopal, sat under the outsize Presbyterian
minister, Patterson; and at the First Baptist he set eyes on a thirteen-
year-old girl. He was not introduced, but remembered the face. Her
name was Emma, and her social standing clearly a cut above his.

There were plenty of other girls. To little sister Lizzie in
Northfield he scribbled: 'When I went out to Uncle Cal's I see
quite a number of fine looking young ladies here is the place for

ladies... I always thought before I came out here there was hardley none but it is not so there is a nuft but they dont seem like the good old New england folks now I tell you I think befor I get married I shall hav to come home and let you pick me out a wife.'

At the end of 1857 Moody left Wiswall for the post of travelling salesman and debt-collector for the wholesale boot-and-shoe house of *C H Henderson*. His brother Luther, temporarily in Chicago, 'thought it was very foolish in my leaving Wiswall but I have got me a situation that is worth five of that and if I have my health and my *God* is with me I shall sucksead better here in Chicago than I ever thought I should.'

He enjoyed the new job 'better than anything I have ever done it is nothing but excitement all the time'. He hustled all over Illinois, and in late February 1858 was in the south of the state, where the scenery was pleasant but he thought scorn of the inhabitants: 'the people are more like heathen they all smok chew swere drink gamble and steel they are shiftless losey ignorant miserable people a Yankey can do well here I think'. Most of his customers lived on the railway. Occasionally he had to hire a horse and trap to cross the prairies, and (or so he tried to persuade George) 'I drove a horse into a slew the other day so nothing but his head stuck out I dint ever expect to see him out a gaine but I maid out to get him my hare stood rite up on I will send you a lock so you will see for yourself'.

He grew 'fat as a pig', a heavyweight at twenty-one who could look quite tall when he remembered to brace shoulders and lift head; and he had a short growth of beard to accentuate his chin and impress defaulting shopkeepers. When the icy winter passed, Henderson sent him farther afield. 'I travel most of the time it is very pleasant traveling at this time of the year in the country as you cross the praries you can see the praries wolf and deer chickens are as thick as grasshoppers in August I was down in Missouri not long ago and also in Iowa Wisconsin Indiana I have not traveled much in Michigan but expect to have to there before long and if I do I mean to call on Isaiah but since January I have not had time to turn around the folks I am now with do a very heavy business the largest business this side of N York so in the busy season we have to jump all hands of us as tite as we can jump.'

At Wiswalls he had slept on the premises. He now lived in a superior boarding-house in Michigan Avenue run by a Mrs Hubert Phillips for the smart bachelors of Chicago. Among them was Levi Leiter, who became a millionaire and the father-in-law of Lord Curzon, Viceroy of India and British Foreign Secretary. Moody used to say that he believed he could have beaten the lot except Marshall Field.

When pausing for breath in Chicago he searched for a Christian activity which could command his whole spare-time energy.

Mother Phillips, a member of the First Baptist Church, suggested trying their Wells Street mission Sunday school on the north side, the poor part of the city. One Sunday morning Moody and another boarder crossed the river and walked up Wells Street to the corner of Chicago Avenue. Moody asked the superintendent for work, 'but I don't think he asked for a class,' Dr Roy of Plymouth Church recalled. 'He said in those days that he could not teach.'

The superintendent, unaware whither his remark would lead, casually told Moody he might go into the alleys and streets and bring in what boys he could.

4: 'Go Fast or Burst'

A ragamuffin called Jimmy Sexton played in the streets with three or four other urchins on a Sunday morning. 'We were approached by a stalwart young man about twenty years of age. He was dressed in a checkered suit of grey clothes – close-cropped hair, a muscular frame, easy though awkward in manner, and might have been taken for a horse jockey or an all round sportsman.'

'Boys, don't you want to go with me to Sunday school?' said Moody in a 'familiar and friendly way'.

'Are you going to have a picnic?'

'Come along with me and we will find out.'

They trooped behind as Moody hurried through courts and alleys until, sweaty and triumphant, he delivered to Wells Street no less than eighteen ragged boys, most of them barefoot. 'That was the happiest Sunday I have ever known,' Moody said. 'I had found out what my mission was.' He had been two years 'trying to find out what my work was before I succeeded. If I could not teach them I could take them where there were those who could teach them.'

Next week he hunted up the same gang, and others. 'We became at once close friends,' Sexton recalled in a letter of 1892. 'Notwithstanding his crude and somewhat uncouth appearance we found him to be a most agreeable companion, good humoured, ready and witty in speech, although awkward in the selection of his words; simple, unaffected and kind, with a charm of manner and a personality so winning and interesting that we all immediately swore allegiance to our new-found stranger friend. His earnestness and sincerity gave us confidence in his loyalty, and soon made us feel that we stood upon an equality with a good fellow. Our boyish chaffing pleased rather than annoyed him.'

'Drumming up scholars', as Moody described it, for the Baptists made this Congregationalist late for the Methodist Episcopal Young Men's class, which he had joined in disregard of the frowns of the Plymouth deacons, who set much store on sectarian exclusiveness. Another member of the class was one of the most successful and wealthy men in the city, John V Farwell, who had first come to Chicago on a load of hay with less than four dollars in his pocket and now, at only thirty-three, controlled the leading big store; he was outranked later by his former partner Marshall Field, but remained a prominent citizen for the rest of his life.

Farwell despised this tardy youth until discovery of the cause, 'and then my criticism turned towards home with tremendous force, and why wasn't I doing something for others as well as this young man?' The incident led to the start of a very great friendship.

One Sunday at Wells Street Moody saw a new teacher for the girls, a young lady with good looks and elegance - and her face was the face he had never forgotten. He wangled an introduction. Almost before he knew it he was paying a call on the Washington Street home of a shipbuilder, Fleming H Revell, a comparatively recent immigrant from England. Emma Revell was only fifteen, looked no older, yet had a quiet maturity, a happy laugh and, incredibly, did not seem to think a fellow crude, uncouth or awkward.

When Henderson again sent Moody into the country the ragamuffins drifted. 'We boys did not like the school on Wells Street,' where the lessons included much dreary learning by rote, 'and as there was no immediate prospect of a picnic, we dropped out.'

Moody was appalled by the endless back-streets of the north side. When first he had reached Chicago he could write glibly: 'we seldom ever see a poor person hear and very little stealing goin on'. He had now been embroiled in the stench and squalor of a great city's backwash: a miserable medley of German and Irish emigrants or American-born newcomers, who had dropped in the mad rush westward to wealth, been ploughed under by the violence of competition or the ravages of whisky, and now crowded in the shanties and tumbledown frame houses of an area known as The Sands. The original 'Sands' had been a concretion of shacks on Lake Michigan foreshore, which in 1857 'Long John' Wentworth had cleaned away violently ('an exhibition of barbarism in the name of high morality').

The 'Sands' were now the slums of the North Side. Their poverty, and that churches did not touch the adults nor Sunday schools the children, startled Moody. As he rattled by train across the prairies, or drove pony and trap 'into a slew', or battled to sell Henderson's shoes at best prices to hardbitten storekeepers, he thought constantly of Jimmy Sexton, Tom Stevens and others wilder than they, of their poverty and ignorance, their restlessness in the formality of Wells Street or its opposite number, the North Star School.

Back in Chicago, early in autumn, 1858, Moody and his architect friend Stillson appropriated an abandoned freight-car on North State Street. He sought out Jimmy Sexton and the gang, 'and invited us to assist him in starting a mission Sunday school. We were to be co-partners, so to speak, or co-labourers, and, as one of the boys expressed it, "the whole thing". The idea that we were to boss somebody and to take part in the controlling of others was too captivating for our youthful ambition to withstand.'

Stillson brought in another young businessman, Carter, who had a fine voice and could sing and lead a rousing song and chorus like the newly written 'Stand up, stand up, for Jesus', though there were few hymns extant that guttersnipes of the Sands could hope to learn or remember.

Next Sunday afternoon anyone walking down that block of North State heard extraordinary noises: shouts, whoops, cheers, a moment of silence, a sacred song in a baritone voice swept up into a shouted chorus. A man's voice (and it was not Moody's) spoke for two or three minutes, until murmurs and shuffling indicated that another song alone could preserve peace.

After a few Sundays, with boys bringing pals to the new adventure until the sides of the old car bulged, Lawyer King got to hear. King thought Moody 'should have a better location to teach the boys in, so I said to him I knew of an empty, one-story-and-a-half frame house on Michigan street', later renamed Illinois Street. It was a disused saloon called the Mansion House, one of the first to have been opened in Chicago, but now rotting and ratty. Moody was given the use of the large front room and a store at the back.

A Chicago minister, G S Savage, remembered how Moody 'went out on the streets with candy and knicknack and got the good will of the children', and by thus being a young, exuberant, rich uncle whose pockets trailed maple sugar he made the school a draw. 'All loved him,' said King, 'because he took such an interest in their welfare. No one forgets the pleasant smile and the cordial handshake, both of which were characteristic.'

Sundays grew noisier by sheer numbers. On week-nights, when in Chicago, Moody sometimes collected smaller parties and that November invited Savage to attend a Thanksgiving Day 'service'. 'There were no gas fixtures in the house and he was trying to light it with a half-dozen candles, but the darkness had rather the best of it. I found him with a candle in one hand and a Bible in the other, and a child on his knee who he was trying to teach. There were twenty-five or thirty children in all, and they were as sorry a lot of little ragamuffins as could have been found in Chicago.'

Moody was hindered by continual absences, since Henderson paid his return to Chicago only one Sunday a month and he could not afford other week-ends if operating far. He had now joined a church on the North Side, the 'New England' congregation which worshipped in a small wooden building near the river and had attempted, unsuccessfully, to work up a Sunday school in the Sands. Church members noticed 'a plump, active, keen-eyed young fellow come into our prayer meeting. Sometimes he had a word to say, very brief, and sometimes he prayed. His voice – how shall I describe it? – had electricity in it.' One who noticed was Colonel Hammond, superintendent of the *Chicago, Burlington and Quincy Railroad.*

Much of the Henderson work lay along the C B & Q line. Moody boldly asked Hammond for a free pass – the first recorded beg of the man who was to draw vast sums into Christian enterprise. Hammond sought the advice of another church member, a doctor called Blatchford, who urged him to agree.

Next Sunday morning Blatchford was driving to an urgent case down Pine Street on the edge of the Sands. 'I thought I saw this man, Moody, and I stopped my horse. He was down, I guess, a block and a half from me. I saw him dart into a house, and in a little while he came out of that house with the children all about him, and the mother and father, perhaps, and then he would dart into another house... When I went to church that morning I said to Colonel Hammond, "Your pass will do good".'

By early December 1858, as Chicago's temperature dropped towards zero, Moody's life seemed set in eternal spring. He relished his spare-time work for boys. His employer, Henderson, 'the truest friend I have met since I left home', showed growing confidence, took 'as much interest in my welfare as he would in the welfare of his own son', and hinted that Moody was being groomed to succeed him.

And there was Emma. Her small brother, Fleming H Revell, Jr, then aged nine, would crouch behind the stove on those winter nights 'to listen to the conversation of this young man who came to see

one of my sisters – in a very democratic company, and a very democratic sort of courting, because I think I never remember his ever
coming alone. Around that little sheet iron stove there was always a
circle of young men, and perhaps it was because there were three
girls.'

Emma Revell had been born in London on July 5th, 1843. Her
father, Fleming Hewitt Revell, was a French Huguenot who had
come to England, married an English girl and built up a shipbuilding business, until illness and financial troubles caused him to
emigrate again in 1849 to Chicago, with his wife and daughters
Anna, Emma and Sarah. A fourth daughter, baby Mary, had to be
left with Mrs Revell's sister, and their son was born in America.

Though Revell never made much, and young Emma earned her
living as a teacher, the Washington Street home close to Moody's
Michigan Avenue lodgings was cultured, hospitable and rather English.

Emma Revell was a complete opposite to Moody. Moody
brimmed with health, strength and energy, an extrovert. Emma suffered already from asthma and headaches, was shy and retiring.
His humour was boisterous, hers deep and quietly playful. 'No two
people were ever more in contrast,' their younger son Paul summed
up long after both were dead. 'He was impulsive, outspoken, dominant, informal, and with little education at the time they met. She
was intensely conventional and conservative, far better educated,
fond of reading, with a discriminate taste, and self-effacing to the
last degree.'

She took on Moody's education. But she never persuaded him
to insert punctuation in his letters – he had no time. His large scrawl
rushed across the page, leaving the reader to guess where a sen-
tence closed, unless the first word of the next had a capital. Spelling was shaky to the end of his life, like that of many countrybred,
self-educated millionaires, politicians and generals of the period.
The later Moody could spell reasonably when he remembered, but
in notes and letters to colleagues, family and intimates he spelt
phonetically ('shure', 'beleave', 'clurk', 'goin', and in a letter to
his mother written in 1879 at the age of forty-two he spelt 'bed' as

if it was 'bread' with the 'r' left out). An English friend asked Moody in middle age why he did not write oftener in his own hand. 'Spelling,' Moody replied. 'But, Inglis, I'm getting over the difficulty. I am always sure of the first letter and the last, and anywhere between may be upstairs or downstairs.' And that is what his letters look like.

They are vivid in the originals, but without punctuation would read tediously in print; and unless his speech also was reproduced in the phonetics of a New England accent his spelling gives a falsely illiterate air. I shall ease the reader's eye henceforth by generally (but not always) inserting essential punctuation and correcting the spelling.

The opening of Moody's mind, the slow polishing of his rough-hewn character, was largely Emma Revell's. Two years were to pass before they could be engaged when she was seventeen, two more to marriage. 'My father's admiration for her was as boundless as his love,' wrote Paul. 'To the day of his death, I believe, he never ceased to wonder at two things – the use God had made of him despite his handicaps, and the miracle of having won the love of a woman he considered completely his superior.'

In the last week of 1858 Henderson died suddenly.

He died intestate, and the firm being reorganized under conditions annoying to the widow, Moody resigned in her support, although 'it would have been for my interest to have stayed with the new house'. He obtained a similar position with *Buell, Hill and Granger*: a year later Mrs Henderson and her daughter begged him to help them unseat the incompetent administrator of the considerable personal estate, collect the debts and wind it up. 'I told them I was not old enough to take such an estate on my shoulders, but they insisted... I feel highly honoured.'

Business life slipped imperceptibly from first place in Moody's interest.

The Sunday school throve. Numbers rose steadily, and according to Farwell, noise and chaos kept pace. Lawyer King heard that the deserted saloon had become too small. 'I became so greatly

impressed with the great work, and [Moody's] earnestness and devotion to it convinced me that I in my humble way should do something in the same direction.' King took Moody to Long John
Wentworth whom 'I knew very well', and if Wentworth was no
longer Mayor, his influence was enough to secure, rent-free, a hall
built on the site of the old North Market.

It was upstairs, 'a great grimy hall with blackened walls and
ceiling, and as bare and uninviting as can be imagined'. Underneath stood the local fire-engine; sometimes in years to come a
school session would be madly distracted by the rush of firemen to
harness the horses and gallop away, clanging the bell and stoking
the engine boiler to get steam to pump the hose.

The North Market Hall was used for the Saturday-night dance
of a German society, who threw all the school chairs, banners and
impedimenta into a heap, and left the floor a mess of cigar stubs,
ash, beer puddles and paper. Moody would not employ labour on a
Sunday. Instead he got up at six, however late back from travelling,
hurried to the hall and alone, or with Jimmy Sexton to whom he
had assigned the task, spent hours rolling out beer kegs, sweeping
sawdust, scrubbing. 'This was,' said Sexton, 'as dirty, disagreeable
and unpleasant a chore as could be imagined. I have never done
any work quite so filthy and disagreeable since, but then I was part
of the machine and considered myself well paid for my labor if I
received an approving word of encouragement from Mr Moody.'

Leaving Jimmy, Moody would rush out into the lanes 'to drum
up the scholars and new boys and girls' (girls now came to; it is
probable that a few had been admitted from the start). If parents of
a boy or girl were fractious he had to persuade them; if he found
them snoring off the previous night's booze he actually washed and
dressed their children.

At two o'clock the service began. For some months the riot was
beyond the wit of Moody, or of his more articulate helpers, to break
into classes – the afternoon was one glorious improvisation of short
talks, songs and chorus. 'The singing was a vent for their spirits,'
said one of the early teachers, 'and such singing I never heard before. The boys who sold papers in the street had an indescribable

lung power, and the rest seemed not far behind.'

When classes could be formed Moody whipped up more of his friends to serve as teachers. To one he said, before the bell rang for the start, 'I want you to take these lambs.'

'Lambs? Wolves, I should say.'

The school rose rapidly to some six hundred. Moody made a banker, Isaac Burch, superintendent, and afterwards John Farwell, but he himself was the driving force. 'I shall expect to have a good time when I get home,' he wrote to one of his brothers when on tour in July 1859, 'for I have been away some time now and the children are so glad to see me when I return. I think I have got the best school there is in the west, anyway it is the largest school there is this side of N York.' He was wrong. John Wanamaker, founder of the great store in Philadelphia, had one bigger.

Somebody said the school made him think 'of those steamboats on the Mississippi that must either go fast or burst'. That described Moody too. 'I am in a great hurry,' he would scrawl in letters home, 'I am in such a hurry tonight you must excuse me for not writing more this time I am in a hurry.'

Moody had thought he could never speak in public until, writes, Emma, in those smaller evening children's meetings, 'he found himself sometimes left without a speaker and would be obliged himself to say a little. Gradually he got so that he could talk to the audience.' He had been intimidated by the polish and length of contemporary sermons.

To tell boys and girls a story or two about Bible characters described as if living in the next block proved easier, and once he broke silence the dam burst; he could not thereafter resist opportunity to release the love and gratitude to Christ that bubbled inside, provided no minister was around, when Moody would start trembling and go tongue-tied.

On commercial tours he discovered place after place without a Sunday school. A small girl, a Miss Warner, went into the grocer's in the country town of Warren. Coming out she saw two men, the larger one on a box preaching at the corner, and stood with other children entranced. 'The railroad train was near-by, en route to Chicago. The other man got behind the speaker, pulled his coat tail and urged him to hurry and catch the train. They did catch the rear car.'

Moody would not preach to grown-ups, but there was something that he could do. He set about it in roaring Chicago fashion, Emma having scarcely begun to tame him.

Late in 1859 he announced that he really would visit Northfield. 'You seem to think that there is some humbug about my coming home,' he wrote to George in November, 'but I think there is no doubt but that I shall be home next month with out fail if not in January shure.' He came during January 1860, having given, in effect, a warning that Unitarian Northfield would soon learn 'there is nothing like the religion of Jesus Christ'.

Uncle Zebulon Allen, Betsey's brother-in-law, felt the force of it. 'My nephew Dwight is crazy crazy as a March hare. Came on from Chicago last week for a flying visit. I had not seen him but he drove into my yard this morning. You know how cold it was and his face was as red as red flannel. Before I could say good morning he shouted 'Good morning Uncle Zebulon, What are you going to do for Christ today? Of course I was startled and finally managed to say 'Come in Dwight and we will talk it over' 'No I can't stop but I want you to think about it' and he turned the sleigh around and went up the hill like a streak of lightning. I tell you he is Crazy.'

Another episode, back on the prairies in the spring of 1860, was less acrobatic.

William Reynolds, a banker of Peoria in Illinois, was in a train 'when a stout cheery-looking stranger came in, and sat down in the seat beside me.' They started talking as American railway passengers will, and the stranger remarked on the pretty countryside they were running through. 'Did you ever think what a good heavenly Father we have to give us such a pleasant world to live in?'

'Yes, indeed.'

'Are you a Christian?'

'No.'

Both knew what was meant; the America frontier in 1860 had a background of piety, family Bibles read at mothers' knees and old camp meetings when an itinerant preacher would stir a place to repentance and faith, and wander on to the next settlement.

'You are not a Christian ? But you ought to be one at once. I get off at the next station. If you will kneel down right here I will pray to the Lord to make you a Christian.'

They knelt. The stranger prayed. The train rattled to a stop and he hurried out, calling back, 'Remember, my friend, now is the time to accept.'

Reynolds, in a daze, ran on to the little platform of the carriage and shouted after him, 'Tell me who you are!'

'My name is Moody.'

Reynolds made inquiries, and one week-night called at the old saloon, still used for smaller meetings, 'and the first thing I saw was a man standing up, with a few tallow candles around him, holding a negro boy, and trying to read to him the story of the Prodigal Son'.

The banker became Moody's ardent admirer. To friends who were puzzled by this sudden conversion Reynolds would tell of the talk in the train. He went to Chicago again, Moody told George, 'to get me to go into the country & talk to the children. Well I went & had a good time. I will send you a peace cut from the paper.'

Moody had leisure for the meetings in Peoria because he now served his firm on a part-time commission basis, confident that energy and astuteness would secure him almost as substantial a salary as if always on the road. He did not intend to abandon trade. His future lay clear: to earn his bread as a quick-time businessman, amassing a fortune to pay for the philanthropic work next to his heart.

And so it might have proved, had not, on a June day of 1860, one of his North Market Hall teachers, a 'pale, delicate young man' staggered up the stairs to Moody's office at *Buell, Hill and Granger*, pushed open the door and 'tottering and bloodless, threw himself down on some boxes'.

5: The Children's Friend

'What's the matter?' Moody said.

'I have been bleeding again at the lungs. The doctor says I cannot live on Lake Michigan, I must go back to New York State. I suppose I am going to die.'

He trembled and looked so upset that Moody asked, 'What is the trouble? You are not afraid of death, you are ready to go?'

'No sir. I am not afraid. But I am anxious for my class.'

Moody knew that class, girls from twelve to sixteen, 'the most frivolous set. They kept gadding around in the school room, and were laughing and carrying on all the while'. He had once taken it in the man's absence sick, and 'they laughed in my face. I felt like opening the door and telling them all to go out and never come back.'

The teacher repeated, 'I am anxious for my class. I've failed. Not one of them has been led to Jesus. And I haven't the strength to do it now. I believe I have done the girls more harm than good. Not one converted.'

Moody was astounded. 'I had never heard any one talk like that before.' His whole concentration in the school had been on numbers: elated at a full attendance, at hundreds of noisy children, cast down when numbers dropped. He had not supposed that any of the little savages could undergo deep personal experience like a grown-up; he had not reckoned them as individuals.

After a pause Moody said, 'Suppose you go round and tell them how you feel. I will go with you in a carriage if you want to go.'

He helped the man on to the street and hired a carriage and drove into the slums. At the tenement home of one of the girls the teacher called her and said faintly, 'I have come just to ask you to come to the Saviour.' The girl listened wide-eyed as he revealed that he must leave Chicago and would die, as he explained why she should put her trust in Christ. And then, said Moody, 'he prayed as I never heard before', and the girl, in tears, promised 'to settle the question then and there'.

The two men mounted the carriage again and rumbled off to

another girl's home. The teacher struggled upstairs for a similar conversation. After three or four calls he was exhausted. Moody returned him to his lodgings.

At the end of ten days 'he came to the store with his face literally shining: "The last one of my class has yielded herself to Christ. The great vital question of their lives is settled. They have accepted my Saviour. My work is done and I am going home".'

'You are not going today. Wait until tomorrow and get the whole class together. Bring them all to tea tonight.'

Moody said afterwards that if he had known what that meeting would do to him he might have stayed away. All came, the teacher spoke and read to them, and they tried to sing a parting hymn. They knelt to pray. The man begged God to deepen the girls' new-found faith. Moody prayed. 'I was just rising from my knees when one of the class began to pray for her dying teacher.'

Astonished, Moody listened to the faltering, extempore prayer of a slum girl whom he had known as an empty-headed scoffer. A second besought her God for power to win others to Himself. One after another the girls stumbled into prayer. As Moody heard these genuine, fervent thanksgivings, these earnest petitions, the hundred thousand gold dollars of his dreams turned to tinsel, the ambition to build a commercial empire showed up tawdry, transient. Better to spend his years as this dying teacher had spent ten days.

Next evening, 'as the sun was going down over the Western prairies', Moody hurried to the Michigan Southern to see off his friend. Without any prearrangement every one of the girls was on the platform. They sang a hymn, and 'as the cars rolled out of the depot we could see his pale hand pointing towards heaven where he wished to meet them'.

Many of the girls became Moody's ardent helpers in the Sunday school. In the early nineteen twenties, when Will Moody had told that story at a service in California, 'a middle-aged lady came up and said, "Mr Moody, I want to meet you. My mother was one of those girls."'

As for D L Moody, that 'beautiful night in June' left him a problem that took three months to solve. Like Matthew of old he had heard a call to leave business. He did not want to leave business. 'I fought against it. It was a terrible battle. But oh! how many times I have thanked God's will.'

To love the prestige of wealth in a city that knew no other criterion of fame, to postpone marriage and then have a mere pittance to offer Emma, to abandon the excitement of commercial warfare, the race to be first millionaire of his set, the power that money brought, all this was the cost that took three months to count.

A day came in the autumn of 1860 when J V Farwell discovered that Moody had left *Buell, Hill and Granger*, had left Mrs Phillips's select boarding-house and was bedding on a settee in one of the rooms used by the YMCA in the Methodist Church block. He ate in cheap restaurants or made do on cheese and crackers, determined to stretch his savings and to spend freely on his school. 'I said to myself, "I'll live on what I've saved. When that is gone and there is no means of support I'll take it as a call to return to business".' Next year, when Moody was appointed an official of the YMCA, the clerk who inserted the Resolution of the Board of Managers wrote '...for the coming year at a salary of $—'. The blank was never filled in. Farwell says, 'I urged him to take a salary, which he refused', because it would shackle his freedom. There would come a renunciation even greater, but this of 1860 was a decision of genius, giving a moral right to beg hard for mission causes.

'No!' confirmed Fleming H Revell in a letter of 1917, 'Mr Moody never accepted a salary after he gave up a business I have always understood yielded him $5,000. His first year after, his income was $150. A test of real faith.'

A close friend, J H Harwood, summed it up: 'That a young man full to overflowing of animal spirits and interest in everyday life, should be able for Christ's sake to put the world completely under his feet and ask for nothing that this world had to give is not to be accounted for on any natural principle.'

Moody now poured himself, recklessly spending the resources of his nearly full-grown mighty physique, into the mission Sunday school. The North Market Hall could hold twelve hundred: it must be filled.

His pockets, as always, were full of toothsome delights. He would offer a prize such as a squirrel in a cage to the scholars bringing the most recruits in a given time. He never failed to keep the children to their promise of attendance. 'If for some reason I broke my promise,' is the memory of one of the girls, 'I would sneak along the streets, in the hope of avoiding Mr Moody and a reprimand. When I had almost reached home, he would stand before me with his hand outstretched and a sad look, and would greet me with, "Why, Jennie, where have you been? I missed you at Sabbath school. I hope you were not ill? Your folks are well? You will not disappoint me this coming Sabbath will you? It will make me very sad indeed if you fail me." '

He mobilized his friends in systematic slum visiting. 'We used to carry with us bread tickets,' wrote J B Stillson, 'and a little money to relieve the sick, widows and orphans, and had an arrangement with several physicians to visit the poor and sick without charge, also to furnish night watches.'

Moody was most persistent. In an upper flat above a store in North Clark Street lived six children who were, in the memory of the people below, 'noisy and ill-bred, and the father (a giant in size) was habitually drunk and violently abusive to his tiny wife, who supported the family as best she could by washing and scrubbing. Mr Moody went again and again to try to convert the drunken father. Almost every day they would receive baskets of groceries, fruit, coal or cordwood.'

On whisky he waged ceaseless war, which Betsey would have approved however she might sigh over Dwight's evangelical fervour. At one slum house, the father absent, Moody found in Farwell's words, 'not only children but a jug of whisky. He took both out of the house, the children to his school, and the jug of whisky to sprinkle the streets with.' Next visit the irate father roared, 'Did you pour away my whisky?', taking off his coat and rolling up his sleeves, 'I'll thrash you!'

'I broke the jug for the good of yourself and family. If I am to be thrashed, let me pray for you all before you do it.'

Moody's heartfelt prayer on the tenement floor was different from the whining cant the man expected from preachers. Shame-facedly he mumbled, 'You had better just take the kids, not a whip-ping.'

Moody was as prodigal in time as in energy. A small girl – the story was all over Chicago – promised she would take Moody home to get her mother's consent to her joining the school; first, said the girl, she must do an errand, if the kind gentleman would wait on the street corner.

The kind gentleman waited no less than three hours, in vain. A few days later he caught sight of her. She fled. He chased. She flew along the raised plank sidewalks, Moody after her, clattering down and up the steps where the levels varied, dodging the horse-drawn tram, scattering dogs and old ladies, until she dived through an alley, Moody after her, into a saloon and up the stairs to a bedroom, Moody after her, and under the bed. Moody, perspiring, breathless, coaxed her out. 'And when,' as one of his friends said, 'he drew that little girl from under the bed, he drew a whole family into heaven.'

This daily extravagance of stamina on indifferent diet brought such frequent shadows under the eyes that John Farwell gave his twenty-three-year-old friend a little piebald Indian pony. Thereaf-ter a mounted Moody clopped by on his rounds, with a basket of oranges behind or small boys riding pillion, and a tail of older boys scraping through the mud on their home-made wooden handslides taking a tow, and the risk that Moody with a burst of laughter might drop somebody's rope. He was on the pony when D W Whittle, fresh in from the Connecticut Valley and afterwards one of his clos-est associates and dearest friends, first saw him. 'As I was passing up Clark Street someone on the sidewalk said, "There goes Crazy Moody". I turned, looked down the street and saw a young man riding a small pony, his trousers in his bootlegs, a cap on his head.'

The pony was a powerful aid to recruitment. Seventeen years later Moody could claim: 'Some of the most active men in Chi-cago were little barefooted boys once picked up in the lanes and the by-ways.' The same element of shameless bribery with best intentions pervaded the North Market Hall. Clara Goldy remembered how 'the children would always find a bag of peanuts, popcorn, apples, and candies, topped with an orange, awaiting them at the foot of the stairs, and it was quite an inducement. A wash basket full of these bags was always in reserve.'

Sparks flew too. There was a boy who made his teacher's life a misery and disrupted neighbouring classes. At length Moody told Farwell, 'I am going to take that boy into the police office below and whip him, and when you see me start for him have the school rise and sing the loudest hymn in the book until I return.' Farwell did so, 'and when Mr Moody returned, his face was very red from this religious exercise. In a month's time the boy became a Christian and a great help to his teacher', and many years later an active supporter of Moody's Chicago Campaign of 1876.

Stories soon clustered round this self-appointed children's missionary: how, when Irish boys broke the Hall windows and beat up scholars in the streets, Moody called on the Roman Catholic bishop, the famous James Duggan, and actually had him praying with a Protestant; how, when drunken fathers rushed at him with shillelaghs, he took to his heels, not trusting his quick temper and hefty fists to remain lamb-like under the blows.

A boy whom he had been asked to secure for the school proved to be the son of a saloon keeper. Moody 'had never been in a saloon in my life. I walked by the door about a dozen times. I said, "I can't go there, people will think that I have come to get a drink."' He looked left and right, saw no prying deacon, and went in. 'The old father was behind the bar, and when I told him what I came for he said, "We won't have any canting hypocrites here", and I went out quicker than I came in. I went in a second time and again he drove me out. I went back the third time and the old man wasn't quite so drunk or quite so cross, but he said he would rather have his sons drunkards and his daughters harlots than Christians.' Having discovered that the fellow edited a cheap rationalist rag, Moody waded through Tom Paine's *The Age of Reason* in return for a promise to read the New Testament.

One Sunday morning Moody said, 'I wish you would go to church with me.'

'I haven't been to church for eighteen years.' He gave a vigorous rub to the gin glass he was polishing. 'No, I won't go. But you may have a church here if you want to.'

Moody was shocked. '*A church in a saloon*?' It was the only way to the man's heart. Afraid of deacons' disapproval, Moody set the hour at a time when they would all be in a proper church. The saloon keeper said: 'I want you to understand, young man, that you are not to do all the preaching.'

'What do you mean?'

'I may want to say something, and my friends may want to say a word. We won't let you preach all the time. We may want to answer back.'

The atheists were allotted forty-five minutes, Moody fifteen ('The fact was, I didn't think I could preach for more than fifteen minutes'), and the press of infidels itching to mince him made necessary a move to a larger room down the street. In support he had brought one of his best boys, very small for his age; but Moody felt 'a scared man. I shook from head to foot.'

'They began to poke questions at me, but I said, "No sir. You have got to preach forty-five minutes."' They did so, until Moody was 'sick and tired of infidelity'. Then he said, 'Let us pray'.

They protested. He knelt. They jeered and sneered as he prayed aloud. He called up his reinforcements, and Moody's instinct was right: the small boy created a sensation when 'with a pleading voice [he] prayed God to forgive these men for talking so against his dear Son'. It was a saccharine scene, but the atheists, silenced, began to steal away. The old saloon keeper said, 'If that is what you teach your children, you may have mine.'

So the school grew. Moody had felt when in business that he 'got the children for one hour in the week and the devil had them all the rest'. The balance was righted. 'I have been holding meetings in my school every night this winter,' he wrote home, 'it has taken all of my time.'

As, from the platform, his eye roved over grateful if dirty 'parishioners', or as he greeted a thousand ragged scholars jostling into the Hall, or mounted his pony to ride the back-streets, or accosted a recalcitrant parent, Moody had no doubt he had found his life's work – the years would be devoured in the confined sphere of the Chicago slums serving generations of children.

6: Drums in Tennessee

Abraham Lincoln, President-elect, spent Sunday, November 25th, 1860, in Chicago. At the invitation of Farwell, who on a brief excursion into politics had been prominent for Lincoln, he agreed to visit Moody's school provided they expected no speech. He attended morning service at St James's Episcopal Church, and left a luncheon early when Farwell called for him.

Cheered to the echo, Lincoln sat through the opening hymns and prayers. He rose to go. Moody then naughtily announced, 'Mr Lincoln has come to see the school on condition that *he be not asked to speak*. But if he wishes to say a word before leaving, we all have our ears open.'

Lincoln strode slowly to the centre of the Hall. He stopped, looked around, and said: 'I was once as poor as any boy in the school, but I am now President of the United States, and if you attend to what is taught you here, some one of you may yet be President of the United States.'

After that, and being from Boston and living in the city of which Lincoln affirmed, 'After Boston, Chicago has been the chief instrument of bringing this war on the country', there could be no two opinions for Moody: he was strong for Union and Abolition, rated Southerners nothing but slave-holding rebels, the Civil War plain conflict between good and evil; and between 1861 and 1865 would probably have snorted at reports of the winds of deep spiritual life that swept the Southern ranks.

When Lincoln called for volunteers after Fort Sumter, seventy-five members of Moody's school joined the colours; Jimmy Sexton rose to be a colonel. Moody stayed behind primarily because he would not abandon his Mission; and he had a somewhat nebulous personal pacifism ('I felt that I could not take a gun and shoot down a fellow being. In this respect I am a Quaker') which did not dampen zeal in recruiting.

At the outbreak of war a military city of tents, barrack huts, parade grounds, guard rooms, to mobilize and train the citizen army flocking in from the north-west, was thrown together a few miles south of Chicago, near the site of the future Illinois Institute of Technology, and called Camp Douglas. Moody and Benjamin Franklin Jacobs, the young real-estate agent who was his opposite number in the North Star Sunday School, were deputed to provide religious ministrations in the Camp by the committee of a new, small, struggling organization the name of which had little significance as yet in Chicago: the Young Men's Christian Association. Its principal activity had been a prayer meeting held daily at noon in the Association rooms at the Methodist Episcopal church block. When in May 1861 Moody put his activities under its wing and was appointed 'Librarian, with the understanding that he shall act as Agent for the Association, and City Missionary', these grandiloquent titles covered the fact that he was 'all there was to it officially'.

At Camp Douglas Moody and his friends began regular services, and reaped the harvest of which they had dreamed. The soil was fertile. The war brought out qualities and defects dormant in the American character. Sheltered lads from farm or forge were thrown into the rough barrack life where excitement and puzzlement, and all the temptations they had been warned against by pious mothers in frame houses or log cabins, swirled around them in a heady atmosphere of manly toughness and boyish simplicity.

'From the commencement the interest in these meetings was very great,' runs the dry account in the YMCA Report. 'To supply an immediate demand for hymn books, an edition of 3,500 was printed from plates of the Sabbath School Union. The work enlarging an Association Army Committee was appointed... The meetings at the camp continued to increase in interest until as many as eight or ten were held each evening, and hundreds were led to seek Christ.' Every night Moody would return with packs of surrendered playing-cards which, rather oddly, he stored away carefully in a corner of the YMCA rooms.

'I am all taken up with this,' he wrote in June to his mother. She had complained of desultory correspondence. 'Oh no Mother,' he replied, 'I think of you as often as ever I did but if I could see you & tell you how the Lord is blessing me in my labors I think you would say God Bless you, go forward... I am drove more now than ever in my life,' for he had Sunday school conventions and his own school too.

Camp Douglas, especially when casualty lists began to appear and the war ceased to resemble a picnic, burned into Moody the sacredness of the individual; each one mattered; each of these cheery boys might be soon a sprawling corpse in some southern wood or wheatfield, each needed the gift and assurance of eternal life.

It faced him, too, with a personal problem: he could not rely solely on Jacobs or others who knew how to preach; as Emma wrote, 'when he was called to meet the soldiers he felt that he must tell them, at every opportunity, of the power of Christ to *save*'. Moody must conquer his shyness in addressing men of his own age or older; he could not stifle the desire to 'talk with you about my Saviour that seems so near me – Oh what would life be without Christ'.

Never had Moody felt more aware of his poor attainments. Daniel McWilliams, a young accountant, a Presbyterian, was present at a small dinner given in the summer of 1861 by Reynolds of Peoria to enable ministers and laymen to meet his friend of the railway carriage. Their dominant impressions, wrote McWilliams, were Moody's 'earnestness in seeking to lead persons to the Saviour, and his intense thirst for the knowledge of the Bible; for the entire dinner time was taken by Mr Moody in quoting verses and in asking the ministers to tell him "What does this verse mean?"'

Farwell said of Camp Douglas that it was Moody's 'kindergarten of training'. He received quick promotion. In the autumn he went, by invitation of the chaplain of an Illinois regiment which masked its city origins with the glorious title of Zouaves, to visit their camp at Elizabethtown in Kentucky, near Lincoln's birthplace. The regimental newspaper reported that 'the active missionary of the YMCA of Chicago... has labored incessantly both day and night in distributing books, papers, tracts, hymnbooks etc' and added, with more truth than grammar, 'His advice and example convinces and converts'. In the improvisations of the Civil War an unordained chaplain was not improbable; but Emma records that Moody's 'friends in Chicago begged him not to join the army as chaplain as some of the soldiers urged, feeling that he could do more for the soldiers by being free rather than to confine himself to one regiment'.

Chicago, sobered by this strange, sad war of brothers' blood, pregnant with fear for sons and lovers, where crêpe hung on doors and maimed ex-soldiers searched miserably for work, where liveli-hoods had been blasted yet profiteers fattened, awarded Moody, for the present, a broad measure of respect and admiration.

He was ceaseless in city and camp. 'I have some 500 or 800 people,' he wrote to his favourite brother Samuel on a bitter January day in 1862, 'that are dependent on me for their daily food & new ones coming all of the time. I keep a sadall horse to ride around with to hunt up the poore people with & then I have a man to waite on the folks as thay come to my office. I make my headquarters at the roomes of the Young Mens Christian Association & then I have just raised money enough to erect a chapall for the soldiers at the camp 3 miles from the city. I hold a meetig down thare evry day & 2 in the city so you see I have 3 meetigs to atend to every day be side calling on the sick & that is not all I have to go into the countrey about every week to buy wood & provision for the poore also coal wheet meal & corn...'

For his preaching, 'I do not get 5 minuets a day to study so I have to talk just as it happens... I do not answer one letter out of 10 that I get - I cannot get time - it is 11 to 12 every night when I retire & am up in the morning at light... I wish you could come in some time about 1 to 3 o'clock my office hours and see the people wait-ing to see me.'

Allowing a discount for Moody's purpose in writing – to show why Northfield letters went unanswered – this discloses the man a few weeks before his twenty-fifth birthday: not slothful in business, fervent in spirit, but with a dangerous assumption, nearly to wreck him a few years later, that godliness must be measured principally in terms of ceaseless action: 'Go to church all you can, as many prayer meetings as you can'. None, however, would quarrel with his motto: 'Do all you can to make the world better than you found it. Do all you can for Christ and then you will make others happy.'

Haphazard voluntary services for relief, welfare and religion in the Federal armies were at length co-ordinated by the formation of the United States Christian Mission, a private organization with official sanction, somewhat a mixture of Red Cross, NAAFI, and auxiliary chaplains' department. Farwell became President of the North-Western Branch. Moody, inevitably, served frequently as one of the delegates to the front (they received expenses but no pay).

In February 1862 when the unknown Grant rose to fame by capturing Fort Donelson on the Cumberland in Tennessee, and coining the term 'unconditional surrender', Moody was down from Chicago among the casualties. 'I tell you you do not know how roughley the poore fellows are treated. I was on the battlefield before they had buried the dead, it was awful to see the dead laying around without being anyone to burrey them.' On return home he was sent immediately with further supplies for the wounded.

The following month Grant fought the ghastly Battle of Shiloh or Pittsburgh Landing, a partial defeat though inducing Confederate withdrawal. An emergency call to Chicago brought a train-load of extra doctors, nurses, medical students, organized by the YMCA for the Christian Commission. 'In the forward end of the car was Mr Moody conducting a prayer meeting', noticed a medical student as he settled for the night; 'in the rear end was a company of men playing cards'.

Shattered limbs, gangrene, amputations often without chloroform, deaths which might have been avoided had medical science and hygiene advanced a little further, sharpened Moody's acute sensitiveness to human want in all its forms, the certainty that his urgent message could make an immediate difference to a man's eternity, his anxiety to get an honest answer to his constant question in the presence of death, 'Are you a Christian?'

'Coming down the Tennessee River we had four hundred and fifty wounded men on board. A good many of them were mortally wounded.' Moody and his companions 'made up their minds we would not let a man die on the boat without telling him of Christ and heaven – we would tell them of Christ as we gave them a cup of cold water.' Moody came upon a youth dying from shock and loss of blood. He gave the boy brandy and water in the hope that he would briefly recover consciousness.

The casualty next on the deck said they were buddies, from the same company, the same town, had enlisted together and that the dying boy was the only son of a widow. Moody knew that the mother 'would be anxious to get some message from her boy, and I asked if she was a Christian. He said, Yes, she is a godly woman.'

At intervals Moody called the lad's name, and at length his eyes opened. Moody gave him another sip of brandy and water.

'William, do you know where you are?'

'Oh, yes,' he murmured, 'I am on my way home to mother.'

'The doctor told me you cannot live. Have you any message to send to your mother?'

'Tell my mother... that... I died trust in Christ.'

Moody's heart leaped – 'it seemed as if I was at the very gate of heaven.' He said: 'Is there anything else?'

The boy's eyes closed. 'Yes, tell my mother and sister... to be sure and meet me... in heaven.'

It was the authentic voice of the old American frontier, deep in simple piety and love of home, speaking to the man who, unknown to himself, was being bred to proclaim the old, sure foundations to the garish age being born.

Emma Revell, who had fallen in love with a prosperous shoe-salesman, become engaged to a children's missioner, and was now about to marry a six-horse Jehu, wondered where it would end.

They married in Chicago on Thursday, August 28th, 1862, and went 'away on my weding tower', as Moody described it.

In June he had been back to Northfield where his heart so often strayed. 'I am homesick' had been a constant theme; 'Tell mother she does not know how good a letter would seem if it was penned with her own hand... As she never was away from her mother she cannot tell how good it seems to get a letter from a mother.' He was always generous to the family, beyond his means, and concerned for their affairs. He yearned to 'see my mother and all my brothers and sisters converted to God'. The 'very pleasant time' in Northfield, supposed to be a holiday, he transformed into a mission which created enough stir for some twenty-five townsfolk to come and see him off at the station. Two of his brothers started a prayer meeting, but Betsey's prejudice deepened because Dwight was about to marry a girl English-born and a Baptist.

They settled in a tiny house on the North Side (Chicago divided itself into the then fashionable South Side, south of Chicago River, and the slummy North Side), where Emma continued at short range the long, slow task of taming Moody, to make him the man she saw he could be. She was 'before everything else practical and orderly'. She threw away those patent shirts he was so proud of that did not, he claimed, need washing for weeks on end. She failed, for the time, to make him eat regular or ample meals. She remained unflustered by the cascade of improbable events which made every day an adventure.

Her achievement may be gauged by the change she wrought, so gently and imperceptibly that he could say at the end of his life: 'she was the only one who never tried to hold me back from anything I wanted to do and was always in sympathy with every new venture.'

Samuel Moody, the ailing, lovable twin with political and intellectual interests, who merely smiled when Moody talked of religion, had come to stay in the autumn of 1862 with a view to finding work in Chicago. 'Dwight is run from morning to night,' he wrote. 'He hardly gets time to eat. Camp Douglas is situated here (there is about 17,000), he holds meetings down there most every night – it is a treat to go down there and hear the soldiers sing, which is about 300 or 400 gathered as they come from most every state. The Rebel prisoners are among them.' These were Fort Donelson men. Moody was quite hurt when they refused to sing out of hymn-books decorated with stars and stripes. And Farwell had 'never seen him so excited' as at the discovery of the famous conspiracy to break out and burn Chicago.

Emma says he went to the front nine times. He was under fire in January 1863, among the wounded at the sanguinary battle of Murfreesboro or Stone River, as Rosencrans pushed for Nashville. He watched the dying find peace as he ministered, until the certainty drilled into his consciousness that a man may know immediate, assured salvation. Moody was reaping a well-sown field, for few of the generation that fought the Civil War lacked a background of basic Christian teaching; but he was under no illusions about the 'evil ways' of men calloused by battle and barrack.

'Chaplain, help me to die,' whispered a casualty of Murfreesboro, in the small hours. 'I've been fighting Christ all my life. I had a praying mother and I disregarded her prayers always.'

Moody, Bible in hand, repeated promise after Scripture promise, 'but he could not see them and I got nearly discouraged'. Moody started to read the story of Nicodemus from St John's Gospel. 'As I read on, his eyes became rivetted upon me, and he seemed to drink in every syllable.'

The comforting Yankee accents cut into the thick atmosphere of the ward. '"And as Moses lifted up the serpent in the wilderness, even so must the Son of man be lifted up: that whosoever believeth in Him should not perish, but have eternal life".'

The soldier feebly put up a hand. '*What's* that? Is that true? I want you just to read that again... That's good! Won't you read it *again*?'

As Moody read the third time, the dim candlelight showed that the man's 'troubled expression had given way to a peaceful smile'. The orderly next morning, by the empty cot, said the man had died restfully, murmuring the words of promise.

Moody, a quick learner where his heart was engaged, was seen to move and speak in the wards 'as though the special study of his life had been the wants of sick men'. Nor was it thus in hospitals only, or distributing magazines and games among convalescents. The diffident amateur of 1861 had become, by the fourth year of the war, a practised if homespun preacher. 'I was bringing together my Fourth Army Corps,' wrote Major-General Oliver Otis Howard, of those spring days of 1864 in Tennessee when Sherman mobilized for the Atlanta campaign and the march to the sea. 'Two divisions had already arrived and were encamped in and near Cleveland. Our soldiers were just about to set out on what we all felt promised to be a hard and bloody campaign, and I think we were especially desirous of strong preaching. Crowds and crowds turned out to hear Moody. He showed them how a soldier could give his heart to God. His preaching was direct and effective, and multitudes responded with a promise to follow Christ.'

An infantryman of the 96th Illinois 'went to the meetings one night and was much impressed with his earnestness. I wasn't at the time a Christian, though the thought had come to me that it would be well to begin the Atlanta campaign a soldier of Christ as well as a soldier of my country. The next morning, or soon after, I went to my dog tent, opened a little copy of the New Testament which some men of the Christian Commission had given to me, and then and there began to read and pray my way into the kingdom of Christ. The joy of salvation came to me after a few days. I have always looked on Mr Moody as my spiritual father.'

Moody did not march through Georgia, nor see Corse's men hold the fort at Altoona, which was to inspire the most famous of 'Moody and Sankey' songs.

Great matters were stirring in Chicago.

7: The Rescue Shop

In autumn 1862 the North Market Hall had been partly burned in spite of the fire engines below. For about a year Moody transferred his Sunday school to the more dilapidated Kinzie Hall. Numbers dropped. The school had to be nursed back to strength.

Moody never ceased to conjure new tricks to win recruits. He picked a dozen or fifteen of the raggedest boys, their names eloquent of their condition: Smikes, Madden the Butcher, Darby the Cobbler, Jackey Candles, Black Stove Pipe; and promised a new suit to each who attended every Sunday until Christmas. He made them into a class under Farwell. All but two won their suits and Farwell called this uniformed set 'Moody's Bodyguard'. Moody had it photographed before and after the issue of suits and circulated the pictures, the first captioned 'Does it Pay?', the second 'It does Pay'. In at least one case it did pay: thirteen years later a colleague of Moody was told by a railway-office manager to go and 'pick out the worst looking one in the lot, and you will see your humble servant, now a church member and a Sunday school worker'. But Moody began to doubt bribery: his City Relief Society was fooled too often. 'I came to the conclusion that a loaf of bread in one hand and the Gospel in the other was wrong.' Succour of the sick and destitute continued to absorb much of his time as a Christian ministry in itself; Moody had no patience with those who preached bliss in heaven while doing nought about misery on earth.

His Sunday school's famous picnics were more an outflow of his own exuberance than a deliberate attraction. He 'loved contests and games of skill', his sons used to say; Farwell only went once because he claimed that the 'physical exercise to keep up with Mr Moody in a race was too much for me'. 'Few at the picnics were his equal in racing, jumping or other sports,' remembers another helper, and Moody liked to show it. He seized a heavy barrel of apples and ran ahead of the horde, tipping out a trail of apples which the smaller boys picked up while the older ones chased him to try for the lot; he kept ahead until a naughty bystander tripped him.

To play a practical joke on Moody was paying him his own coin. The teachers once wanted a swim in the Lake, nicely secluded but reached only by wading through a bog. A young dandy shirked the mud. 'Finally, Mr Moody, with a mischievous twinkle, said, "Mr C, you get on my back and I will carry you across." All went well until the middle of the swamp, when Mr C with white vest and lavender pants, was unhorsed and had to help himself to terra firma.'

A joke with a streak of cruelty was sport to Moody right to the end of his life. As Paul Moody wrote: 'While the tenderest-hearted man in the world, he would enjoy laughing at something the victim did not consider so excruciatingly funny.' And when young Paul (at a time when Moody must have been in his late fifties) had a fracas with infuriated bees, 'worse than the stings of the bees was the sight of my father actually rolling on the ground with laughter, but at a safe distance.' There was a grain of truth in the family proverb: 'No Moody ever laughs at anything unless blood is drawn.'

On December 26th, 1863, Emma wrote to Sam, 'The building for the Sunday School is almost completed, the plastering is being done now and we hope to get in the building in a few weeks. We need it badly for the hall gets worse every Sunday. We expect to have good meetings when it is finished as several prominent clergymen from different cities have promised to come and preach for us...'

This new building, the first to be owned by the Mission School, was erected in Illinois Street between La Salle and Wells, two blocks from Kinzie, at a cost of $24,000 subscribed by Farwell and many others, with pittances from parents and scholars. It was opened in the early months of 1864, 'a queer looking brick building' with some resemblance to a church. 'Houses crowd it on either side so as to scarcely leave room for it to stand upon. It looks almost as if pains had been taken to make it as plain as possible so that no one, however poor, might be driven away by any outward display.' On the right side of the entrance stood a gilt sign: 'Ever Welcome To This House of God Are Strangers And The Poor', and a notice, 'The Seats Are Free'. The interior was decked with texts 'neatly done in scroll and panel', the wall behind the platform proclaimed 'God is Love'. On entering 'You faced the classes, which were chairs in a circle, the teacher's chair being designated by a silken banner bearing the number of the class and also a Scripture verse. These banners were in different colors, their poles being fastened to the chair-back so they would stand upright. With the sun shining in the room, these banners of many bright colors and the rosy, happy faces

of the children surrounding them, made a most beautiful picture.'
It is doubtful if the slum children's faces were rosy.

Flanking the doorway, two Bible class rooms, one for each sex,
had glass partitions which could be thrown back to enlarge the hall.
Above, another glass partition made an area for an infants' class or
for a reception room where guests could watch proceedings below
while the superintendent (as Moody was in name now, as in fact)
extolled his system and pointed out his teachers. He had a small
library upstairs too, where he could interview.

On either side ran a gallery. Charley Morton, a discharged soldier in his twenties who had lost his right arm at Williamsburg and
drank heavily to deaden the pain, was idling with two or three pals
one Sunday afternoon when they happened to pass the building.
'People seemed to be going in, men, women and children, as though
they belonged there, and we turned in too, to see what it was.' The
usher said, 'The gallery is for young men.'

They found themselves under an assistant whose 'hair was very
long, his trousers very short, and he was nervous. He talked very
loud in teaching the lesson, and I saw very soon that he didn't know
very much about the lesson himself. The boys wanted to leave, but
I said, "Let's see this out".' Charley Morton never forgot the impact of the whole school singing, 'Do you know any little barefoot
boy?' and its doggerel chorus, which evokes the very atmosphere
of Moody's Mission:

> *Go bring him in, there is room to spare,*
> *Here are food and shelter and pity;*
> *And we'll not shut the door*
> *'Gainst one of Christ's poor*
> *Though you bring every child in the city.*

Morton looked down as they sang, 'and I noticed most of the
boys and girls were poor looking, some barefoot, and most of the
teachers seemed to be well dressed and altogether different from
the scholars, and I said to myself "Well, there isn't much looking
after money here. They won't get much pay for looking after those
boys and girls", and I made up my mind I would come again, and I

did. And it was not long after before I put my hand in Jesus Christ's hand, where it has been ever since.'

Farwell once asked a small boy why he walked three miles every week to Illinois Street when there was a school near his home. He replied: 'They love a fellow over here.'

When Moody went south in the spring of 1864 before Sherman's Atlanta campaign, his Mission in Chicago not only had a new home, but was developing alarming possibilities.

In North Market Hall days adults had attended on week-day evenings at the old saloon and there, in Emma's words, 'many souls were born of God'. Moody exhorted converts to join city churches, but 'some of the poorer ones felt strangely in the more beautiful church buildings'. When the Mission secured a permanent home and held meetings every night they wanted to make that their church. The 'gathering' of a new church was neither unusual nor difficult under Congregational custom. Moody hesitated. His Mission was not Congregationalist but united, its one formal link being to the YMCA. Constantly he would say: 'If I thought I had one drop of sectarian blood in my constitution, I would open a vein and let it out.'

The converts pressed. For them it must be Illinois Street, or they would be sheep scattered and unfed.

Moody yielded. It would seem that Sunday evening services were held that summer. At the end of 1864, on December 20th, 'a meeting of the most interested in the movement was held', so runs the official *Manual of Illinois Street Church* printed in 1867, 'and the opinion was unanimous that a church should be formed. All were agreed that it must be independent of all denominational connection, since those already gathered in the work represented nearly every evangelical denomination. It was therefore voted that the church be an Independent Church.' A half-hearted scheme to entrust the oversight to some Council of Chicago Churches came to naught. Moody and two friends drew up a simple doctrinal statement, and articles of organization based on Congregational custom. At Emma's behest a baptistry as well as a font allowed adult or infant baptism.

Moody invited students from the Chicago Theological Seminary (Congregational) to fill the pulpit until, in Farwell's memory,
'one of them failed to appear, when I suggested that it was provi-
dential, and that he must take the pulpit himself. He finally consented, and from that time he was wanted every Sunday'. Students
preached in the mornings, Moody in the evenings; he found a formal sermon alarmingly different from extempore talking to troops
or children. 'It was hard work for him to preach in those early days,'
a Chicago minister remembered. 'One day I found him in his room
trying to get up a sermon. He had thrown off his coat and was
struggling with his Bible and a concordance, while the sweat ran
down his face.' (This may have been back in July 'sixty-four, when
he had written, 'I have gained 20 lbs since last summer – I am so
fat that I have to sweat a good deal for it this hot weather.')

The Seminary desired to regularize the ecclesiastical position
by having Moody ordained at once as a Congregationalist minister, bad grammar and all. He could then administer the sacraments
himself.

'What do you think about my being ordained?' he asked his
ministerial friend G S F Savage.

'Don't,' replied Savage. 'If you are ordained you will be on the
level with the rest of us. Now you are a preaching layman and that
gives you an advantage. You are on the right road, keep to it.'

Moody declined the Congregationalist offer. In 1865 he enrolled
as a student in the newly-formed Baptist Theological Seminary.
How many lectures he attended is obscure; he did not proceed,
never was ordained. Had he become a minister of one denomination he would not, in that generation, have attracted from ministers
of other denominations the broad support where lay much of his
secret. As Farwell commented, 'He had more power as a layman,
and as such he was more welcome in union meetings, which were
his ambition and delight.' Certainly neither the Church of Scotland
nor the Church of England would have co-operated. He would not
have become a national influence in Britain or in America, but
remained unknown to history.

He stayed lay pastor until 1866, when a young man was or-

dained to the pastorate and Moody retained the title of superintendent, and effective control.

The making of the Illinois Street Independent Church symbol-
ized that Moody's Mission no longer was a Sunday school with
extensions, but an all-age rescue shop within a yard of hell. Eccle-
siastically, however, it could have formed the basis of the new denomination which Moody in years to come was urged to found,
and refused; or might have sidetracked him into a 'No Church'
movement like the Plymouth Brethren. It did neither. Instead, it
was a useful proving ground for methods later to be used among
the tens of thousands drawn to meetings in London, Philadelphia,
New York, which to Moody were Illinois Street writ large.

There is no evidence that he sported a clergyman's white necker-
chief, but he worked himself somewhat into the image, his sermons
clerical, his tone strident, his theme smelling of brimstone to an
extent that made even Emma admit that she 'cringed' as he painted
terrors of divine judgment. While a children's missioner Moody
had not been face to face with degradation in those he sought to
save; it formed their background only. As a missioner to all ages he
was confronted, inescapably, with human nature at its worst, and
reacted in the way traditional to mission preachers of his day. 'I
preached that God hated sinners; that he was standing behind sinners
with a double-edged sword, ready to cut off the heads of sinners.'

A dichotomy appeared in D L Moody. From the pulpit he stressed
stridently the wrath of God, in the tradition of the old camp meetings. In personality he remained genial, buoyant, bubbling with
love and merriment. Watts de Golyer, a deacon at Illinois Street,
said, that in the Moody home 'it was not an infrequent occurrence
to hear peals of laughter over some joke administered mainly by
the host, or somebody trying to get even with him. I well remember a rule adopted and passed by himself that hereafter any person
failing to hang up his hat or coat on the rack would find it in the
yard, and the result was, shortly afterwards that I was busily employed finding and separating my belongings in the yard. I would
not have you think that the sole and only topic discussed or thought
of in the minds of those composing it was that of religion, but it

was as much the absorbing theme and desire, as to temper and sweeten everything else.'

Meanwhile, on October 24th, 1864, the first child had been born, and named Emma Reynolds. 'Both of her little fingers are as crooked as mine,' Moody told his mother in December. 'They all say she looks like me but I must say I cannot see any resemblance.' Emma could. The resemblance grew. When the child was two: 'She is so full of mischief. You would certainly think she was a second edition of D L Moody in his childhood.'

Before the baby was six months old Emma left her temporarily in the care of Mrs Revell and accompanied Moody to Grant's army for the climax of the Civil War. They were at the great base of City Point, near Hampton, as casualties flowed from the last battles in Virginia. Moody claimed to be among the first to enter fallen Richmond, ministering to the wounded of both sides, freed slaves, and Federals liberated from the horrors of Libby Prison.

8: 'Brutally Ridiculed.'

Discharged soldiers streamed into Chicago. The city leaped to seize fortunes out of Reconstruction. Moody flung himself more deeply into the work of the YMCA, long one of the apples of his eye.

At the noon meeting he was a familiar figure except for his whiskers, which he had altered three or four times as if to ape the latest war hero, until he settled on a smart, short, rounded beard, lengthened in the early 'seventies to the dark, wavy forest that Great Britain came to know. 'A stocky, bustling Simon Peter sort of man standing at the door and shaking hands with all who entered,' a student described him. A country boy attending commercial school was 'miserable, lonesome and homesick in the great city amid its great throngs who passed me by in restless haste and left me alone. Even in my boarding-house no attention was paid to me. In my desperate loneliness I dropped into the noonday meetings. I can never forget that Mr Moody was first to grasp my hand and inquire all about me.'

They sang. They had a brief Scripture reading. They prayed extempore, 'no long speeches or prayers tolerated' – a breath of fresh
air which Moody was to blow upon wider fields of American and
British religion. Requests poured in from city and countryside, to
be read out by Jacobs, Moody, Major Whittle or whoever was leader
for the day. At an affecting plea from some mother whose son had
succumbed to city temptations, Moody would weep unashamedly;
in him lay always something of the impressionable child, never far
from tears, never far from laughter. 'Mr D L Moody is so earnest,
aggressive and regardless of all namby-pamby notions of propriety
in his work that he occasionally shocks the exceedingly proper people. At other times he is known to betray them into a laugh, a veritable guffaw right in prayer meeting.'

Moody and his friends of the YMCA were not pietists; they sent
the State Legislature a petition for the establishment of a Board of
Health, they set up a committee to investigate the flouting of Sunday liquor laws. But the introduction of so much as a chess set had
to await the next decade. Activities were centred on bringing their
constituency to face the issues of heaven and hell, belief and unbelief. And to urge action. 'I want a faith's got legs 'n c'n run around,'
Moody would say. The Chicago YMCA published and distributed
tracts and a four-page paper; administered charity, helped in a chol-
era epidemic, Moody risking his life again and again. And he ran
an informal bureau to trace prodigal sons lurking in the Chicago
underworld.

In 1866 the Presidency of the Chicago Association was offered
to a prominent businessman, an energetic, able supporter. He refused. 'We have been talking about a building,' he said. 'We need a
man who has the time, the holy purpose and the faith in God to
make this project a success. I nominate Dwight L Moody for President and John V Farwell for Vice-President.'

Some members said: 'Many of our church people count Moody
as too radical.' But, at twenty-nine, he became President.

Without delay 'Moody was on the warpath securing subscriptions' – thus they described the energy with which Moody badgered the worthy and wealthy of the city; he revelled in turning the

dollars of the rich into an institution which should, in a favourite phrase, 'do good'. Each subscriber was to receive stock and be repaid over ten years, it was hoped, from rents received by the YMCA for offices to be let in this magnificent new building, subsequent profits to go to city charities.

Cyrus Hall McCormick, a Presbyterian, inventor of the combine harvester which revolutionized prairie farming and brought him great fortune, promised no less than $10,000, and within a month the full sum of $199,000 had been pledged, Farwell, McCormick and George Armour the meat king being among the trustees. McCormick regarded 1866 as the year when he 'became sure of Mr Moody's great worth'. The Moodys were invited frequently to the millionaire's mansion. A contemporary describes 'points of similarity in the characters of these two men. Both had great earnestness and great sincerity, and both hewed out their career by hard strokes... Both of them were bright and cheery.'

Once in the late 'sixties (the year is uncertain) Moody rushed into the study of a Chicago minister, Harsha, with a sealed envelope. 'Open that!' he cried. 'Open it! There is a cheque for $2,000 in there.'

'How do you know? Have you seen it?'

'No. But I asked the Lord for it, and I know it's there! I came all the way across Chicago that you might prove my faith in prayer.'

Young W T Harsha 'stood by my father's side as he tore open the envelope. Truly enough, there was a $2,000 cheque within, payable to the order of Mr Moody and signed by Cyrus H McCormick.'

Moody bubbled out his story. He had gone to the millionaire: 'Mr McCormick, the Mission School is in dreadful straits!'

'Why, you are striking me rather hard of late. I gave you something not long ago.'

'I want a thousand.'

'A thousand! Why, surely you don't mean that, after all I've given you of late?' But he went upstairs to write the cheque.

'And then,' continued Moody, 'I thought to myself, what a fool I was not to ask for two thousand! And I fell on my knees there in the parlour, and asked for two thousand. Mr McCormick came downstairs with this sealed envelope. I thanked him, and rushed over to you. Isn't my faith confirmed?'

Old Mr Harsha was so bemused that he asked McCormick, 'Can you recall the inducements or influences acting on your mind leading you to make the cheque for twice the amount asked for?'

'Well, as I remember, I went upstairs to my desk and took out my cheque-book. I wrote in "D L Moody", and then I began to think of the noble work he is doing in our city, and what a splendid fellow he is. Finally I concluded to make the cheque for the amount I did.'

Long afterwards at Northfield the younger Harsha asked Moody about the incident. Moody replied: 'God gave me the money that day because I needed it. And He has always given me money when I needed it. But often I have asked Him when I thought I needed it, and He has said: "No, Moody, you just shin along the best way you can. It'll do you good to be hard up awhile." '

Whatever McCormick thought of him, Chicago's wartime respect for Moody had dissolved. 'He was often most brutally ridiculed and buffeted and persecuted,' recalled de Golyer. 'His language, his looks, his methods of work were made objects of ridicule and burlesque, and the most cruel remarks were passed from mouth to mouth about him.'

A journalist, then with the *Chicago Tribune*, Frederick Francis Cook, deploring Moody's 'early excrescences of manner', wrote that 'the established pulpit, especially in its higher or formal ranges, contended that he lowered religion. While the man about town judged him from the standpoint of ordinary social intercourse, and resented his intrusions... Aye, what a hustler he was in early days!... Always on the go, except when he might halt a stranger anywhere, to interrogate him on the state of his soul; and even when his amazed or abashed victim was gathering his wits to frame an answer suited to the astonishing occasion, off he would be to startle somebody else into "fits of salvation".'

'"Are you a Christian?" became an arrow point directed to every man, woman or child in Chicago,' wrote Farwell's daughter Abby,

then just out of the schoolroom and, like her father, Moody's devoted slave. 'He shouted it from the platform, he whispered it in
the narrow passageway, seated at your side at the dinner table, as
he joined you on the sidewalk, in fact, everywhere.'

He kept a vow in these years not to pass a day without speaking
to someone of Christ. 'Seeing a man leaning up against a lamp-
post, I went up to him and said, "Are you a Christian?" He damned
me and cursed me and told me to mind my own business.' The man
told a mutual friend that he had never been so insulted. Three months
later Moody was knocked up after midnight, 'and there stood this
stranger I had made so mad at the lamp-post', to confess that he
had known no peace: 'Oh, tell me what to do to be saved.'

Moody would not be intimidated. A Presbyterian called Potwin
happened to walk north up Wells Street 'just behind a big powerful
fellow, when Mr Moody, coming from the north, stopped him with
the question, "Are you a Christian?" The stranger was enraged, drew
back, and would have hit him a powerful blow had I not caught his
arm.' The *Tribune* shorthand clerks were interrupted (Moody had
come to insert a YMCA notice) with the abrupt question, 'Is Christ
among you?' In the startled silence, a middle-aged Scot slowly
removed his pipe and answered: 'Na, Maister Moody. He was here
a bit ago, but he's just stepped oot to see a friend round the corner.
He'll be sorry to miss ye. Will ye wait?'

Moody never laughed on such occasions. Nor would he betray
that he was sensitive to mockery: 'The most banal sallies left him
wholly unscathed.' William Reynolds told Whittle some years later
'how he used to be alone with Moody and often Moody would cry
at the abuse heaped upon him by those who misunderstood and
opposed him', but he had 'made up my mind to keep sweet ... you
cannot do any good unless you keep sweet.'

Farwell was urged, even by his wife, 'Why don't you tell him he
does more harm than good by shouting at people at every turn?'
When Farwell did so, Moody replied, 'You are not my boss. God is
my boss.'

Moody was heckled in the stockyards, was guyed and catcalled
outside the Court House. At the back of the crowd a young doctor

impressed by the preacher's 'dauntless manner' asked who he was. A bystander 'glanced at the speaker with a contemptuous smile and then said, "Why, that's Moody!"'

Moody drove his frame to its limits. 'I wish you would learn to eat your meals regularly,' Mrs Farwell would scold. 'You will undermine your health.' Emma must have said the same. He would not listen – then. Afterwards he admitted, 'I was an older man before thirty than I have been since.' In his frenzy to carry the city for Christ he was redeemed by humility – a willingness to listen, to learn, to experiment; by basic common sense, although not always obeying its dictates; and by Emma. But Moody was wrapped in the one ambition 'that every soul be saved'. He did not mind much what happened further, except that the saved be put to save others. 'I lived in Chicago knowing but *one* truth and thinking that the only necessary one, ignoring all related truths till I built up a wall of prejudice all around me.'

It would have been hard to imagine that Crazy Moody in a few years would hold the respect of Gladstone and President Grant, the affection of the Lord Chancellor of England, the gratitude of the Princess of Wales and the attention of millions of all sorts and conditions in Britain and the United States.

9: The Little Lancashire Lad

Had it not been for Emma's asthma Moody would have been a proof of Shakespeare's dictum,

> *...violent fires soon burn out themselves...*
> *He tires betimes that spurs too fast betimes.*

In occasional pauses on Moody's breakneck gallop he had brooded on visiting England. Conscious of spiritual and mental lack, knowing that in Chicago he never could detach himself from ceaseless scramble, there were three in England he yearned to meet.

George Williams, a London wholesale draper, was founder of the YMCA. George Müller of Bristol was the elderly German who prayed, and without capital or asking a soul for a penny maintained a large orphanage and numerous overseas missionaries (and lived to be ninety-three). Charles Haddon Spurgeon was Moody's senior by three years only, yet a preacher of fame; like him a rustic, virtually self-taught, jovial, rather stout. Spurgeon's sermons at the Metropolitan Tabernacle, his Baptist church in South London, fluttered all over the world; their homely language, fund of anecdote, humour, grasp of Scripture, made Moody greedy: 'everything that I could get hold of in print that he ever said, I read'.

Nothing would have come of Moody's hankerings for England had not asthma so pained Emma during the early winter of 1866-7 that the doctor advised a sea voyage; somehow Moody found the money. Mrs Revell promised to keep little Emma. On February 24th, 1867, D L Moody, just thirty, and his twenty-four-year-old wife steamed out of New York in the *City of Washington*, 'which is considered a very fine boat'.

Emma loved it, but, she wrote to her brother-in-law, 'Mr Moody was sick more or less from the time we started till the time we landed at Liverpool which was two weeks.' She was the sole lady among sixteen cabin-class passengers and had 'plenty of attention', even if 'rather a gay crowd' had 'no scruples about drinking champagne and wine and playing cards and even gambling for money at which I was much surprised and shocked'.

On reaching England the woebegone Moody, affirming that 'one trip across the water is enough for me', perpetrated one of the most exploded prophecies of the nineteenth century: 'I do not expect to visit this country again.'

They landed on a Sunday. Moody sermon-tasted. Emma contented herself with a Sunday school, 'which I thought rather a dull formal one and the room was very gloomy and dark'. Next day they sped from Liverpool to London by rail 'much faster than in America, at the rate of from 40 to 50 miles an hour and the cars do not stop to get water but scoop it up from a sort of ditch as they rush by without stopping'.

From Euston they took a growler 'a very long distance' through the City and the East End slums, where they saw barefoot boys in streets more grim than Chicago, to Poplar. Emma's uncle was a postmaster and lived at No 3 Pennyfields, near the West India dock, and here Emma and her younger sister Mary met after eighteen years.

The Moodys' first English surroundings were scarcely choice, and it rained or snowed most of that week. Early impressions made them both inclined to sniff, and forget that Emma was a Londoner. Moody wrote to his mother, 'I do not like the old country as well as our one, I must tell you how glad I am I was born and brought up in America.' He missed the informality, thought England must be a 'horrible place to live in'. Emma considered the City as sooty as Pittsburgh, the Bank of England timeworn, St Paul's Cathedral 'a very grand building but seemed to me more appropriate for any other kind of performance than for church service'.

Next Sunday they went to the Metropolitan Tabernacle. They had no tickets, but bluffed their way up to the gallery. Moody marvelled at the congregation of nearly five thousand, and as Spurgeon 'walked down to the platform, my eyes just feasted upon him, and my heart's desire for years was at last accomplished'. 'His manner is very simple,' Emma described the sermon, 'and he is a very plain looking man but had the undivided attention of his whole audience... And then the singing... So many voices mingled together in such harmony and good time seemed perfectly grand'. Moody longed to preach like that, to see singing led like that.

Moody duly visited Bristol to imbibe a heady draught of Müller's faith. In London he met George Williams, was invited to the annual breakfast of the original YMCA in Aldersgate Street, and prodded them into beginning a daily noon prayer meeting on the Chicago pattern; it was maintained unbroken until the First World War.

Through Frederick Hartley, secretary of the Sunday School Union, who had visited Illinois Street, the Moodys received several social invitations. They were taken to a House of Commons debate by an MP; Emma saw over Newgate Prison and the Bank. London seemed prettier with spring, 'in some parts most beautiful,

especially the parks and the square gardens'. By early May Emma
'liked the English better than when I first came. I do not think
them as reserved as I expected them, but do not think them as free
and open as Americans.' Moody enjoyed the sensation of being
appreciated. Episcopalians in Chicago had passed by on the other
side, or called him names; but Church of England clergy and laymen whom he met were kind. Evangelicals, Anglican and Nonconformist, took to him. His expansive geniality, his sincerity and drive
caused a religious newspaper to remark how with an unknown name
he had swiftly won his way 'deeply into the affections of a multitude of Christian brethren'.

May, in the Victorian age, was sacred to 'May meetings', that
sober succession of anniversaries for every mission and charity.
Moody wanted, American tourist style, to 'do' as many as possible,
and even hurried Emma across to Dublin and north to Edinburgh
where, on this first brief visit to the city that would, surprisingly,
become so familiar, she thought the wynds and street stairs and old
stone houses 'quaint'. In London he addressed the May meeting of
the Sunday School Union, at that Mecca of Evangelicals, Exeter Hall
in the Strand. He was allotted the moving of thanks to the chairman, the great philanthropist, Lord Shaftesbury. At the appropriate
moment the vice-chairman announced: 'We are very glad to welcome our American cousin, the Reverend Mr Moody of Chicago...'

Moody rose. He looked at the serried ranks of the godly, the
ladies' bonnets and crinolines, the whiskers and formal black of
the men; all sleepy and surfeited with speeches on a warm May
afternoon and thinking an American a sort of colonial who was not
quite English and had a vulgar accent.

Moody said: 'The vice-chairman has made two mistakes.' The
audience sat up. 'To begin with, I'm not "the Reverend Mr Moody"
at all. I'm plain Dwight L Moody, a Sabbath school worker. And
then I'm not your American cousin. By the grace of God I'm your
brother, who is interested, with you, in our Father's work for His
children. And now about this vote of thanks to the "noble Earl". I
don't see why we should thank him any more than he should thank
us...'

The audience gasped. Lord Shaftesbury, who had a great sense of humour and no pomposity, was delighted. Emma made a mental note to scold Moody — it is certain that five years later he never would have committed such a solecism.

The stuffy atmosphere had been too much. And he had cleared it. A young customs clerk, Tom Bond Bishop, soon to help found the Children's Special Service Mission, 'heard Mr Moody for the first time... I well remember how it thrilled the audience', as he urged them to have done with colourless catechisms and tedious verse-learning, and to act on the belief that children could trust in Christ as a Friend.

Both Moodys had strange experiences in Britain. Emma, travelling alone by train, entered what she supposed an empty compartment in which someone had left a bundle of old clothes. The train started. Out of the bundle a man's voice said, 'Do you know what I would have done with my wives if I had been Henry the Eighth?' He slid across to her side, leering. No trains had corridors in the eighteen sixties. The next stop lay twenty minutes on.

Emma, unrattled always, merely said, 'No, do tell me.' The maniac recited blood-curdling details, with strong hints that he intended to test his theories on her. When he paused to enjoy the effect of his words, she briskly said she knew better ways of execution, and each time he suggested a horror she capped it, keeping him still and absorbed until the train stopped and she escaped.

Moody's experiences were less macabre. A wholesale butcher in West London, Henry Varley, much of his own age, had become an evangelist and a Plymouth Brother, preaching at a mission hall with such force that his 'assembly' numbered several hundred. 'I visited that man to find the secret of his success. At home he prayed for the meeting. After supper we took a fly, and as we were rattling along the rough stone streets of London he said, "Now, brother, let us have prayer for that meeting",' and knelt on the swaying floor of the fly, among the wisps of straw. Moody had never tried praying aloud on the floor of a carriage: 'rattling through the streets wasn't exactly a comfortable place in which to pray'. After the service he watched (or so he embroidered the tale in America afterwards) 'seventy butchers with tears streaming down their faces gathered round that man of God', and knew that prayer was Varley's secret.

Through Varley he was invited to speak at other Brethren halls. And it was in Dublin, at the close of a service, that he heard a voice at the level of his shoulder: 'Ah'm 'Arry Moorhouse. Ah'll coom and preach for you in Chicago.'

Moody turned and saw an insignificant, beardless little man. 'He had a boyish appearance, did not seem to be more than seventeen years old.' Quite unaware that this was one of the significant confrontations of his life, Moody hid his disdain under a kind smile. 'Ah'm 'Arry Moorhouse,' the fellow repeated, 'Ah'll preach for you in America. When d'you go 'ome?' Moody told him he didn't know, and told himself he would not have revealed if he had known.

He had heard of Harry Moorhouse, a Lancashire lad, out of the gutter, a converted pickpocket, the Boy Preacher. Moody did not believe such a stripling could preach. Moody soon forgot him.

After ten days in France in June to see the Exposition (and start a little daily prayer meeting at La Salle Evangélique) the Moodys returned to England for a farewell dinner. Emma's asthma had gone. They were now pining for America and little Emma. Moody said he had to jump 'to keep from getting homesick, and whistle to keep up his courage'. The fortnight's seasickness on a gentle summer ocean was not a high price to pay.

Back in Chicago the first excitement was the gift house. 'Mr Farwell is building me a house to live in,' Moody had written from London to his brother George. 'It is about three blocks from where I used to live. I don't know if it will be brick or stone – I have not heard.' Farwell, developing land as an investment, had decided to put the Moodys into one of the houses rent free, inviting mutual friends to help him furnish it. When the travellers returned they were taken to this pleasant home in State Street; and in pride of place were their two portraits, that of Moody having been done without fee by the most famous American portrait-painter of the day, G P A Healy, a Chicago resident and a Roman Catholic.

The next excitement was the opening of the new YMCA hall in Madison Street in the heart of the business centre; testimony to the power of organization and fund-raising. It had been designed by a member, W W Boyington, architect of Crosby's Opera House, the Sherman and the Grand Pacific hotels, city churches, the new waterworks. It could justly be claimed as the first building in the world to be erected by a YMCA, and the scale was magnificent. Five stories high, it had a marble façade, the largest auditorium in Chicago on the first floor, five shops for letting at street level, a library, reading room, lecture rooms; a gymnasium, and a dormitory for forty-two; and, ironically in view of its swift fate, the spare office space was rented by the fire, police and health departments. The YMCA intended to name it Moody Hall. At the grand dedication on September 29th, 1867, Moody carried by acclamation his motion that the place be Farwell Hall. 'The only mistake,' said Farwell gallantly, 'Mr Moody ever made in connection with this enterprise.'

The opening of Farwell Hall appeared to crown Moody's achievement in Chicago. He was a leading, if much abused, citizen. A description in a religious newspaper of November 1867 shows that by now he appeared shorter than actually he was, and not, to Chicago at least, ill-educated: 'Mr Moody is rather below the medium height, and inclined to fleshiness, not corpulence. As he goes to the platform with a quick, nervous step that means business, you notice that he has a round, ruddy and good humoured but earnest face, but back of it a busy brain... When Moody speaks, everybody listens, even those who do not like him. His remarks are short, pithy and practical, and his exhortations impressive and sometimes touching even to tears. He is aggressive and his remarks always have a martial ring...'

Unexpected irritant, came a letter from Harry Moorhouse to say he had arrived in New York, would preach in Chicago if Moody wished. Moody wrote him a note: 'If you come West, call on me' – and 'thought I should hear no more about him.'

Harry Moorhouse, who was twenty-seven, had served time in

gaol before he was twenty-one, and afterwards stumbling on a back-street mission had heard an ex-prizefighter and coalminer preach on the Prodigal Son. Moorhouse was transformed, slowly: he had to wear thick gloves for a while to keep him from picking pockets. He became a respectable auctioneer, married a childhood friend, then moved to a tiny cottage on the outskirts of Manchester to give his whole time to preaching – preaching with a difference.

A whimsical, gentle creature, self-effacing, whose burning sense of mission was balanced by a strong sense of humour and an ability to prick any bubble of pretension or cant, he had Moody much in mind during the Atlantic crossing. His first reaction to New York was absurdly like the Moodys to London. He thought it a horrible place. 'Everybody seems to think he is better than everybody else and it is hard to get a civil word from anybody.' It was also most expensive. 'Ten shillings for a coach to bring my luggage to the hotel, five minutes' journey; fifty cents, or two shillings, for hair-cutting...' Soon he was taken in by a rich Quaker, William Kimber, who wrote, 'I spent many hours with him over Murray's grammar etc, that he might correct the grammatical errors which at first marred some-what the public delivery of his wonderful gospel messages.'

Moody knew nothing of that. He thought, by New Year, that he had heard the last of this peculiar character. He soon had some-thing else to try him.

On January 7th, 1868, shortly before midday, fire broke out in Farwell Hall, still shining with new paint. No police, health or fire department on the premises could save it in the city of strong winds. Members, bystanders and firemen rescued furniture, all the records, five hundred books. A young boarder, David Borrell, subsequently a famous preacher, had reached the doorway with his trunk on his shoulder, smoke filling the street, flames crackling, fire bells clang-ing, when he heard a voice, 'Put it down.' He saw Moody. 'Borrell, throw it away and help me. We want to have a prayer meeting in the Methodist Church.' The noonday meeting took place. 'Scores wept as though their own home burned,' the minutes recorded. That af-ternoon secretary and committee 'ran about among the merchants in the city for subscriptions: "Our hall is burning, sir. There is no hope. We shall want a new one. Let us have money enough to begin at once."' Thousands of dollars were subscribed before the rubble cooled. Insurance had been incomplete; three months later McCormick had an appeal from Moody 'struggling to raise the balance of the funds necessary to rebuild our hall'.

Some weeks after the fire Moody to his annoyance heard again from Moorhouse, that he was coming to Chicago and would like to preach.

Moody scribbled a note, 'If you happen to come West, drop in on me,' and thought 'that would settle him'. Moorhouse's reply gave the date and time of arrival.

Reading it, Moody blew an impatient puff. The man could not preach; and on that day Moody must be in St Louis for the Missouri Christian Convention. He asked Emma to put Moorhouse up, told the deacons, 'Try him – and if he fails I will take him off your hands when I come back,' and boarded the train for St Louis.

He had been in demand in the north-west for conventions designed to draw together ministers and lay people of differing denominations, or of opposing sympathies in the war. Men who had served on the Christian Commission and now sought to continue the amity bred in wartime, knew Moody of Chicago as a man to stir sluggish saints, differences forgotten, into united assault on the unbelief, apostasy and indifference fast gaining ground in a nation absorbed in material advance. At Missouri he was nominated chairman, and made a strong speech: 'We can carry this state and hold it for Christ,' he said, using a political simile in a presidential election year. 'The power lies buried in the Church, and the question is, how to get it developed.'

It was easy to forget Moorhouse.

Seventeen-year-old Fleming Revell, boarding with his sister and brother-in-law, was the first to see him. Revell had expected 'some long-bearded, stately, dignified man'. 'I went to the door and saw a little stripling standing there, an insignificant-looking little Englishman, he was. He said, "I am 'Arry Moorhouse." "What, sir?" "I am 'Arry Moorhouse. This is Mr Moody's, isn't it?" We asked him in and the little fellow toddled in.'

With much misgiving that Thursday night they set him a trial run at a small meeting in the Illinois Street basement. 'We didn't quite know what to make of it. He talked differently from anybody we had ever heard. He seemed to have a different message from anything we had ever heard, and the deacons got their heads together at the close of the meeting, and while the hymn was being sung, and agreed that we would announce that 'Arry Moorhouse, as he called himself, would speak the next night.'

Returned on Saturday, Moody asked Emma about Moorhouse.

'They liked him very much,' she replied. 'He preaches a little different from you. He preaches that God *loves* sinners.'

Moody puffed impatiently, having 'concluded that if he preached different from me I would not like him. My prejudice was up.' 'He is wrong,' said Moody.

Emma said: 'I think you will agree with him when you hear him, because he backs up everything he says with the Bible.'

At Illinois Street on Sunday morning Moody noticed his congregation were all carrying Bibles. He had never told them that persons in pews should bring Bibles. 'It was something strange to see the people coming in with Bibles, and listen to the flutter of the leaves.'

Moorhouse announced his text: 'John 3:16: God so loved the world, that He gave His only begotten Son, that whosoever believeth in Him should not perish, but have everlasting life'. Instead of dividing the text into firstly, secondly, thirdly in ministerial manner Moorhouse, Moody noted, 'went from Genesis to Revelation giving proof that God loves the sinner, and before he got through, two or three of my sermons were spoiled'. Moody's teaching that it was the sinner God hates, the sinner as well as the sin, lay shattered at his feet. 'I never knew up to that time that God loved us so much. This heart of mine began to thaw out; I could not keep back the tears.' Fleming Revell remembered all his long life the sight of Moody drinking it in on that Sunday morning, February 8th, 1868, and how 'on Sunday night little Harry Moorhouse stood swaying from one foot to another in his seeming awkwardness, but you forgot all about it as you heard the message coming from his lips'.

The text was the same. 'God so loved the world...' unfolded once again from Genesis to Revelation, by a different route, his address not a sermon so much as a string of related texts or passages, briefly commented upon to form what came to be known, rather oddly, as a 'Bible Reading'.

At the end Moody jumped up. 'Mr Moorhouse will speak every night this week. Everybody come. Tell your friends to come.'

Night after night Moorhouse announced, 'God so loved the world...' and drew his hearers by a fresh line through the Bible: 'My friends, for a whole week I have been trying to tell you how much God loves you, but I cannot do it with this poor stammering tongue...'

Outside, in the sharp February air, Chicago life rolled on unawares. Merchants dined and wined, the poor huddled half-frozen round smoking stoves, sailors from iced-up ships lechered or boozed or brawled. At Illinois Street among that crowd of humble citizens and a few new immigrants and a sprinkling of the rich, the spirit of love ran unfettered. And D L Moody turned in his ways, to become from that time forth an apostle of the love of God, the dichotomy resolved.

Day by day, too, in the State Street house presided over by the Healy portrait, where Moorhouse had become a firm favourite with his little ways and comic sayings and Lancashire accent, Moody was learning a lesson as compelling as the lesson of love. Moorhouse taught him how to read and study the Bible.

Moody had always looked on the Bible as text-book and weapon. He was unaware as yet, and for years to come, of critical problems and disputes which had scarcely penetrated even the theological world of Chicago. To him it was the Word of God. But he had regarded it as an armoury of well-worn texts whereon to peg talks and sermons, or to throw at individuals. He was curiously ignorant of much that the Bible taught. Moorhouse told him he didn't know his Bible, showed him how to treat it as an entity, to trace the unfolding themes of Scripture, made him see that 'it is God's Word, not our comment upon it, that saves souls', warned him that he should take time to receive more than he gave out. Moody began to rise before the household was astir (being a man who needed little sleep), would light and trim the oil lamp in the study, and pore for an hour or more over his big Bible, scribbling notes in the margin.

Harry Moorhouse was of the Plymouth Brethren. Moody never denied their influence, eagerly bought their commentaries. His common sense kept him from selling out to theories or speculative allegories which marred their attempts to allow Scripture to interpret Scripture, and he had no truck with the separatist or fissiparious tendencies of some of them, 'eating their gingerbread all by themselves in a corner', as he expressed it. In his relations with the Brethren Moody showed his knack of drawing strength from a movement without becoming its slave.

Fleming Revell wrote: 'D L Moody had great power before, but nothing like what he had after dear Harry Moorhouse came into our lives and changed the character of the teaching and preaching in the chapel.' John Milton Hitchcock, who became one of Moody's closest assistants, first heard him soon after, in the summer of 1868. It was of then that he wrote: 'the most impassioned, powerful, incisive, pathetic and effective appeals I ever knew him to make were before he had acquired a reputation beyond the shadow of his own chimney.'

And Moody, addressing the Illinois State Sunday School Convention at Du Quoin that same summer said: 'Be kind – conquer by love. If a man has his heart full of love and a little common sense, he will succeed.'

10: Sankey on a Soapbox

The years 1870-71 were decisive. They brought Sankey; put Moody on the right path of several he was attempting to travel at once; and gave unlooked-for strength to fulfil his commission, ringing down the curtain on 'Crazy Moody'.

Moody had long been conscious of the power of song. He himself, as his later associate singer George Stebbins wrote, had 'no

more idea of tune or time than a child. He was one of the unfortu-
nates who had no sense of pitch or harmony, and hence are unable
to recognize one tune from another or to sing in unison or harmony.' That did not prevent him making a noise like 'one of the
notes of the organ sounding when it ought to be silent'.

He could be powerfully impressed by a hymn. It is true, as his
daughter-in-law discovered, that if he asked for 'Rock of Ages' and
she played 'Yankee-Doodle' slowly with soulful chords, he would
wipe tears from his eyes; but a sacred solo or the sweep of a congregation caught up in a chorus of praise could move him profoundly, not only by the impact of the words. He saw too that singing
created a mood of worship and response, especially among the semi-
illiterate poor, and whereas, like others cradled in Puritanism, he
suspected oratorio and counted opera devilish, he wielded hymn-
singing as a weapon. 'You sing over there!' he would cry, 'Now
you sing. Now you sing down there. And now everybody sing.'

'Why do you want them to sing that way?' Robert Weidensall, a
YMCA leader, once asked him. He replied: 'Weidensall, they will
forget what I say, but if they learn "Jesus, Lover of my soul", and
sing it to themselves, they will get it in their mouths at least, and
they will get the Gospel along with it.'

During the 'sixties Moody was somewhat vaguely searching for
a song-leader. He worked occasionally with an older man, Philip
Phillips, known as 'the pilgrim singer', but Phillips did not live in
Chicago. In the summer of 1869 Moody met a Pennsylvanian of
nearly his own age, Philip Paul Bliss who, according to their mutual friend D W Whittle, 'crystallized' Moody's sense 'of the power
of singing in Gospel work'.

By all expectation Bliss, already a fertile composer and versi-
fier, and a spirited singer, should have been Moody's Sankey. He
had been based in Chicago since 1865, travelling for a musical
publisher to give concerts and teaching in north-western cities, but
they had not met. 'To think,' said Moody in 'sixty-nine in a hurt
tone, 'that such a singer as Bliss should have been around here for
the last four years and we not known him.' He was lovable, a cheerful man with beautiful manners and many 'curious conceits so pi-

quant and varied'. And he could write hymns that children and the
semi-illiterate picked up easily.

Bliss helped Moody on Sunday evenings when in Chicago. In
May 1870, having heard Major Whittle describe the defence of
Altoona during the Atlanta campaign, when Sherman signalled his
famous message, 'Hold the fort. I am coming', Bliss wrote the
words and music of the hymn that would sweep Britain and America.
But in July he became choirmaster of the First Congregational
Church, and was lost to Illinois Street.

That same July, Moody went to the YMCA International Convention (held alternately in Canada and the United States) at
Indianapolis, Indiana.[1] He met there a twenty-nine-year-old delegate from Pennsylvania, Ira David Sankey.

Moody was announced to lead an early prayer meeting at seven.
Sankey, a fastidious dresser, arrived late, every hair of his handsome mutton-chop whiskers in place, and sat near the door. A windy
delegate was praying. Sankey's neighbour, a Presbyterian minister
from his own county, whispered, 'The singing here has been abominable. I wish you would start up something when that man stops
praying, if he ever does.'

When the wind ceased, Sankey began 'There is a fountain filled
with blood'. The congregation joined in, and the meeting thereaf-
ter moved with pace.

The Presbyterian introduced Sankey to Moody. Moody, as his
manner was, sized him in a second.

'Where are you from? Are you married? What is your business?'

'New Castle, Pennsylvania. I am married, two children. In Government service, Revenue.'

'You will have to give that up.'

Sankey records: 'I stood amazed, at a loss to understand why

---

1. Moody intended at Indianapolis to change the whole character of the North American
YMCA, having got it into his head that it would be a good idea to merge YM and YW in
one glorious and most un-Victorian Youth Association. The international chairman made
short work of him. 'Mr Moody got thoroughly whipped by Mr Brainerd, for Brainerd just
wiped that away, and he did not take very much time to do it, because the boys were
schooled on that question' (Robert Weidensall).

the man told me that I would have to give up a good position. "What for?" I exclaimed.'

'To come to Chicago to help me in my work.'

To Sankey's protest that he could not abandon his business Moody retorted: 'You must. I have been looking for you for the last eight years.'

Sankey obliged Moody by joining him briefly in the vestry to pray, 'but as yet I had no thought of giving up my position'. He was, however, aware that only a day or two earlier the singing of another delegate had been 'a revelation to me of the marvellous power there was in a simple Gospel hymn when the singer put his whole heart and soul into it. I shall never forget how the great gathering was thrilled by the wonderful pathos of the singer's voice. It was an entirely different style of singing from that which I had so often heard in many churches where I attended. Every word could be distinctly heard in the remotest part of the building.' Under the influence of this hymn there had arisen 'a great desire in my own heart that I might some day be able to use my voice in like manner'. He had not expected his desire to be fulfilled so quickly or so literally.

Next afternoon he received a crisp note commanding attendance at a street corner. As factory crowds streamed homewards Moody told Sankey to get on a soap-box, an undignified posture for a smart young man. Sankey smoothed his whiskers, straightened his bow-tie and somewhat gingerly mounted. He sang a martial solo. Moody watched as Sankey's voice drew a crowd; this swelled to a mass when Moody began to talk, and Sankey saw how 'The people stood spellbound as the words fell from Moody's lips with wonderful force and rapidity.' After twenty-five minutes Moody said they would continue in the Opera House rented by the Convention. Sankey and his friends led the way 'singing, as we marched down the street, "Shall we gather at the river". The men with dinner pails followed closely on our heels instead of going home. The Opera House was packed to the doors. Moody first saw that all the working men were seated. His second address was as captivating as the one delivered on the street corner.'

Sankey left Indianapolis undecided: 'I presume I prayed one way and he prayed another. However, it took him only six months to pray me out of business.'

Ira David Sankey had been born on August 28th, 1840, at the village of Edinburg in Western Pennsylvania, and had lived since 1857 in the town near-by, New Castle; a curious foreshadowing: international reputation was to come at Edinburgh in Scotland, Newcastle-upon-Tyne to be the birthplace of the Moody and Sankey hymn-book. Son of a bank president and State Senator, Sankey always had about him a faint air of colonnaded bank and senate plush; he was 'rather given to frock coats and silk hats', Paul Moody writes, 'thus presenting a good deal of a contrast to my father's more informal appearance'. Sankey was 'a very jovial man', of the sort that delighted in puns and elaborate comic stories; he could skylark when under Moody's influence, but whereas Moody even in old age frolicked with the abandon of a schoolboy, Sankey would be distinctly avuncular. Sankey lived on the verge of being pompous, while Moody could not have been pompous had he tried.

Sankey was a Methodist. He had been Sunday school superintendent, helped to found the local YMCA, was church choirmaster. Serving briefly in the Civil War he is said to have owed his life to his voice: he was on sentry duty at night when he began to sing a favourite hymn. A Confederate sniper who had him in his sights was so moved by the singing that he lowered his rifle. Sankey's baritone never received professional training; he sang in church, at Sunday school conventions, in local churches in Western Pennsylvania and Eastern Ohio.

Back in New Castle after meeting Moody in Indianapolis, he discussed the future with his wife Fanny, daughter of another State Senator. She had been a member of Sankey's choir whom he married young in 1863, as lovely as her husband was handsome; shy, too, and retiring like Emma Moody. It was much to ask Fanny Sankey to accept the extinction of her husband's career in the Civil Service, that he might aid a missioner based on the slums of Chicago with occasional flings to other cities.

Sankey consented early in 1871 to a trial week with Moody. At its end he resigned from the Revenue, but reserved an option in that he did not bring Fanny but set up bachelor quarters in the rebuilt Farwell Hall. 'Thus we commenced work together, visiting poor and needy ones of Mr. Moody's little flock, singing and praying with the sick, speaking and singing at the daily noon prayer meetings.'

Sankey's advent was unheralded. 'A comparatively obscure man,' John Hitchcock noted, 'his presence amongst us was not regarded in musical circles as a great acquisition to their forces.'

11: Fire

The Moody whom Sankey joined was Moody in a jam.

After Moorhouse he had become an apostle of love in public speech as in private life, and knew how to draw waters of wisdom from the well of Holy Writ. But he stood uncertain at the crossways. While post-war America dragged its moral anchor, worshipping money in the north, resentment in the south; while Britain lay half-bogged by smugness laced with hypocrisy, half-stirred by spiritual quickenings and missionary adventures that needed to be knit together, the man of the hour dithered.

He might remain primarily a Sunday school worker. Moody, J H Vincent the future bishop, and B F Jacobs the businessman, all three still in their thirties and living in Chicago, formed a triumvirate that led the north-west, and the north-west led American Sunday schools. Moody was President for 1869 of the Illinois Convention, at Bloomington. His mission school was famous and he held the reins: 'He is a man that does a great deal of hard work himself and surpasses all men in finding something for others to do. Sluggards don't like him and he doesn't like them... Much of his success is due to the *personality* of his efforts.'

He might remain primarily a city missionary, an American William Booth. It was as a successful slummer that he had held the attention of the great national convention at the Marble Church in New York in 1868. Some of the elders had protested: 'The idea of

putting Mr. Moody on with Dr. John Hall and Henry Ward Beecher!'
Moody spoke at the end of the day. 'He claimed attention at once,
and I believe you could have heard a pin drop all through that hour.
Why, it seemed to me that he just grew larger and larger... Mr.
Moody was a revelation to us on "How to reach the Masses". He
told his simple, straight story of how he had done the work.'

The YMCA claimed as much of him. He gloried in being an
Association man in days of rapid expansion.

There lay another opening – to Congress. In 1868, an election
year, he had led a Christian Convention at Leavenworth, the then
capital of the young state of Kansas. A group of politicians called
on him.

'See here, Mr. Moody, you come out here and run for Congress.'

'I have got a higher service than that!'

They left him in disgust. One politician exclaimed, 'I think that
is one of the strangest of men. Just think of it! He could just as well
go to Congress and I believe we could make him Governor.' And if
Governor, it is not beyond bounds that, with the powers he developed of administration, command and speech, D L Moody eventu-
ally could have run for President.

Sunday school, city mission, YMCA: in each he evangelized.
He was not, nor intending to be, a full-time itinerant evangelist. He
loved a dash to some city of Illinois, Michigan, Wisconsin or farther afield for a revival in a church or YMCA, but he belonged to
Chicago. The rest were secondary. Chicago, too, held his home,
doubly dear since March 25th, 1869, birthday of William Revell
Moody. Here he could romp. Here was little Emma's enormous
rocking horse, made in gratitude by a man Moody had helped. Here
was that latest idea, a bathroom, where Moody could take his cold
bath winter and summer in the built-in tub.

A delicate, home-loving wife, two small children: no background
for a peripatetic preacher.

This dithering yet dynamic Jack-of-all-trades had one major
defect of character. Certainly he was not introspective, nor gloomy;
indeed, a journalist with him in a train wrote of 'D L Moody who
with all his real piety is sometimes *unbearably* funny'. He had com-

passion, kindness, and under Emma's gentle pressure a growing courtesy, though formalities of handing ladies to their seats, of 'please', 'thank you', 'you're welcome' generally were crowded out. Despite his quick temper (with his intimates he could be brusque, even snappish), he flared rarely under deliberate provocation, scurrilities, baitings, misrepresentations. 'I suppose if Jesus Christ could eat the Last Supper with a Judas Iscariot I ought to shake hands with you,' he said when a persistent heckler offered his hand. Once Moody knocked a man down the steps at Illinois Street who had vilely insulted him or probably had made a filthy insinuation about Emma. Within five minutes Moody had made public apology, with never a word of the insult.

Moody's grave defect was another violence, a vehemence that sought to carve a kingdom for Christ in Chicago by sheer expenditure of energy, as in the two hundred calls on a New Year's Day remembered by Hitchcock, who was with him and the church officers as they trotted briskly from State Street in a hired omnibus immediately after breakfast. 'On reaching a family belonging to his congregation, he would spring out of the 'bus, lead up the stairways, rush into the room, and pay his respects: "You know me: I am Moody; this is Deacon De Golyer, this is Deacon Thane, this is Brother Hitchcock. Are you all well? Do you all come to church and Sunday school? Have you all the coal you need for the winter? Let us pray." And down we would all go upon our knees, while Mr Moody offered from fifteen to twenty words of earnest, tender, sympathetic supplication that God would bless the man, his wife, and each one of the children. Then, springing to his feet, he would dash on his hat, dart through the doorway and down the stairs throwing a hearty "good-bye" behind him, leap into the 'bus, and off to the next place on his list; the entire exercise occupying about one minute and a half.

'Before long the horses were tired out, for Moody insisted on their going at a run, so the omnibus was abandoned and the party proceeded on foot. One after another his companions became exhausted with running upstairs and downstairs and across the streets and kneeling on bare floors and getting up in a hurry; until the tireless pastor was left to make the last of the two hundred calls alone; after which feat he returned home in the highest spirits, and with no sense of fatigue, to laugh at his exhausted companions for deserting him.'

This violence was a symptom of inner tension. Another was his passion for crowds. Every Sunday evening, rather to the distaste of the regular ministry, Moody preached in the rebuilt Farwell Hall under its two hundred gas jets, its biblical frescoes, and could boast 'I have an audience of about 1,200 to 1,800', mostly young men. If the hall was nearly full he would 'be lifted up at the sight of so many people before me'. If numbers dropped his morale dropped. Another symptom, mixed with a general sense of adventure, was the restlessness that took him with Vincent and Philip Phillips that spring of 1871 by the new Pacific railway to visit California, through wild west lands where the train dared Indian attack, through desert and mountain, to hold a Sunday school convention on the rough-and-tumble coast where, Moody observed, gold, fast horses, to-bacco and rum held high carnival.

At the other end of the scale lay a moment of stark discouragement, if the unsupported evidence of B. F. Jacobs' brother, Will, be accepted. Will Jacobs claimed (in 1911) to remember Moody coming to their office on a 'cold, cold day in that winter of 1870-1' without an overcoat, his jacket nearly threadbare. 'I stood listening, and this is what Mr Moody said. "Jacobs, I do not know but I will have to give it up after all... I left my wife and children this winter morning without a mouthful of food at home, and without a dollar to purchase any. Jacobs, I would not care for myself... But, oh" – and the great form shook with agitation – "it is hard for a man to leave his wife and children without a morsel of food."' Moody never remembered, or never revealed, such a moment of destitution; and during that winter Fleming Revell still boarded and lodged with the Moodys, earning good pay at a printer's. Did he go without breakfast?

There is no disputing that Moody was empty in his soul, and refused to admit it.

He was dissatisfied with the multiplicity of administrative duties. The YMCA had become a hive of activity with Moody Queen
Bee. There was the tract campaign, 'what I am trying to do for the
people who do not attend church', scattering a million pages a week,
'and I can't tell you how much good they are doing'. There was
fund-raising, badgering McCormick for $2,000 towards an organ
for Farwell Hall ('the singing is horrible without it'), and organizing the 'Yokefellows' who would frequent saloons, boarding-houses,
street corners, to whip in for the Farwell Hall services. Every week,
Moody claimed, 1,500 different young men came to the YMCA
rooms, and over 5,000 had been found employment in a year – but
Moody's figures generally suffered from his countrymen's complaint of hyperbole. It all meant office work. 'I was on some ten or
twelve committees. My hands were full. If a man came to me to
talk about his soul I would say: "I haven't time: got a committee to
attend."'

Moody knew that he should choose, once for all, whether to be
a social-religious organizer or an evangelist. What is more, by early
1871 he perceived, but pretended he did not, that 'God was calling
me into higher service, to go out and preach the Gospel all over the
land instead of staying in Chicago. I fought against it.'

He was, therefore, becoming as sounding brass (certainly not a
tinkling cymbal), not because he had not charity; nor, since
Moorhouse, did he lack wealth of Bible lore. But the inner tension,
his half-recognized rebellion, tangle of objectives and utter lack of
integration ensured that his speech and his preaching were not any
longer like St. Paul's, 'in demonstration of the Spirit and of power.'

Two women in his congregation noticed this.

Sarah Anne Cooke was a recent immigrant from England –
English influence again on the one so to influence England – a
Buckinghamshire woman, only ten years older than Moody but
generally known as Auntie: Moody always thought of her as elderly. Her husband was in meat-packing and she was a Free Methodist, a woman of intense earnestness, 'continually going to every
kind of religious gathering within her reach', who could speak only
in the language of Zion, probably lacked a sense of humour, was

full of good works and buttonholed the unwary to exhort them to flee from the wrath to come.

At a camp meeting in June 1871 'a burden came on me for Mr Moody, that the Lord would give him the baptism of the Holy Ghost and of fire'. With her friend, a widow called Mrs Hawxhurst, she settled in the front pew, and while Moody preached they prayed in an obvious manner.

'We have been praying for you,' they said afterwards.

This nettled him. 'Why don't you pray for the people?'

'Because you need the power of the Spirit.'

'I need the power?' And Moody puffed.

He had not a chance. 'No opportunity was lost after that in urging upon him his great need.' They pursued like the Hound of Heaven; in the mist of tears he hid from them, and under running laughter; they found 'little conviction of his need' at first, but their unhurrying chase 'set me thinking. I asked them to come and talk with me, and they poured out their hearts in prayer that I might receive the filling of the Holy Spirit. There came a great hunger into my soul. I did not know what it was. I began to cry out as I never did before. I really felt that I did not want to live if I could not have this power for service.'

It would not come: because he refused to admit to himself that he was called 'to go out all over the land'.

In September he invited Auntie Cooke and Mrs Hawxhurst to pray with him every Friday afternoon in his room at Farwell Hall. They each prayed aloud in turn. On Friday, October 6th, 'Mr Moody's agony was so great that he rolled on the floor and in the midst of many tears and groans cried to God to be baptized with the Holy Ghost and with fire.'

Rolling on the floor in prayer was un-Moodylike enough to render suspect Auntie's evidence, put in a letter to S B Shaw twenty-eight years later, were it not for D W Whittle, reliable observer and Moody's close friend, who mentioned in his private diary only five years afterwards that Moody at that time had been 'continually burdened and crying to God for more power. He was always wanting to get a few praying ones together for half a day of prayer and would groan and weep before God for the baptism of the Spirit.'

The heavens remained brassy as the sky in that memorable Indian summer. Day after day had passed in drought and high wind. Prairie and city were dry as tinder, dry as Moody's heart. Moody leaped and cried like a prophet of Baal, but there was no voice nor any that answered. For Moody would not place himself on the altar, would not yield in his determination to stay in Chicago. How could he desert the thriving mission building in Illinois Street? Who else could hold sway in that fine monument to his organizing zeal, Farwell Hall, with its two hundred gas jets, its monster reflectors, its seats for 2,500, its splendid organ? Nothing should move him from these two dear buildings. The still, small voice, 'go out and preach the gospel all over the land', could not be from heaven.

On that Friday, October 6th, Moody 'cried to God to be baptized with fire'.

On Sunday evening, October 8th, Farwell Hall enclosed a capacity crowd. Moody spoke superbly. Sankey at his little organ began a final solo, 'To-day the Saviour calls'. He reached the closing words of the third verse: '...and death is nigh', when 'my voice was drowned by the loud noise of the fire engines rushing past the hall and the tolling of bells, among which we could hear the deep sullen tones of the great city bell, in the steeple of the old court-house close at hand, ringing out a general alarm. Tremendous confusion was heard in the street, and Mr Moody decided to close the meeting at once, for the audience was becoming restless and alarmed.'

Moody and Sankey went out at the back and saw an angry red smudge to the south-west, upwind from the main part of the city. They separated, Sankey to help at the scene, Moody to cross the river for home to reassure Emma and the children. As he walked the south-west wind rose almost to hurricane force, the sky became a fireworks display as sparks blew and house after house caught fire. Moody's first words to Emma were: 'The city's doomed.'

By midnight much of Chicago was a holocaust of roaring flames, crashing buildings, wild neighing of terrified horses, the shouts of fire-fighters and refugees. Sankey hurried back to Farwell Hall –

'several times I had to shake from my coat the falling embers' –
and rescued a few belongings before the pride of the YMCA went
up in flames. He made for the lakeside.

In the quarter where the Moodys lived a temporary sense of
security was shattered in the small hours when police knocked up
those who had gone to bed, and urged flight. Moody may have
gone round to Illinois Street: his secretary, Katherine Abbott, helped
to move valuables from his office. He was back at home before the
flames engulfed the Mission Church and all its street. Emma had
woken the children. 'If you will not scream or cry,' she said, 'I'll
show you a sight you will never forget.' She dressed them in two of
everything, and took them to the french windows in the first-floor
drawing-room.

While the Moodys hastily threw things together, little Emma
wandered to the front door. The scum of the city were running wild
for loot. A filthy hag saw the well-dressed little girl and beckoned.
Emma, bewitched, started to run out but her dress caught in the
door, or she would have been lost.

The flames consumed a neighbouring block. Moody arranged
for a neighbour who owned a horse and buggy to take the children
with his own through the panic-mad streets to safety with friends
in a northern suburb, then pushed Bibles and a few valuables into a
pram. Emma begged him to save the Healy portrait. 'Take my own
picture!' he laughed, 'that would be a joke. Suppose I meet some
friends in the same trouble as ourselves and they say, "Hullo Moody,
glad you have escaped. What's that you've saved and cling to so
affectionately?" Wouldn't it sound well to reply, "Oh, I've got my
own portrait!" '

He would not touch it. Looters had entered. One of them politely cut it out of the frame and handed it to Emma.

The Moodys after abandoning State Street did what they could.
'Mr Moody, please save my doll!' cried one little girl from a window or door of a house lapped by fire. He carried the girl to safety.
At last, exhausted, they reached Emma's sister Sarah Holden and
her attorney husband in their safe western suburb.

Throughout the next day the fire raged. Homeless thousands

streamed out of the city, thieves looted, martial law was proclaimed, buildings blown up to make a fire-break. For twenty-four hours Moody and Emma did not know whether their children had been trapped or saved: Emma's hair began to turn grey. They could not tell if Sankey had been burned to death.

In fact, he had spent the night by the lakeside with his precious bundle of belongings, and much of Monday in a boat by himself out on the lake. In the evening 'I went back into the burnt district. Farwell Hall was gone, and every building in that part of the city had disappeared. The paved streets [were] covered with hot bricks and long coils of burnt and twisted telegraph wire.' He found a railway station still functioning and took a train to Pennsylvania. 'As we left the city it seemed as though the whole country was on fire; in all directions we could see huge banks of flame sweeping across the prairies, and the air was filled to suffocation with smoke.'

By Wednesday the fire had burned out. Chicago lay prostrate. Relief, badly organized, flowed from neighbouring states.

A fortnight afterwards Moody drove the family, as young Emma records, 'to the ruins of our house. Father went over everything in the ruins with a cane. The only thing of value he found was a toy iron stove of mine in perfect condition.'

New York, November 24th, 1871

My dear Sir,

You know something of the sad state of things in Chicago so far as the spiritual work is concerned. Fifty churches and missions are in ashes and the thousands of men, women and children are without any Sabbath home. The temporal wants of the people are well supplied but there is no money to rebuild the churches and missions. The churches in the part of the city that was spared can do nothing. Their moneyed men are either bankrupt or as badly crippled as to prevent them from helping outside enterprises. My mission school and Free Church, on the North side, went with the rest. One thousand children and their parents are looking to me for another building. I have no earthly possessions and apply to those in sympathy with God's work who have the means of helping. My plan is to raise $50,000 and put up a Tabernacle to accommodate seven or eight burnt out Missions. It is for this purpose I have come to New York on a hurried visit. In a very short time there will be 50,000 Mechanics and others back on the North side. The grog shops are already rebuilding and some are doing business. The theatres are helping the theatres... Will you help us?... Yours respectfully,

D L MOODY

He met generous response in Philadelphia from George H Stuart and John Wanamaker; in a Massachusetts coastal city a man took him round rich neighbours; in New York – Moody hated it: 'My heart was not in the work of begging. I could not appeal. I was crying all the time that God would fill me with His Holy Spirit.'

His prayer remained unanswered because he fought the will of God. Farwell Hall and Illinois Street were in ashes, the ten or dozen committees had scattered like dying embers, nor could Moody face the weariness of reorganization. Had God, then, burned him out that he should 'go all over the country', perhaps the world? Moody said 'No.' The chains that bound him to Chicago had snapped, all but one: his own will.

Yet he craved power. He began to pace New York streets at night, wrestling, panting for a Pentecost.

In broad daylight he walked down one of the busiest streets, Broadway or Fifth Avenue – he scarcely remembered which, while crowds thrust by and the clop-clink of cabs and carriages was in his ears and the newsboys shouted. The last chain snapped. Quietly, without a struggle, he surrendered. Immediately an overpowering sense of the presence of God flooded his soul. 'God Almighty seemed to come very near. I felt I must be alone.' He hurried to the house of a friend near-by, sent up his card, and brushed aside an invitation to 'come and have some food'. 'I want to be alone. Let me have a room where I can lock myself in.'

His host thought best to humour him. Moody locked the door and sat on the sofa. The room seemed ablaze with God. He dropped

to the floor and lay bathing his soul in the Divine. Of this Com-
munion, this mount of transfiguration, 'I can only say that God
revealed Himself to me, and I had such an experience of His love
that I had to ask Him to stay His hand.' Turmoil of mind glided into
peace, conflict of character snapped into integration. That master-
ful strength which had hammered at the gates of hell and charged
full tilt at the world, the flesh and the devil was melted and re-
moulded, to leave him gentle as a babe, utterly dependent on a
power beyond his own. Not for him to see and choose his path, nor
pride to rule his will. God must lead, and God supply. Moody need
never thirst again. The dead, dry days were gone. 'I was all the time
tugging and carrying water. But now I have a river that carries me.'
The clock of a near-by church chimed the quarter, the half, three-
quarters, the hour, the hour again.

Crazy Moody became Moody the man of God.

Part Two

THE MAN FROM THE WEST
1872-5

12: The Unanswered Letter

London on a Sunday in the summer of 1872. A butler off duty walked, fast as dignity allowed, by Westminster Abbey and the Houses of Parliament, up almost deserted Whitehall until he reached Downing Street. He did not turn left to the house of the Prime Minister, Mr Gladstone, but along Richmond Terrace towards the river, as yet without Embankment.

The butler hurried down the area steps of No 5 into the basement, took off his billycock hat, changed, and waited impatiently until he heard his young master and mistress, Mr and Mrs Quintin Hogg, return from church. He walked upstairs, coughed politely and said: 'Excuse me, sir, but there was a wonderful American gentleman preached at Chelsea Chapel. Real powerful, he was. He would do our lads a power of good, sir.'

'What was his name, Edwards?'

'Mr Moody of Chicago, as I heard, sir.'

'Moody? The man whose Sunday school I visited on our honeymoon last year, before that awful fire?'

'It must be him, sir. He preaches again to-night, if you would please to give me leave, sir.'

Quintin Hogg went too. An Old Etonian 'of twenty-seven, son of a baronet, partner in a sugar firm, athlete, he spent much time among rough slum boys in the alleys and warrens of Charing Cross where he had started a Ragged School and a home for destitutes, helped by his butler, his coachman and a couple of Old Etonian friends. It grew into the London Polytechnic. He was the British counterpart of the man Moody might have been had he remained in business. Hogg had much in common with Moody – love of poor boys, a complete absence – rare in England of the 'seventies – of any sense of social barrier, so that he brought ragamuffins into his house by the front door; partiality to fun and practical jokes.

He listened to Moody that night with delight. 'He spoke with much power,' Hogg wrote to a co-worker in the Ragged School, the Honourable Tom Pelham, 'and I was glad to find that he was going to a hotel, which enabled me to secure him as a guest. On the Mon-

day following we closed school, and I invited the home boys and
your class to come to tea here on Tuesday and then go to hear Moody
at Chelsea Chapel. They did so, and every single boy there was
broken down more or less. Eleven professed to find peace that night.
The following night I asked any who liked to come again and fifty
boys came to the chapel and we had a special service in the school
room for them. I went around after the gas went out and prayed
with each alone...'

It was odd that Moody was preaching at all. 'I went to London in
1872 just to have a few months of rest and study the English Christians. I was determined not to get into work if I could help it.' The
previous winter Moody had returned to Chicago in November 1871
with a modest $3,000 to construct a less ambitious 'tabernacle' of
pine boards, the first building in the devastated section. He had
sent for Sankey, opened it on Christmas Eve as a centre of relief
and evangelism, and with his assistants slept there (they had to
place their boots over the cracks to keep out icy draughts), while
Emma and the children lodged with her sister.

A young man who slipped into the Watch Night Service on Sunday, December 31st, recorded his impression: 'Consider the deso-
lation all about. The midnight, the midwinter stillness, the yawning
cellars and gaunt walls, one had to pass walking southwards for 45
minutes before reaching buildings and inhabited houses again. Ten
below zero, a clear sky, a full moon overhead and absolute quiet.
At last I came to Moody's Tabernacle just built among the ruins. It
seated 1,400 and I found it nearly full. Mr Moody was just finish-
ing an address. Another preacher followed whose uproariousness
made no impression except in contrast to Moody's quiet ways. Then
Mr Sankey followed with his organ and extremely sweet voice singing some of his hymns. Mr Moody was last and ended with saying
that it was a few minutes off twelve. He called for silent prayer.
Presently the complete silence was broken by his wishing us a Happy
New Year.'

Moody had accepted that he should restart his Mission, but would
not entangle himself in committees. Chicago no longer held him.

He must be an evangelist; and presumably would discover where
to begin. He went east again in January. In Brooklyn a casual remark led to a series of meetings in the new mission chapel of a
famous church, after which a wealthy layman, Morris K Jessup,
wanted him permanently in New York. 'The more I see of Moody
the more I like him,' Jessup wrote to Farwell on January 17th, 1872.
'I believe God is making him the instrument of a great work among
the people. Moody and I had quite a talk about getting hold of the
masses in this city and he quite cheered me up... Moody is the man
to come here... I should be willing to take the expense on my shoulders.'

Moody did not intend to cast off from Chicago merely to anchor in New York.

The Moodys had gone on to Northfield. And the best portrait of
D L Moody in these months of pause on the verge of fame comes
through the eyes of a Northfield child, Eva Stebbins Callender, on
a Sunday morning in the Trinitarian Congregational Church:

'After the service had begun there was ushered into the first
pew a stout pleasant-faced man and a lady. Mother whispered they
were Mr and Mrs Dwight Moody of Chicago. I had heard of the
Chicago Fire and wondered if they too were burnt out. Probably
had been because Mrs Moody wore a very pretty bonnet, a flat
three cornered affair trimmed with quite small black feathers and
black velvet ribbons, but made of straw, white straw, which was not
the usual material for bonnets in wintertime, so perhaps her real
winter bonnet was burned. Our old minister came down from the
pulpit and cordially greeted Mr Moody while the choir were singing the second hymn. Then Mr Moody briskly arose and followed
up the three steps into the pulpit, taking off his overcoat as he did
so and threw it carelessly on the long shelf behind the desk. Quickly
turning he said, "If the ushers will open the windows we will sing
again, Number – ". He seemed to have entirely forgotten they had
just sung the second hymn of the morning, and now another – surely
he was different.'

The sermon usually bored Eva, though she was forbidden to
fidget. 'As soon as Mr Moody began to talk I found to my surprise

that I could understand him and I liked it. He told stories – and it was Sunday too – stories when he knew people could not help but laugh, and then it might be a story when the grown ups would cry. I would have cried too but was too busy watching this very enthusiastic preacher who talked with his hands and feet as well as his mouth, as he paced up and down the narrow platform. No, he didn't preach, he only talked using the simplest language, sometimes with a loud voice as he denounced wrong doing but always holding the attention of the hearers. I distinctly remember in one part that, to give emphasis to his remarks he brought both hands down in no gentle manner on the cushion on the pulpit desk. A cloud of dust immediately arose and it also seemed as though a small feather flew into the air...'

In summer, with Chicago fast rising from its ashes, the Tabernacle mission working well, Moody left Emma for the British Isles.[1] He attended conventions and conferences, occasionally being prevailed upon to speak, always stuffing the roomy pockets of his Scotch tweed suit with notes and pumping his British friends for sermon illustrations. Near Dublin a wealthy Plymouth Brother opened his mansion for a 'Believers' Meeting', and here Moody met 'Butcher' Varley again. Together, with some twenty of like fervour, they spent one entire night in prayer. Next morning as the two, sleepy but elated, rambled in Bewley's well-tended shady pleasance, Varley let slip a remark which flashed an inspiration to Moody. It was a remark unpremeditated, casual – Varley forgot it instantly until reminded more than a year afterwards.

Varley said, 'Moody, the world has yet to see what God will do with a man fully consecrated to Him.'

The phrase startled. Moody made no comment at the time but devoured Varley's words, sucked at them, digested, regurgitated them for days and weeks: 'The world has yet to see what God can do with and for and through a man who is fully and wholly consecrated to Him... A man! Varley meant any man. Varley didn't say he had to be educated, or brilliant, or anything else. Just a *man*.

---

1. A curious transposition in W R Moody's *D L Moody* (1930) has given rise to the belief that Moody was in Britain in 1870. The incidents noted therein belong to 1872.

Well, by the Holy Spirit in me I'll be that man.' Back in London, in the gallery of the Metropolitan Tabernacle, Varley's remark and Spurgeon's preaching focused into 'something I had never realized before. It was not Spurgeon who was doing that work: it was God. And if God could use Spurgeon, why should He not use me?'

It was then that the visit to Britain got out of hand.

A Congregationalist minister persuaded Moody to preach at Arundel Square near Pentonville Prison, in a lower-middle-class district. And Sunday morning's smug, stolid drowsiness made him rue his irresolution in accepting.

Unknown to him a woman hurried back to her younger sister, a mere slip of a girl but permanently bedridden, Marianne Adlard, and broke the news that Mr Moody of America had preached. Marianne exclaimed: 'I know what that means! God has heard my prayers!' She drew from under her pillow a newspaper cutting crinkled and faded, and together they looked again at the account of this unknown American's activities in the slums of Chicago which had caused Marianne, day after day, to pray, 'O Lord, send this man to our church.'

That evening, from the moment Moody mounted the pulpit, the congregation listened hushed and alert, his every word seeming charged as with electricity. At the close he asked any who wanted 'to have your lives changed by the power of God through faith in Jesus Christ as a personal Saviour', wanted 'to become Christians', to rise, that he might pray for them. People rose all over the chapel. Surprised, Moody thought either they or he had made a mistake and told them to sit. He repeated what he meant by 'becoming a Christian', and asked that those who wished should withdraw to the adjoining hall or school room. He watched, astonished, as scores of men, women and older children made their way quietly to the connecting door. The school room had been prepared as an Inquiry Room by placing out one or two dozen chairs. Many more had to be sent for.

Moody addressed this second meeting with the utmost care, enlarging on repentance and faith. The whole room rose when he put his question the third time. He told them to meet their minister, who was as dazed as he, next night. Moody had to leave London in the morning. He was telegraphed for on Tuesday because more had come to the minister's Monday-night meeting than had been in the room on Sunday. He returned and spoke nightly all that week and the next. 'Four hundred were taken into membership of that church,' wrote, fifty-three years later, a Baptist minister in Somerset, James Sprunt, 'and by the grace of God I was one of that number.'

After that experience Moody could not refuse to hold the short mission for the Anglican incumbent of Chelsea Chapel where Quintin Hogg's butler had heard him. Hogg even postponed his holiday in Scotland, sending ahead his wife and baby, the future Lord Chancellor Hailsham, while he made the most of Moody's influence on wild street-arabs and urchins.

A few days later Moody called at an hotel where his friend the noted Presbyterian preacher, Cuyler of Brooklyn, was staying.

'They wish me to come over here and preach in England,' Moody said.

'Do. These English people are the best people to preach to in all the world.'

'I will go home, secure somebody to sing, and come over and make the experiment.'

Henry Bewley had evidently said at Dublin that he would help with expenses, so Moody understood. Cuthbert Bainbridge, a rich, elderly Methodist layman of Newcastle-upon-Tyne was explicit in promise of funds. The invitation of predominant importance came after Moody's return to America, from William Pennefather, the outstanding evangelical Anglican of those not yet on the bench of bishops, a man of saintly character, of authority, insight and drive, whose parish of St. Jude's, Mildmay, had an influence far beyond London. Pennefather had his finger on the pulse of British religion and, wrote his close friend and biographer, 'was strongly impressed with the conviction that Mr Moody was one for whom God had prepared a great work'. Pennefather, though only fifty-seven, was a sick man. From the Black Forest during a tour abroad for his health he wrote, in the third week of August 1872, 'a letter of invitation to Mr Moody, telling him of the wide door open for evangelistic effort in London and elsewhere, promising him a warm welcome if he would come over and help'.

Moody, American fashion, sent no reply.

There followed the most extraordinary behaviour by the man who was afterwards to be not evangelist only, but an efficient, decisive administrator. Because of Moody's uncharacteristic inaction, Britain's greatest religious revival since Wesley would begin so haphazardly as to exhaust human explanation for its success.

Moody made plain to Chicago during the winter and spring of 1872-3 that he was off. 'I did all I could,' Farwell wrote, 'to persuade him to stay and help build up from the ruins of the fire along religious lines, but to no effect.' He backed the fund for the third Farwell Hall, launched an appeal for a permanent replacement to the Tabernacle, secured the site at the corner of La Salle Street and Chicago Avenue which has been linked with his name ever since and set builders to work. That was all. His heart was across the sea. 'I want,' he told a great meeting at the Second Presbyterian Church in the spring of 1873, 'to dream great things for God. To get back to Great Britain and win ten thousand souls!' 'Are you going to preach to the miserable poor?' Auntie Cooke asked. 'Yes, and to the miserable rich too!'

No word came from the United Kingdom. Moody seems to have imagined that three men of different denominations living in widely separated parts who probably were unacquainted, Bewley, Bainbridge and Pennefather, to whom he had not bothered to reply, were organizing an evangelistic tour. He may have been reluctant to push himself. He was certainly true to his countrymen's belief that plans may fructify in a vacuum of unanswered correspondence.

A letter came: from a young chemist in the cathedral city of York, George Bennett, founder-secretary of the local YMCA. They had met at a breakfast in Leeds, and he wrote to say that if Moody were over again, would he please speak at York? Moody sent no reply and continued to prepare for his visit to Britain.

Sankey, who had brought his family to Chicago, and J H

Harwood, the official pastor, were ordered to look after the Tabernacle for the six months Moody expected to be abroad. The then famous, now forgotten, Philip Phillips was invited to be singer for the tour: he knew Britain well, had lately returned from a hundred nights of sacred song. Phillips refused; he was arranging a tour of the Pacific coast. Indeed, Phillips made Sankey 'a very enticing offer, including a large salary and all expenses, if I would go and assist him'. Sankey, to whom money meant much, was tempted; but decided to stay with Moody's Tabernacle at the price, it seemed, of certain fortune and possible fame.

Moody turned to Bliss. Bliss regretfully declined because he could not afford, with a young family, to abandon professional engagements. There was no alternative but Sankey the amateur. Moody gave Sankey a personal guarantee of one hundred dollars a month.

No word came from Britain except another letter from young Bennett of York. Moody had occasion to write to Morgan and Scott, religious publishers in London. Through them he sent Bennett a non-committal message. Bennett wrote again in late spring, to receive a cautious reply direct from Moody, 'saying he thought of coming and as I seemed earnest about it, he might commence at York and would bring someone to lead the singing'. Moody's thoughts were on more influential sponsors than a tradesman of York; no doubt these were carefully preparing, and on the strength of such expectation he booked steamship passages for himself, Emma, little Emma (aged eight and a half), Willie (just four), and for Sankey and Fanny, their two children to be left with grandparents.

Still no money, or letter, from England; nor is that a wonder.

The afternoon of farewell from Chicago, John Farwell brought a gift of five hundred dollars. Moody kept fifty and asked him to invest the rest, as all expenses were to be paid from the moment of leaving America. The fifty dollars took them to the coast. The *City of Paris* was due to sail on June 7th. From New York Moody had to wire Farwell, who released the four hundred and fifty dollars, not knowing that without them the party would have been stranded on the quay. The last English mail brought nothing. A letter from the persistent Bennett, promising to make arrangements in York if

Moody would state his wishes 'and when he would be likely to be here', missed the Moodys and was sent in pursuit.[1]

Across the Atlantic Moody, as usual, was seasick. From New York he had alerted Moorhouse, who on June 17th came on board at Liverpool to tell them that Pennefather had died in April, Bainbridge in March. And Bewley must have forgotten. There were no engagements, no committee, no funds.

The Americans were stranded three thousand miles from home. Moody turned to Sankey. 'God seems to have closed the doors. We'll not open any ourselves. If He opens the door we'll go in. If He don't we'll return to America.'

They went to the North Western Hotel. Putting the children to bed the Moodys rejoined the Sankeys and Moorhouse in the lounge to mill their problem, and there Moody recalled the York invitation which he had treated so airily. 'This door is only ajar,' he said.

Next morning, Wednesday, June 18th, 1873, George Bennett, who in view of Moody's vague answer and subsequent silence had told no one except the doctor at the lunatic asylum, was horrified to receive a telegram from the secretary of the Liverpool YMCA: *Moody here are you ready for him.*

13: White Elephants

'I have no doubt that if I had known when I reached England of what was before me I would have been frightened.' Thus Moody, two years after.

He waited in Liverpool throughout Wednesday, June 18th, 1873, for a reply from York. A ship-owner interested in the YMCA, Richard Houghton, took the Moodys to his mansion for the night, while Moorhouse carried off the Sankeys to the Manchester cottage. The Moodys left for London and on to Leytonstone in Essex, the home

---

1. This disposes of the oft-repeated legend that Bennett's one and only letter was found by Moody unopened in his pocket after arriving at Liverpool. Bennett gave a full statement of the whole affair to W R Moody in a letter of March 12th, 1900, after reading the inaccurate account in the hurriedly produced *Life of Dwight L Moody*. Extracts from this letter have never before been published.

of sister Mary, now Mrs Alfred Sharpe, where on Friday morning a
telegram forwarded from Liverpool arrived from Bennett: *Please
fix date when you can come to York.* Moody tossed his head at such
dilatory planning. He wired back: *I will be in York to-night ten
o'clock stop Make no arrangements till I come.*

He travelled north alone. On stepping from the train he said to
Bennett: 'How far is it to Manchester? I might have meetings there
first before York.'

'Sixty or seventy miles. But you can't go now. You must come
with me for supper and the night anyhow, and then we can talk it
over.'

Bennett, to Moody's amusement, appeared dazed as they walked
the short distance beside the city walls, through Micklegate Bar to
the chemist's shop in New Bridge Street. Over supper Moody made
up his mind: 'Every man has to make his own way, so I propose we
make arrangements to-morrow, Saturday, to commence meetings
Sunday. You telegraph Mr Moorhouse to have Sankey here sometime tomorrow.'

Bennett's account continues: 'We mapped out there and then
matter for posters to be printed and posted next day, and knowing
he was tired I showed him to his bedroom. I apologized for the
bedcurtains being covered up – we had not had time to put them in
apple pie order. Mr Moody replied, "I don't think the Lord Jesus
had any curtains to His bed. What did for Him will do for me."'

Sankey on Saturday afternoon found Moody alone and in high
spirits. 'I say, Sankey, here we are, a couple of white elephants!
Bennett is away all over the city now, to see if he can get us a place.
He's like a man who's got a white elephant and doesn't know what
to do with it.'

Bennett returned discouraged. Ministers were suspicious:
'*Americans?*' 'Why do they want to come to York?' 'What's the
YMCA up to?' 'Whoever heard of a mission in mid-summer?' He
had booked the large and ugly Corn Exchange for the afternoon,
and the Congregationalist deacons had grudgingly promised the
morning pulpit at Salem Chapel because their new minister was
away. Young men were scouting the city to inform likely persons

that this would be a meeting for 'Christian workers'; detailed posters were printing.

That first Sunday morning cut little ice with the staid Dissenting congregation of tradesmen in sober black, their ample wives, numerous children; a footman or two from the Deanery and the Canons' houses, a few soldiers from the barracks, a sprinkling of washerwomen and railwaymen up from back-to-back streets beyond the station. In the afternoon, as the Americans walked with Bennett towards the Corn Exchange, Moody stopped at the YMCA and filled his arms with Bibles.

'Now, Sankey, you bring a pile of Bibles.'

Bennett said: 'What do you want to do?'

'Oh, I shall have your hair standing straight on your head before I have finished in York!'

Some eight hundred people waited in the Corn Exchange, which could hold more. Moody briskly distributed Bibles here and there, in each copy a slip with a number and a reference, and ordered, 'Read the text out when I call your number.' The resulting 'somewhat novel but very profitable Bible lecture on "God is love",' as the *Yorkshire Gazette* called it in a brief paragraph on 'Mission Work' between notices of a banquet and of a court case over a local Dotheboys Hall, caused interest.

All week at evening meetings in chapels 'the spiritual atmosphere seemed at zero and little result was effected'. So thought Bennett. Beneath the surface, however, in the hearts of men and women for whom chapel-going was essentially an emblem of respectability, something stirred. Sankey could make them sing new, rousing songs utterly unlike the dirges thought proper to divine service; even the strait-laced as they went about their daily business found it hard to resist humming 'Hold the Fort'. When this charming American sat at the little harmonium his solos, every word distinct, lifted hearers to worlds unknown, faced them with Christian teaching that had lain blurred in a haze of tacit, impersonal acceptance; and if tears were inclined to run too easily, this was a lachrymose age.

Moody's informal preaching shocked, then intrigued. His hearers noted that he did not seek to score by denigrating the regular ministry; indeed, he let it be known unequivocally that he 'prefers preaching in chapels, and so strengthening existing causes, to commencing a new work in public halls, etc.'. In their cage of convention they were warmed by his emphasis that religion was a friendship: '"To as many as received Him," he would quote, "to them gave He power to become the sons of God" - *Him*, mark you! Not a dogma, not a creed, not a myth, but a *Person.*' They noticed the blend of reverence and affection with which he would speak of 'the *Lord Jesus*'.

Behind the scenes Moody had started a noon prayer meeting in the YMCA's 'small ill-lit room' in Feasegate. 'I can see Mr Moody standing there to lead it,' wrote one of Bennett's friends in old age, 'little realizing that it was seed-germ of a mighty harvest.'

For on the second Wednesday, July 2nd, the movement broke surface. Moody spoke at the Wesleyan chapel in the heart of the walled city, on 'Redeemed with the precious blood of Christ'. Bennett wrote: 'The Holy Spirit's power was mightily manifested and anxious souls were all over the building, in the body as well as in the gallery. The aged superintendent of the Chapel seemed paralysed by astonishment, he could do nothing but weep for joy.' That night had been the last of their invitation to the Wesleyan chapel, and they moved south of the Ouse to Priory Street just within the walls, to the new Baptist chapel, its dark-brown varnish still glossy, its imitation Early Decorated exterior bright and clean.

Moody had preached there the previous Sunday morning, his second in York. The starchy young minister, Frederick Brotherton Meyer, consulted by Bennett on Moody's telegram, was puzzled as to what an evangelist did that he could not do himself, being correct in doctrine, painstaking in preaching, a most worthy young man; but with only the slightest curl of his classical nose he had invited Moody to his pulpit. He listened unmoved to the story of that dying Sunday school teacher in Chicago. But the woman who taught the senior girls' class had been so gripped that she missed her midday dinner to pray. At teachers' tea Meyer asked casually, 'Well, Miss Lines, how have you got on this afternoon?'

'Oh, I told that story again and I believe every one of my girls has given her heart to God!'

That had shaken Meyer, who now watched, night after night, his moderate-sized chapel, 'vestries, lobbies and pulpit-stairs crowded!' And in the minister's parlour at the close of each evening he saw subdued citizens of York seek the way of release.

Towards the end of his life, a leading Nonconformist in London, past president of the National Free Church Council, social reformer, preacher, author of seventy books of which, according to the *Dictionary of National Biography,* five million copies circulated, F B Meyer declared of that mission in York, 'For me it was the birthday of new conceptions of ministry, new methods of work, new inspirations and hope... I had been brought up in a holy home. I had been in business for a little, then took my degree at college, but I didn't know anything about conversion, or about the gathering of sinners around Christ, and I owe everything, everything in my life, I think, to that parlour room where the first time I found people broken hearted about sin. I learned the psychology of the soul. I learned how to point men to God.'

The revival stayed parochial, scattered, the churches not united, the stirrings limited to a 'parcel of dissenters'. One or two clergymen of the Established Church offered Moody and Sankey verbal encouragement, but the canon-in-residence as he robed for the daily services in the Minster remained unaware of their existence. Had good Archbishop Thomson, 'the People's Archbishop', been told at Bishopsthorpe that in less than two years his brother primate of Canterbury would write a long earnest letter about them to the Lord Chancellor, he would have been amused.

Mrs Sankey had already joined Sankey. Emma and the children arrived on July 4th, the day before her thirtieth birthday, guests of Dr Hitchings of the Friends' Retreat, a private lunatic asylum. He let the children play with harmless inmates, rather to Emma's disquiet; when the Moodys were roused in the middle of a night by a scream from Willie and found his bed empty, there followed frantic searching of house and asylum until he was discovered beneath his own bed, having fallen out, screamed, rolled over and gone fast asleep out of sight.

The Moodys and the Sankeys were homesick. Moody implored Farwell to send full details of the YMCA and Mission in Chicago. Sankey complained that the sun would not go to bed at a civilized hour: nor would it, for a man from a place on the latitude of Rome who worked in midsummer on the latitude of Edmonton or parts of Labrador.

Sankey was agitated by a summons to Sunderland. A Baptist minister, an ex-sailor called Arthur Rees, wanted the evangelists, but doubted whether an unknown soloist of sacred song would prove acceptable to the northern shipbuilding town, whose Nonconformists had an almost Scottish suspicion of music in worship.

Sankey was dispatched by train in a state of nerves. He was at once taken to the back parlour of a butcher's shop, where the butcher's wife proudly displayed a dilapidated harmonium which, six years before, had been played by the great Philip Phillips. The instrument was out of tune, a stench of meat and blood percolated from the shop.

Sankey sang. Rees sat entranced.

Sankey returned to York, the evangelists moved on July 19th and found that Rees had neatly dodged local prejudices by announcing that Mr Moody would preach, and 'Mr Sankey will sing the Gospel'. The Sunderland campaign (Moody carried forward the terminology of the Civil War just as Billy Graham seventy years later adopted Eisenhower's word 'Crusade') was a disappointment. At the end of its five weeks the Moodys, Emma noted in her diary, 'had a feeling that one minister had done much to hinder blessing among others'.

Methodists, however, had persuaded Newcastle-upon-Tyne, a dozen miles north-west, to offer a hearing to the Americans. When Moody entered the great coal seaport on August 25th, he determined to stick there until prejudice died.

At the end of September a Scottish minister of the United Presbyterians in Berwick-on-Tweed, John Cairns, a brilliant theologian in his fifties who held a part-time professorship in Edinburgh, passed through Newcastle.

He wrote to his sister: 'There was a great crowd at Mr Leitch's church. At the meeting, which was opened by Mr Leitch and myself, the chief peculiarity was the singing of a Mr Sankey with harmonium accompaniment, under the direction of a Mr Moody, an American gentleman who has been labouring in Newcastle for five weeks. The singing was very impressive, the congregation striking in at the choruses with thrilling effect. The address by Mr Moody though thoroughly Yankee was deeply earnest and produced a great impression. It was on the grace of God, and had many happy strokes though here and there grotesque. The audience was fairly carried away at times by this mingled impulse of singing and appeal, and at the close a good many persons, impressed for the first time, waited to be spoken with.' He added that the movement had spread all round Newcastle and into the countryside, that he had discussed it with many acquaintances 'who all speak warmly of its results'.

Moody and Sankey had jumped from the obscurity of York to being the talk of the greatest city in the north of England.

The Newcastle campaign started among the well churched middle-classes. It spread slowly upwards and downwards. Rich merchants, shipbuilders, coal-mine owners began to attend, encouraged by a vigorous commendation from a local Member of Parliament whose *Newcastle Chronicle* praised the 'wonderful religious phenomenon', its lack of sectarianism, the single-mindedness of Moody, and especially that 'the jingle of money is never heard at these meetings'. The 'Geordies', sallow and stunted from overlong hours underground on scanty diet, the people of the slums who lived in a lifelong atmosphere of coal dust, the 'masses' whom Moody longed to reach, held aloof – until he tried a mothers' meeting. A baby in arms had yelled until the irritation of the audience drove to tears its working-class mother, at which Moody, in contrast to a nearly twentieth-century evangelist who refused to continue until a noisy baby was removed, charmingly announced on the spur of the moment a women's meeting at which no one would be admitted unless carrying a baby. His supporters, delicate ladies (there was sharp distinction in the 'seventies between 'women' and 'ladies') went, Emma recorded, 'to the poorest, meanest streets and told the women to come and bring their babies with them. Such a squealing!... But the poor women listened while the tears ran down their faces and Mr Sankey and Mr Moody were both able to continue their talks remarkably well.' Enlarging attendance brought a demand for copies of the hymns Sankey sang, especially of 'Jesus of Nazareth passeth by', an affecting ballad on the healing of blind Bartimeus, written by an American in New Jersey ten years before, which struck home to hearers left unmoved by Moody's preaching. The happy, stirring or sentimental hymns of Bliss likewise were the rage. As Sankey said, it was now 'that we began to realize the wonderful power there was in these Gospel songs'. Families wanted to sing them as they gathered round pianos in parlours, but the only copies in England lay in Sankey's personal scrapbook.

He wrote to the English publishers of Philip Phillips' collection, used at the meetings, offering his own selection without charge if they would print it as a supplement. They refused, and threw away a fortune. Moody promised another publisher, Richard Cope Morgan (of Morgan and Scott, whose weekly *Christian* had been the evangelists' warm friend) that he would guarantee an edition of a sixteen-page pamphlet of Sankey's selection.

On September 16th, *Sacred Songs and Solos* in its first short form, at sixpence a copy, or a penny for words only, to be used in alliance with Phillips' book, was on sale.

Moody and Sankey had brought a warm breeze into the fusty religion of Nonconformist churches in the north-east corner of England, though churchmen held aloof from preachers lay and unaccredited. But other American visitors sponsored by Nonconformist chapels had come in years past, and flown forgotten as a dream. Would Moody and Sankey be different? They planned to move to Darlington for nine days in mid-October, had accepted a week in Bishop Auckland, where lay the Bishop of Durham's palace, and after that would give one or two days to several small towns on Tees or Tyne. Two-thirds of the six months which Moody had allotted to Britain would be gone, and despite numerous invitations to scattered parts of the country, the mission seemed in danger of fizzling out.

One autumn day changed the prospect.

In the Newcastle suburb of Walker, where the leaves were falling already, Moody, as he dealt with inquirers in a chapel vestry, noticed a clergyman who introduced himself as 'the Reverend John Kelman, minister of the Free Church of Scotland, at Leith, the port of Edinburgh'.

Kelman put a startling proposition. 'Come to Edinburgh,' he said, 'and I and my friends of the Free and Established Churches will form a committee. We will prepare the ground and I believe that every presbytery will support you. Win Edinburgh, and you will win Scotland. Scotland needs you.'

Moody was aghast. Edinburgh, the Athens of the North, where his lack of formal education must appear an impertinence? Able Presbyterian theologians, dry scholars of intense earnestness, grave, discriminating, rigid, would be on the platform. His racy torrent of anecdote and informal Bible teaching might shock or irritate. As for Sankey, most Scotsmen considered offensive the singing of 'human' hymns, those other than metrical versions of the psalms. Moody lamely suggested accepting a prior invitation to Dundee. Kelman was emphatic. 'Edinburgh *first*. Then you will reach the nation.'

Moody did not give an immediate answer. This was a decisive moment, his first opportunity to work in a capital city prepared by a representative committee. Edinburgh's leading men of religion, Kelman asserted, would rally behind him. That, Moody reflected, was only an opinion.

If he accepted, it would be at the risk of being laughed out of Britain, never to return.

14: Surprise in the North

Moody and Sankey slipped into Edinburgh, which Emma considered the most beautiful city in the world, on a dismal, storm-swept Saturday night, November 22nd, 1873, and from Waverley Station took cabs for hotels, until run to earth by the committee. The Sankeys were carried off to the manse of the veteran hymn-writer, Horatius Bonar, the Moodys to stay with Professor William Blaikie, the friend of Livingstone. 'D. L. Very hoarse,' noted Emma in her diary. 'Prof Simpson sent for.' He diagnosed acute tonsillitis.

Prominent Presbyterians, mostly of the Free Kirk, had risked good repute to sponsor unknown, unordained Americans and hold six weeks of preparatory meetings. 'I've just had a letter from one of the most eminent ministers there,' a Scotsman had told Emma early in November, 'and they are most enthusiastic over Mr Moody coming.'

On the opening day, November 23rd, despite the rarity of evening services in the Scotland of 1873, the Sabbath calm of Princes Street was broken with the tramp of countless feet, the rumble of a few carriages defying the current interpretation of the Fourth Commandment, to say nothing of folk who had come in by train, paying the double fare by which the railways quieted their Sabbath conscience.

The committee tended to hazard wild guesses at attendance figures, but on this first night Sankey could see the city's largest hall 'densely packed to its utmost corners; even the lobbies, stairs and entrance were crowded with people, while more than two thousand were turned away'. Sankey felt nervous. He had overheard carpings about his use of 'human' hymns, even more against the 'kist o' whustles', as they were pleased to dub the little American organ, and moreover, the chairman's first words, greeted with gasps of disappointment, announced that Moody was too unwell to attend.

Sankey had the sense to begin by inviting the congregation to unite in a familiar 'praise', the Old Hundredth. When he sang 'Jesus of Nazareth passeth by', 'the intense silence that pervaded that great audience at once assured me that even "human hymns", sung in a prayerful spirit, were indeed likely to be used of God to arrest attention and convey Gospel truth to the hearts of men in bonny Scotland, even as they had in other places.' The address was given by James Hood Wilson of the Barclay Free Church, whom Moody had honoured at once as a man of love, vigour and military precision. Sankey wound up with 'Hold the Fort', and to his delight the congregation joined in the chorus lustily.

Moody spent the day spraying his throat from the latest invention, since Professor (Sir) Alexander Simpson 'had taken a handspray with me, for medicine had just entered on the microbial era'; and in heeding Professor Blaikie, who initiated him into the mysteries of a land that wore an impressive cloak of piety and good conduct, but where love lay expunged by law, joy and religion were divorced, and most men believed it blasphemy to claim certainty of heaven, saying that though Christ had died, none knew whether he or she be predestined to salvation. In this severe, chilling Calvinism the 'Guid Book' had less authority than the Westminster Confession. Industrial areas, moreover, held a widening circle of the 'lapsed mass' who never attended kirk; university and divinity schools were lapped by ripples of 'Doubt'. And the nation was weakened by schism: the Disruption of thirty years before had left a legacy of competition, mistrust, disputation. Movements towards reunion, either of the Established Church with the Free, or the Free with the older Secession church, the United Presbyterians, had bred merely an unhappier atmosphere.

Then Blaikie spoke of those who like himself, Hood Wilson, Kelman, Professor Charteris, sighed for a Divine wind. The Revival of 1859 from Ulster and the United States had blown little beyond Scottish country districts, yet with all its extravagances had been a sign to those who could discern. And now, fourteen years later, an aged saint, R S Candlish, shortly before dying that very autumn, had prophesied a great blessing, which should not be despised though it came strangely.

The newfangled throat-spray enabled Moody to attend the second night of the mission, in the Barclay Church, where the evangelists arrived to find the 'kist o' whustles' left in the concert hall. A committee man jumped into a cab, galloped into the night, and

twenty minutes later came a cry outside and a crash – the cabby
had rounded the corner too fast and spilled on to cobbled street
committee man and 'kist'. Sankey shook his head sadly. Repair
must take a day and he would not sing without his 'kist'. Moody
heard one Scotsman say to another that it 'all had a gr-r-and tendency to break up any scheme the evangelists might have in their
working together'. From the third evening the mission could run
its course.

'The church was crowded in every part,' wrote Hood Wilson,
within a week, 'every spot of standing ground was occupied. A
number have come to peace in believing – some of them the most
unlikely. Night after night... all sorts of people from all parts of the
city. Many have come in from the country, ministers and others. I
have felt much stirred up and hope to get a blessing. We have a
busy time before us.'

Moody, thirty-six-years old, swept from obscurity to fame.

Surprise was the keynote of those fantastic seven weeks. Moody
marvelled that staid Scots should listen to the torrent of his 'pro-
fuse diction which stops neither for colons or commas' (Simpson
said Moody could pronounce 'Jerusalem' in two syllables), should
tolerate his Yankee accent, forgive him for sometimes deliberately
making them laugh in church. His audiences were surprised by
joy: no sudden break as at York, but a steady brightening, like some
spring sunrise dispelling the chill November murk as men and
women grasped the astonishing fact that God loves sinners; they
had believed He loved only saints.

'A young man,' they heard Moody say, 'told me last night that
he was too great a sinner to be saved. Why, they are the very men
Christ came after! "This man receiveth sinners, and eateth with
them." The only charge they could bring against Christ down here
was that He was receiving bad men. They are the very kind of men
He is willing to receive. All you have got to do is to prove that you
are a sinner and I will prove that you have got a Saviour. And the
greater the sinner, the greater the need of a Saviour. You say your
heart is hard. Well, then, of course you want Christ to soften it. You

cannot do it yourself. The harder your heart, the more need you
have of Christ. The blacker you are, the more need you have of a
Saviour. If your sins rise up before you like a dark mountain, bear
in mind that the blood of Jesus Christ cleanses from all sin. There's
no sin so big or so black or so corrupt and vile but the blood of
Christ can cover it. So I preach the old Gospel again: "The Son of
man is come to seek and to save that which was lost." It was Adam's fall, his *loss* that brought out God's love. It was his fall, his
sin, that brought it out. A friend of mine from Manchester was in
Chicago a few years ago – ' and Moody was off on an anecdote.

His hearers hardly believed their ears. It sounded so simple.
'Scotch preaching,' wrote a layman signing himself 'Onlooker' in
the correspondence column of the *Scotsman,* 'has for fifty years
been little else but a reiteration of doctrines which, to me, at least,
are an unintelligible puzzle. The whole ingenuity of our preachers
has been to convince us that we are the subject of God's wrath,'
who could gain forgiveness only by believing in 'a complex theological puzzle...' 'Onlooker' begged the clergy to learn a lesson
from the two strangers who had come to 'sing and recite the declaration of God's goodness and forgiveness... Throw aside that complex system.'

Moody's addresses seemed brief to an age of sermons an hour
long or more, and often he interspersed them with silent prayer, or
a song from Sankey. He made 'no attempt to awaken excitement or
sensation', an Edinburgh divinity professor noted with satisfaction; provoked 'no articulate wailings, no prostrations, no sudden
outbursts of rapture which we have heard in former revivals'. But
he preached for decision. He would not trim his message to suit
Calvinistic hesitancy, which feared lest appeal for a definite step
of faith overrode predestination, a word Moody could not pronounce; 'I preach the Gospel to *every* creature,' he cried.

Moody, said Blaikie, placed his emphasis 'upon the doctrine
that Christianity is not mere feeling, but a surrender of the *whole*
nature to a personal, living Christ'. And thus, as at Chicago, the
inquiry room or after-meeting was the very hinge of the campaign.
It was not new to Edinburgh. Indeed, the Secretary of the Carubber's

Close Mission, which did for Edinburgh slums what Illinois Street did for Chicago's, asserted that Moody had picked up the idea during his visit of 1867, but few had seen one, and ministers suspected the inquiry room to be an emotional forcing-house or a complete surrender to an unbalanced doctrine of free will, or even a dark imitation of the Roman Catholic confessional. Fears were soon quieted. The *Daily News* reported ministers 'finding their difficulties melting away by personal contact with the work', until Moody noticed pews or benches, in church or parish hall used for after-meetings, dotted with black-coated, white-neckerchiefed, bewhiskered figures, Bibles open, talking earnestly to inquirers. Moody urged upon his 'personal workers', as he called them, *'patient* and *thorough* dealing with each case, no hurrying from one to another. Wait patiently, and ply them with God's word, and think, oh! think, what it is to win a soul for Christ, and don't grudge the time spent on one person.' He had come far from breakneck Chicago days.

The inquiry room drew a cross-section of Edinburgh, young men especially: medical students from the university, sons of generals or lawyers from spacious Georgian squares, and rough fellows from huddled wynds of the old city who stood out by their shabby homespun. To work among all of them Moody conscripted theological students of the Free Church's New College: and thus met Henry Drummond.

Moody and Drummond were a contrast, for the twenty-two-year-old Drummond, future author of *Natural Law in the Spiritual World,* had a supple, incisive mind powerfully educated in natural science and theology, was cultured, refined, a little of a dandy, a fine sportsman; quiet, with what a fellow-student called 'a perilous sense of humour'. The soul of Drummond knit with the soul of Moody, who recognized in him a high quality of leadership, knew him at once as a 'humble, unselfish and cheerful friend'. Night after night men marked Drummond walking back through the gas-lit streets in swirling mist, a green and black tartan plaid thrown over head and shoulders, his arm through that of some youth he had helped.

By mid-December all Edinburgh was awake, amazed. 'If,' said Professor Charteris, 'anyone had told us that our decorous city would be stirred to the depths by two strangers, we could not have believed the tale.'

Moody and Sankey had put a match to the well-laid dry sticks of Scottish religion. They had done more. Charteris continued: 'If anyone had said that the sectarian divisions which are so visible not only in ecclesiastical concerns but in social life and in private friendships, would disappear in the presence of two evangelists who came among us with no such ecclesiastical credentials as we are accustomed to value most highly, the idea would have seemed absolutely absurd.'

It was this 'most blessed and precious result' that at once gave Moody a place in Scottish history. Dimly, after weary years of wrangle, Scotland perceived that the road to unity lay through service, that what discussion failed to promote, mutual devotion to Christian mission could produce almost unawares. It would be twenty-six years to the first major reunion, and fifty-five to the great though incomplete reunion of 1929; but already Blaikie could comment: 'We all seemed to be lifted above our usual sectarian limits,' and, a year later, an Edinburgh man told his London brethren: 'We have rather a character of being theological porcupines, but a vast number of the quills have been drawn and there has been a warmth and kindness between the various ministers and denominations such as I have never witnessed before.'

Nor was that all. Stiff, conservative Edinburgh took from Moody and Sankey what they would not from their own kin. Thus, the Committee had started a noon prayer meeting before the mission. Moody sat through a few prayers, long, Scriptural, doctrinal, obliquely controversial, comprehensive and quite indefinite, and banged his fist on the table. 'I tell you, friends, some people's prayers need to be cut at both ends and set fire to in the middle.' As a Scotsman declared, 'Only he, at that date, could have done it and lived!' Sankey's personal conquest was even more extraordinary. In early days he could almost smell disapproval of his 'kist', and one night in the Free Assembly Hall was startled in the midst of a solo by a shrill female from the gallery: 'Let me oot! Let me oot! What would John Knox think of the like of you?' At the end of the solo he crossed to the overflow meeting in the Tolbooth Church. 'I had just begun to sing when the same voice was again heard, "Let me oot!..."'

By December 22nd Blaikie could write, 'It is almost amusing to observe how entirely the latent distrust of Mr Sankey's "Kist o' Whistles" has disappeared.' None rejoiced more than the veteran Horatius Bonar, whose hymns 'Fill Thou my life', 'I heard the voice of Jesus say', 'Go labour on', and many others, were banned by the elders of his own parish kirk.

The Church of Scotland's hymn-book of the previous decade had little use. Scottish conscience had jibbed at Bonar, refused the immortal organ music of Bach or Handel except as secular entertainment. Astonishingly, it surrendered to the 'kist o' whustles' and Sankey's 'touching pathos'. The hymns he popularized (he himself had only written one, to words of Bonar, since arrival in Edinburgh, 'the first Gospel song I had ever composed') were now heard everywhere.

By New Year, 1874, word of happenings in Edinburgh had sped across Scotland like some latter-day fiery cross.

An Appeal for Prayer, signed by leading Edinburgh ministers and laymen, went to every minister of every denomination in Scotland. A specially raised fund of £2,000 provided a weekly copy of the *Christian* for each minister throughout the British Isles, carrying special reports. Eye-witnesses hastened to highland glens and lowland burghs and villages.

In a village on the Firth of Clyde, Inverkip, lived a young railway servant called John McNeill. 'Quiet little village; quiet little Free Kirk; worship of the quiet stereotyped sort. No frills, certainly not. When suddenly there's a stir! Our minister has been to Edinburgh; he has heard a preacher, an American called Moody, and a singer called Sankey, and according to him Edinburgh's on fire! There's a revival on – whatever that may mean. The sough of it is on our minister's breath, his prayers and his preaching. We young folks begin to talk to each other, quietly, about the deepest things; we begin to seek, and we find.'

The minister called a 'testimony meeting, on a Sunday night; unheard of thing in our wee quiet village. Folks mightily stirred; gathered round the doors.' McNeill and two other lads got up in turn. 'They hammer and they stammer, but they're out with it. They have taken Christ to be their Saviour, and mean henceforth to live for Him.' All three remained sturdy Christians, McNeill a spectacular evangelist.

Inverkip was one of dozens of parishes and towns set spiritually ablaze. Invitations poured in to Moody and Sankey. They were able to make a day trip on January 12th to Berwick-on-Tweed where, a fortnight later, John Cairns was still 'occupied from morning till night in seeking out persons who either come to our inquiry meetings, or whom I expect to find anxious or willing to be conversed with on personal religion. The Corn Exchange is filled, and sometimes crowded every night... Our noon-day prayer meeting is attended by from one hundred and fifty to two hundred ... It has been hard work but I never came anything so near the souls of men. If the half hold, it will be the most wonderful experience by far I have ever passed through.'

15: Glasgow Conquered

Sudden fame made Sankey a little heady, his step more jaunty. His wife remained her retiring self, 'very pleasant and friendly', looking forward to the arrival of her two children from America and – though this, of course, in hushed tones with no stranger near – to a little arrival of a different sort.

Emma scarcely noticed fame, and Moody, consciously the mere instrument of a higher power, was too aware of the worth of men around for a swollen head. And too occupied. He barely had a moment to scrawl a letter to Illinois Street: 'I am lonesome often when I think of you all but I shall soon be with you for the weeks go like days when I am busy.'

After three weeks in Dundee they came to Glasgow on February 7th, 1874. A special United Evangelistic Committee had prepared assiduously, massed choirs had practised, prayer meetings drew hundreds daily, tickets to hear Moody were distributed through parish ministers to prevent unsafe overcrowding, the great industrial city and neighbouring burghs were agog, fed by reports of nightly services in Edinburgh continuing unabated since the evangelists' departure.

And instead of a white elephant in the half-prepared bedroom of an obscure chemist, Moody, with his family, was the honoured guest of a leading minister, Andrew Bonar, Horatius' younger brother, a superb Bible teacher who entered at the exact moment when Moody, after six months' preaching, with an indefinite stay in Britain ahead, was in danger of drying up. Moody sucked out the rich reserves of Bible knowledge and insight. 'Come and join us,' he would cry if a friend dropped in to Lynedoch Place, 'we are having a dig in the Rock.' To an American afterwards he said that in all Britain Bonar was one of the two men who helped him most.

It was a happy house, with a nursery for the children, the one defect being that as in similar British homes there was no built-in bath. A hip-bath by the fire, filled by steaming cans lugged up steep stairs by the housemaid, was all very well for Emma. Not much good for a fellow who wanted a cold dip (in February), especially when he was almost the same diameter as the tub!

The campaign opened at nine on 'Sabbath' morning, February 8th, in the City Hall, before three thousand Sabbath school teachers.

One of them, David Russell, in old age recalled how, after the Old Hundredth and Andrew Bonar's prayer, Sankey announced he would sing 'I am so glad that Jesus loves me', a Sunday school ditty by Bliss in peculiar measure, with chorus; to Russell as to most, unknown. Sankey enraptured him. 'I had never heard such magnificent singing. The great consecrated voice, the glad face of the singer and the almost childish simplicity of the words overcame me, and I found tears streaming down my face. I felt ashamed lest anyone should see my weakness, but ere long I noticed tears on other faces. Mr Moody needed no introduction ... On the platform beside him were many of the leading ministers and laymen of the city. Mr Moody's manner of holding his Bible in his right hand was significant of his hold on it and its hold on him. For a few minutes I thought I would not like him. The American accent, and what to me at first appeared to be a lack of reverence and dignity, jarred upon my sensitive Scotch nature, but a pathetic story told in his inimitable way caught me and bound my soul to him. It was a great, inspiring meeting, and I believe that there that morning Mr Moody conquered Glasgow.'

Moody did not have to 'make his way'. He was borne on a surge. Week after week through bleak winter into spring the meetings continued in churches, the City Hall, and at last in the Kibble Palace, an enormous glass exhibition building generally called the Crystal Palace. On foot, by horse-tram, by train, in trim carriages and creaking cabs the people came; from shipyards and mills and grimy tenements of the Gorbals where the air was heavy with soot and bitter winds swept cheerless streets; from sumptuous houses near-by in Hillhead; very many from middle-class homes where *Sacred Songs and Solos* lay on every cottage piano. 'People were thoroughly roused, either to opposition or sympathy,' noted Jane Mackinnon, a ship-owner's wife, who had come up from Campbeltown in Kintyre for the duration. 'It was the subject of conversation everywhere, and everyone had a position to take up, for or against. It was an easy thing to show one's colours.'

Moody forged into Glasgow with every tough ounce of a frame still burly rather than portly, with Sankey manfully pacing him. 'The mind experiences a sense of fatigue in detailing their efforts,' remarked a newspaper when the campaign was at its height. A weekday's first engagement would be the monster prayer meeting at noon, for an hour. 'One to two o'clock, conversation with individuals; four to five o'clock, Bible lecture, attended by some twelve or fifteen hundred; seven to half past eight, evangelistic meeting, with inquiry meeting at close; nine to ten o'clock, young men's meeting.' Sabbath morning held an extra session in the City Hall and a sermon at some other church, but the afternoon was free from twelve-thirty to five. 'He had strength and used it unsparingly,' commented one of his Scottish friends, 'but people seemed to think it had no limit.' He kept one day a week for relaxing, normally Saturday.

Bible lectures and young men's meetings were alike remarkable. The former being at four o'clock drew the more fashionable, since servants and shopkeepers, factory hands and their wives were immersed in the daily grind. 'All around one, people were intensely interested,' wrote Jane Mackinnon. 'Three or four ministers in the pulpit itself and others on the stair, Mr Sankey and the choir on the precentor's platform, and every inch of sitting and standing room occupied.' Bible readings of the Moody-Moorhouse style awakened the People of the Guid Book to their ignorance of it.

This simple teaching of Sunday school sort for adults filled a void left by involved exegesis that flowed ponderously from pulpits. Ministers swallowed pride and introduced Moody's method; in 1900 Sir George Adam Smith, the Biblical scholar, could write, 'In Scotland we owe to Mr Moody a powerful revival of our Bible classes.' The young men's meetings at the end of an exhausting day brought out the very best in Moody, and that of Tuesday, February 24th, became known across Scotland as the 'Hundred-and-One Night'.

While Moody still preached at the City Hall, in Ewing Place Church, 'packed from floor to ceiling', five Edinburgh students led by Henry Drummond gave 'brief, solemn stirring appeals'. Hood Wilson followed on 'Why not to-night?' Moody slipped in. The moment that Hood Wilson stopped Moody said, quite quietly, 'All those who are *sure* they are Christians, stand up!...' 'Sit down again, please! The three pews in front here. I want them cleared. Anyone who wants to take Christ as their Saviour, you all come forward now, so we can pray for you. Let us bow our heads as they come.'

There was extraordinary movement in a tight silence that could be felt. 'From every part of the building a stream began to flow.' Moody lifted his eyes, prayed aloud, and to one of the Edinburgh students, James Stalker, 'the sense of Divine power became overwhelming, and I remember quite well turning round on the platform and hiding my face in my hands, unable to look on the scene any more'. The front seats filled. Moody cleared the next pew, and the next.

An usher counted one hundred and one come forward. 'Christian friends remained conversing with the anxious till about twelve o'clock.' Towards the end a youth who said he 'had been seeking Christ a long time', was going away 'without relief; Mr Moody came up and took me kindly by the hand. He looked at me – I might say he put his two eyes right through mine – and asked me if I would take Christ now. I could not speak, but my heart said, Yes.'

Back in their hotel the Edinburgh Five sat long into the small hours 'discussing the remarkable scene we had just witnessed', and Henry Drummond presented each afterwards with a finely bound New Testament which they all signed; his own copy he used in the next years until it was 'worn to rags'. One of the Glasgow ushers, William Oatts, who had the list of names and addresses of all the hundred and one, kept in touch with most of them for years. 'Did these young fellows stand? Did the decision mean reality?' Over half a century later he claimed that for many it did; he met them, active Christians in Glasgow, London, Australia. And most of the hundred and one in the months immediately following that night worked hard among their generation of all ranks. For a Moody campaign, as men had remarked already, was a spiritual incendiary – always igniting spiritual fire which burned long after the evangelists moved on.

'For the last 3 months I have had to refuse money all the time. At Edinburgh they wanted to raise me two or three thousand £ but I would not let them I told them I would not take it.' Thus Moody wrote to his Chicago friend Whittle on March 7th, 1874.

Any unprejudiced observer could see that Moody had not 'yielded to the temptations that powerfully assail his class. He does not give himself out to be coddled and petted by well-meaning but injudicious admirers.' Letters appeared in the papers asserting the whole campaign to be a glorious hoax organized for gain by Barnum, the American showman. 'Of course I have a good many enemies over here,' Moody told Farwell, 'who say I am a speculating Yankee.' He refused to allow collections for campaign expenses, telling the committee to raise sufficient privately; in Scotland he

appears occasionally to have accepted personal gifts 'to myself for
my own use', beyond hospitality and expenses, but sent much of
what he received across the Atlantic to enable Whittle and Bliss to
abandon business and tour America as another Moody and Sankey.
'If you have not got Faith enough launch out on the strength of my
faith,' he exhorted Whittle. 'Has not our God got as much money
as the Watch Company & all he want of us is to trust Him?' Glasgow
pocket-books had opened wide; Scots who proverbially kept tight
fists on sixpences itched to give pounds. A thirty-year-old chemi-
cal manufacturer called Campbell White, whose father owned the
beautiful estate of Overtoun, asked Moody how he should use his
growing fortune; a young ironmaster, John Colville, asked the same.
Moody need only lift his finger for money to flow. Where should
he point? He had spoken at some of the big shipyards, warehouses
and factories, but knew the force of his detractors' jeer that the
poorest of Glasgow seldom came near his central services: the committee's ticket system tended to debar them. He had glimpsed ex-
tremes of destitution and unemployment. He knew whisky ruled
the slums.

Moody turned the eyes of White, Colville and their like, to consider the cry of Glasgow's poor.

Nor was it a matter merely of money. A text he used repeatedly
was, 'To every man his work.' The result was a surge of activity,
spiritual and social, through channels old and new. The United
Evangelistic Committee perpetuated itself as the Glasgow
Evangelistic Association to begin a long, honourable career in
evangelism and philanthropy – Poor Children's Day Refuges,
Temperance Work, Fresh Air Fortnights, the Cripple Girls' League,
the Glasgow Christian Institute, and a tent on Glasgow Green where
on Sunday mornings young men brought in 'the sleepers-out and
other human derelicts... dejected hungry and wretched-looking'
for a free breakfast (if it was only tea and bread) and a service. A
'Poor Children's Sabbath Dinner' started soon afterwards in co-
operation with an existing agency; a permanent hall rose, and by
1918 five and a half million free meals for adults and children had
been provided.

Economically this was amelioration, not cure, as socialists were quick to point out with scorn at the end of the century when Lord Overtoun (as Campbell White became) collided with Keir Hardie. Moody and his friends in 1874 could not grasp the roots of poverty when modern economic theories were almost unheard. Moreover, they believed that once a man's heart was purified and empowered by the Spirit of God, he could rise above the worst circumstance.

For Glasgow's destitute children, the pathetic orphans of the inebriate, 'hundreds of budding lives anchored down to vice', Moody brought in a munificent gift to William Quarrier's recently formed Orphan Homes of Scotland. Wherever he went 'Mr Moody gave great attention to Young Men's Christian Associations, and at the height of the movement secured very large subscriptions for their foundation or expansion'; Sir George Adam Smith's testimony is valuable because he held no brief for Moody, differed from him theologically, and worked in Glasgow fifteen years. In 1898 he summed up one of the most important facets of the impact on Scotland: 'We have forgotten how often Mr Moody enforced the civic duties of our faith. Yet read again his addresses and articles of the time, and you will believe that in the 'seventies there was no preacher more practical or civic amongst us.'

Moody stayed unmoved by 'some very nasty letters' in the Glasgow press. 'The enemy is thoroughly roused,' Emma remarked. Apart from jokers and the scurrilous, the letter-writers either objected that 'the American brethren virtually and for the time being have superseded the pastors in the city'; or complained that 'Calvinism is in abeyance'.

During early spring Moody detected a change of attitude among strangers, especially from the Highlands. It was reflected in some of the letters in his heavy daily post-bag and in that of Hood Wilson, whose library had become 'a perfect sea of letters, which were not only an inch deep on the large round table in the middle of the room, but covered chairs and shelves in every corner'. Both men knew that a pamphlet to damn them, by the influential Highland preacher John Kennedy of Dingwall, had circulated among extreme

Calvinists and dour conservatives of the remote depopulated northern and western Highlands. *Hyper-Evangelism: 'Another Gospel'
though a Mighty Power* argued that 'the present movement ignores
the sovereignty and power of God', that the emphasis on faith hindered the work of the Holy Spirit and denied 'the utter spiritual
impotence of souls "dead in trespasses and sins".' Dr Kennedy
blasted the inquiry room, the singing of 'human' hymns, the use of
organ music ('unscriptural, and therefore all who have subscribed
the Confession of Faith are under solemn vow against it'), and asserted that prayer meetings had been turned into 'factories of sensation'.

Such diatribe was expected of rigid High Calvinism. Moody said
he could have pointed out more faults in his work himself. This
pamphlet would not account for the subtly poisoned atmosphere.

John Kennedy, a dignified prophet preaching with Celtic fervour sermons massively erudite which simple Highlanders treated
with the utmost veneration, knew Shakespeare, the poets, the Puritan divines – and was an authority on cricket. He had charm, was
widely travelled, lately returned from America. To Kennedy, of the
Free Church, Presbyterians of differing churches who united to work
with Moody appeared betrayers of Calvinism. Not content with his
pamphlet, he cast around for means to cramp the movement, until
a letter from a Chicago acquaintance dropped into his lap. Genuine
Christian though he was, Kennedy distributed manuscript copies
utterly unverified.

Weeks passed before Moody saw a copy and understood the
puzzled glances, shrugs, half hints.

The long letter from a strict Presbyterian lawyer in Chicago, an
emigrant from the Highlands, John Mackay, contained a legitimate
if far-fetched polemic against the YMCA and Moody's teaching.
'... He evidently wishes to get the people of Scotland drifted quietly from their moorings...' But its core had quite another taste,
and Moody skimmed the pages amazed: '...Mr Moody came to
Chicago a poor lad... he called at the office of a pious and wealthy
merchant of this city (now a client of mine) and begged him as a
friend and Christian to give him a place in his office as he wanted

to get away from profanity and ungodliness... Mr Moody with his proverbial audacity and loud Christian professions worked himself into the confidence of the house. His employer had a lawsuit pending in the Court... it transpired that the opposing parties were possessed of secrets of the house. Suspicion at once rested on the saintly Mr Moody... proved him the guilty man... Moody stoutly denied the charge... Undeniable proof... he confessed and was summarily discharged... Soon afterwards publicly declared his determination to discard all worldly pursuits, and to devote himself wholly to the Lord's work. Possessed of great vigour and unlimited cheek he very soon...' etc, etc.

Moody wrote promptly to Farwell from Glasgow on May 7th. 'I heard a few hours ago of a letter that has been written from Chicago to a Dr of Divinity in Scotland making me out a bad man.' He begged Farwell to ask young Henderson (the then head of the house, a nephew of Moody's benefactor) for a letter 'expressing confidence in me... If I did anything unchristian while I was with Henderson I am not aware of it... I was young and might have said and done things that I would not now, but I am grieved to think anyone in that house could say I am guilty of what his letter accuses me of... No one knows me here and if my friends in Chicago do not stand by me, who will, for everyone in this country who is opposed to my preaching and revivals are doing all they can to break me down. I wish you would write me at once.'

A formal request 'for a thorough investigation into the truth or falsehood of these charges' reached Farwell from Kelman, chairman of the Scottish committee: 'If the allegations contained in this letter are quite unfounded, please telegraph per cable to this effect and write to me more fully by post.' Kelman foresaw an uninhibited effort by Kennedy to pillory Moody as a rogue at the imminent General Assembly of the Free Kirk.

Farwell had no difficulty in securing the signatures of thirty-five Chicago ministers to an endorsement of Moody's 'Christian character', which he cabled to Edinburgh. Henderson wrote, 'For fifteen years since Mr Moody left us I have watched him, assisted him and believed in him,' and told Farwell that the conversation upon which Mackay based the slanders was 'intended to raise Moody in his estimation and could only be used as he used it by a wilful perversion of its true intent'.

Farwell demanded a retraction, and since the 'muleish Scotsman' would not retract, threatened Mackay with the law. Moody refused to prosecute. Farwell was disappointed. 'I really think it would be a charitable act to make him pay $5,000 or $10,000 for his slanders, to be expended in evangelizing Dr Kennedy's district in Scotland!'

Kennedy could not kill the Glasgow campaign. A meeting on one of the final days packed the Crystal Palace with registered converts, mostly under twenty-five and of the more educated classes. And on the last Sunday the Great Western Road had been black for three hours with a living stream of all sorts and conditions of men and women, mostly on foot, because 'vehicles were not easily to be had on a Sunday'. Under the strong evening sun of a Scottish May Moody preached in the Botanical Gardens from the box of a carriage to a crowd estimated at twenty or thirty thousand. No one could know the exact figure, which probably lay around fifteen thousand, and if through lack of a wind Moody was not audible to the edges, the singing was unforgettable. To an age when vast meetings were less common it all appeared amazing.

16: Racked Hearts

On the morning of Wednesday, May 20th, 1874, the Americans, 'much fatigued by our incessant labours', went down to Queen Street station without fuss or farewell deputation. Because they were to plunge into two days of Edinburgh meetings before leaving for a heavy itinerary in the North, the two men 'sought the seclusion and rest which a first-class railway carriage in Great Britain affords'; their women and the Moody children seem to have been parked thriftily in second or third class during the short journey, for the evangelists had a carriage to themselves.

Sankey had selected at Menzies' newspaper stall a penny weekly, the *Christian Age,* which specialized in American preaching, and while the train swayed and rattled through Glasgow suburbs scanned it eagerly, to find nothing to interest him except a sermon by Henry Ward Beecher. He gazed out at dull slag-heaps and chimneys. Moody was immersed in Chicago mail. Shortly before Edinburgh Sankey idly took up his paper again to look at the advertisements. 'For sale: A pretty Iron Church (including fittings, etc)... Ambrosial Tea – the most valuable tea ever grown... Shelford's Pianos, from 20 guineas upwards on EASY TERMS... Electricity is Life: Pulvermacher's Patent Galvanic chain Bands, Belts... Hodder and Stoughton's Publications...' He ran his eye down this vitally important book list: 'Dr Wheldon's new commentary... Rev Paxton Hood's new work... One Thousand Gems from Henry Ward Beecher... The New Sunday School hymn book.' He looked across at the next column, on the opposite page, and saw an unsigned poem, 'The Lost Sheep'. It was in bold type and sat on top of Beecher's sermon, but Sankey had missed it the first time. He read the lines carefully.

'Say, Moody. Here's a poem would make a fine evangelistic hymn – if it had a tune.'

Moody glanced up. 'Read it, Sankey.'

Sankey did so 'with all the vim and energy at my command. After I finished I looked at my friend Moody to see what the effect had been, only to discover that he had not heard a word, so absorbed was he in a letter. My chagrin can be better imagined than described.' Sankey popped the poem in his scrapbook. During the press of meetings in Edinburgh that afternoon and evening a phrase or two of possible tunes formed half-consciously in his mind. Next noon in the Free Church Assembly Hall the theme was 'The Good Shepherd'. Several ministers spoke, then Moody as chairman, then white-haired Horatius Bonar, who dwelt briefly but eloquently on the 'Shepherd Work of Christ', carving a deep impression on his sympathetic audience. Moody in the pulpit turned to Sankey at the harmonium: 'Have you a solo appropriate for this subject, to close the service with?'

Sankey had not. 'Greatly troubled', he dismissed the thought of singing a metrical version of the Twenty-Third Psalm because it

had already been used twice at that meeting, and would be no solo:
'I knew that every Scotchman in the audience would join me... At
this moment I seemed to hear a voice saying: "Sing the hymn you
found on the train!" But I thought this impossible, as no music had
ever been written for that hymn.' The seconds ticked. Moody waited.
The audience stirred. Again came the thought, 'Sing that hymn!'

'Placing the little newspaper slip on the organ in front of me, I
lifted my heart in prayer, asking God to help me so to sing that the
people might hear and understand. Laying my hands upon the organ I struck the key of A flat and began to sing:

> *There were ninety and nine that safely lay*
> *   In the shelter of the fold;*
> *But one was out on the hills away,*
> *   Far off from the gates of gold –*
> *Away on the mountains wild and bare,*
> *   Away from the tender Shepherd's care,*
> *   Away from the tender Shepherd's care.*

'After the first verse I was very glad I had got through, but
overwhelmed with fear that the tune for the next verse would be
greatly different from the first. But again looking up to the Lord
for help in this most trying moment, He gave me again the same
tune for all the remaining verses, note for note.'

As the impromptu melody, pibroch-like, redolent of moor and
mist and forest, rose little by little in pitch and tension to its peak in
the fifth line, falling right back in half the last line to point rest,
every man and woman saw the Good Shepherd leave the ninety
and nine, climb the rough road, cross the deep waters and thorn
thickets of the storm-racked mountain, to find His one lost sheep,
'sick and helpless and ready to die'. Then Sankey's voice rang vi-
brant with triumph:

> *But all through the mountains, thunder riven,*
> *   And up from the rocky steep,*
> *There arose a cry to the gate of heaven,*
> *   'Rejoice! I have found My sheep!'*
> *And the angels echoed round the throne:*

> *'Rejoice, for the Lord brings back His own!*
> *'Rejoice, for the Lord brings back His own!'*

Sankey records: 'As the music ceased, a great sigh seemed to go up from the meeting.' Moody, greatly moved, brushing tears from his eyes, hurried from the pulpit and picked up the slip of newsprint.

'Sankey, where did you get that hymn? I never heard the like of it in my life!'

Sankey – with half the audience – in tears, the Victorian's inevitable release from emotional tension, replied solemnly: 'Mr Moody, that's the hymn I read to you yesterday on the train, which you did not hear.'[1]

'The Ninety and Nine' swept Scotland. A short time afterwards Sankey received from a woman a note of thanks for singing the poem of her deceased sister. It had been written in 1868 by Elizabeth Clephane, daughter of Andrew Clephane, late Sheriff of Fife, at the age of thirty-eight; 'she had died the following year. She was left an orphan in childhood with two sisters and a brother, George, a wastrel who was packed off to Canada as a 'remittance man', the contemporary method by which black sheep of 'good' families were given an allowance dependent on their remaining in the colonies. George fell in a drunken stupor on a country road late at night in May 1851, near Fergus in Ontario, to be found dying the following morning. Elizabeth had liked to fancy that in his last hours this lost sheep of a brother 'had found pardon and peace through the Cross'.

When, sixteen years after, a cousin had begged for a poem to print in *The Children's Hour,* Elizabeth recalled her grief and hopes, and wrote the five stanzas. Though copied by one or two other papers it remained little known until Sankey discovered it. Her single other hymn, 'Beneath the Cross of Jesus', also carries one of

---

1. The late Samuel Chadwick told some dinner guests, about 1925, of hearing Moody point out the railway train in the tune of 'The Ninety and Nine'. Chadwick then sang it, emphasizing the *tumpety-tum, tumpety-tum.* Perhaps the germ of the tune passed across Sankey's subconscious mind as he read the verses in the carriage.

the few Sankey tunes to survive, written at Dr Barnardo's house in the East End during the London campaign of 1875.

'The Ninety and Nine' was not Sankey's best, but his most popular, still to be found in representative hymn-books, including the *English Hymnal.* With it, he and the hymns he introduced were woven warp and woof into the Britain, and later into the America, of the 'seventies and after. They spread round the world. *Sacred Songs and Solos* and its American counterpart, *Gospel Songs,* were said to have sold between fifty and eighty million copies in the first fifty years. If greatness were to be estimated by this, or by the tally of persons decisively influenced directly or indirectly, Sankey was great. It has been suggested[1] that fewer people listened to actual performances of Bach's works during the entire nineteenth century than heard Sankey sing in the year 1875.

The music and the musicians of which Sankey was the archetype are derided. The name, if remembered, is mud.

He is judged in the twentieth century for his hymn-book and compositions, and not, as in fairness he should be, for his singing. Sankey essentially was a singer, composing and arranging being a secondary activity. To him the melody was all. Without formal training in choral writing, accustomed to accompany himself on the simplest instrument, he showed little interest in arrangement, and his harmonies were drab, stilted, and limited generally to three basic chords: the tonic, dominant and sub-dominant. They reflected the tinkling taste of the age, the nadir of English music.

Yet many intensely lyrical songs of Sankey or Philip Bliss imply more than they disclose, and if reharmonized create for a generation of a more educated ear the profound impression which they wrought on the late Victorians. 'Grace, 'tis a charming sound', 'Thou didst leave Thy Throne', 'Whosoever heareth' can make good congregational music, while a voice approximating to Sankey's timbre may give Bliss's finest composition, 'Man of Sorrows', a pathos as genuine as that of Handel's 'Behold and See'.

It is said that 'Gospel songs' formed the folk-music of hym-

1. Robert M Stevenson: *Patterns of Protestant Church Music*, Duke University Press, 1953.

nody, that Sankey was the Stephen Foster of sacred music. His was not a conscious use of folk-tunes. But Sankey, Bliss, Bradbury and the others lived close enough to ordinary folk to reflect their feelings. 'Much of it is so Scottish and Irish in its construction,' wrote a Glasgow journalist, 'that to our people, familiar with such music, it is sometimes difficult to realize that what we hear is sacred song... Is it not possible that this may be why these simple songs have found such a direct and wonderful entrance to the Scottish heart?'

Most of Sankey's songs began as solos, each with a chorus which could be memorized by the masses of his hearers who could not read. For congregational singing he would choose established hymnody – metrical psalms in Scotland, in England Watts, or Wesley and hymns of the Evangelical Revival, or the recent hymns of Lyte and Havergal. Popularity forced solos into a choral frame for which they were not designed. The effect was worst when attempted by a small congregation. Sankey music needs one singer – or massed voices. 'Even the critical musician,' wrote a London musical paper in 1875, 'will allow its prodigious grandeur – a grandeur far different from that of a Handel Festival, but more impressive, as it is natural, spontaneous and enthusiastic. No puerility in the words, no consecutive fifths or solecisms in the music, affects those who sing; and the infantile tune becomes magnificent in the surge of ten thousand voices.'

Yet the next generations remembered and judged Sankey as strummed endlessly by amateurs at cottage pianos.

Like all composers Sankey and Bliss wrote more bad music than good. Most composers bury the bad, but the Gospel hymn-writers could not do this – the bad had been collected and perpetuated by popular demand before time weeded out the chaff. And popularity often sprang from non-musical factors; hymns were judged by their effect, which might be caused by social situations that were merely temporary.

The songs were written with a limited purpose: what Sankey called 'preaching and teaching in song'. 'I wish people would get the distinction,' he once said, 'that one class of hymns are to teach, and the other, such as "Praise God from whom all blessings flow"

and "Jesus Lover of my Soul" are hymns in which the whole congregation can praise God.' In the teaching hymn, a development of
the Sunday school music emerging during the 'sixties in America,
words are vital. Sankey 'sings the words and brings out their full
meaning and expression. The music is made subservient, and in
time and accent is constantly varied so as to *fit the words.'* He was
as genuine a preacher as Moody and singing was his natural medium: 'I sang from childhood, and was literally full and running
over with music.' Sankey sang as Moody preached – to implant
simple truths, evoke response. Professional musicians who claimed
that he demeaned music from a fine art by using it as a means to an
end were virtually decrying the use of any art for religious purposes; the fact that his taste was no better than his contemporaries'
is immaterial.

Sankey created a vogue. A host of imitators arose, not all sincere, to stir emotions and soften audiences and make bad music a
substitute for prayer or good preaching. Posterity has judged Sankey by the imitators or by his third-rate interpreters. But the impression he made upon Britain and America can be understood
only by seeing him as man, singer and evangelist.

As man: 'polished, pleasant, sunshiny'; 'very friendly in his
manner'; easier to know than Moody, less impatient, less brusque;
jovial, deeply spiritual but engagingly human – with a touch of the
absurd never far away: 'Sankey,' said Moody at dinner in an English hotel one night as Sankey was about to start on his favourite
dish of steak and fried onions, 'Sankey, do you expect to speak to
anxious souls to-night?'

'Why, yes.'

'Then put down those onions!'

A pause. 'Well! I like my onions, but I like to lead souls to
Jesus, so I guess the onions will have to go.'

His untrained baritone voice, of moderate compass, slightly
rough but round and full and with that quality of 'sweetness' much
prized in his age, had what Hitchcock of Chicago called an 'indescribable quality which, with his sympathetic nature, seldom failed
to reach the most hidden recesses of the heart'. It was this capacity

to penetrate, to create spiritual longing, soften prejudice, bend wills, that was Sankey's distinctive gift. 'He racked the hearts of all classes, rich and poor,' wrote an Englishwoman. Quality of voice cannot explain this; had he come before the public as a concert performer he would have made small stir. Nor may it be dismissed as a trick. Sankey, like Moody, had a horror of consciously whipped-up emotion. Probably he did sometimes force the emotional temperature, for the line between devotional awareness and mental excitement is thin, but his aim was to teach, to confront; to draw his hearers to God.

He was pre-eminently an evangelist, with the true minister's power of submitting himself to be a vehicle of the Divine. 'Mr Moody had just given an impressive address,' wrote a Scots lad, a trained singer, 'and as he closed, a sigh of relief from nervous tension seemed to pass over the gathering. Mr Sankey took his seat at the little harmonium, sounded a few chords and said "There were ninety and nine". Not a sound was heard as he unfolded the story. The people forgot that he was singing – he was telling an old story with a new charm. It was enthralling. As he uttered the last words Moody's hand was up, and heads and hearts were bowed before God, while sheep who had wandered were gathered into the fold.' 'Mr Sankey sings with the conviction that souls are receiving Jesus between one note and the next,' wrote an Edinburgh woman. 'When you hear "The Ninety and Nine" being sung you know of a truth that down in this corner, up in that gallery, behind that pillar which hides the singer's face from the listener, the hand of Jesus has been finding this and that and yonder lost one, to place them in His fold.'

17: The Road to London

Through that whole summer of 1874 revival burned over Scotland. 'Across all the years,' John McNeill wrote poetically half a century on, 'my heart still kindles at the glory of that time. I got my soul and my Saviour out of it. I feel like crying out to the dwindling survivors of that generation; crying out to remind ourselves of that mighty rush and sweep, when all over the land the souls of men were bound before the Lord, like the standing corn in a harvest wind!'

Moody, using a different metaphor, said he was merely shaking the trees: the fruit had long ripened under faithful teaching by the churches. Once the shaking began, the harvest wind to blow, the effect reached far beyond where Moody and Sankey happened to be; indeed, the 'greatest results comparatively have been reported from districts which they have not visited'. Henry Drummond and other students were sent – casually but effectively – to places the Americans had no time for in Scotland, and to northern England where they had been already, and local clergy passed on the fiery cross. Andrew Murray of South Africa, returning to Scotland a few years after Moody's visit, noticed 'very distinctly the influence of Mr Moody's work. There is much more readiness to talk out, and much more warmth... The whole religious tone of Scotland has been lifted up and brightened most remarkably.'

Sankey went south early in August 1874 to rejoin Fanny, the new baby, Ira, and the older children fresh from America, but from late May until early September Moody worked in the north of Scotland until, upon their twelfth wedding anniversary, feasting on the views, the Moodys with their children steamed down Loch Ness and the Caledonian Canal (even Moody could not be seasick) to preach at Oban. Next day they sailed through the glorious scenery of the islands. Late in the evening, after a carriage drive of forty miles, 'very, very tired, Willie fast asleep, [little] Emma nearly so', they reached the home of Peter and Jane Mackinnon at Campbeltown.

Now that they had Moody 'in our very home, to know him and talk to him in ordinary life', Jane scribbled notes of all he said and did and was. She fell in love with ten-year-old Emma because she reminded her of their own dead child; this may have been the first step towards becoming Mrs Moody's greatest friend on either side of the Atlantic. Peter Mackinnon, who was a partner of the British India Line, in course of years became to Moody 'more of a father than any man that has crossed my path'.

Of the Campbeltown mission Jane treasured most the little incidents and facets: how Moody came back after a meeting on a windy night remarking 'the gas made such a noise, it roared and I had to roar, and it was a battle between us, but I think I won'; how when the beadle kept opening a door which Moody shut because a draught interfered with the inquiry work, he locked it and put the key in his pocket; how he would inspect a church for ventilation before speaking; 'he had all his wits about him, even for the smallest details'. She noticed his decisiveness – 'You just listen to me, and do what I tell you.' And his adaptability in the services: 'He said he never knew, even a few minutes before, what he was going to do... I suppose he asks guidance at every step, and is sure he gets it.'

Jane Mackinnon found both Moodys good companions. 'I liked the combination of playfulness and seriousness in Mr Moody... It was delightful having him at leisure; he is so simple, unaffected and lovable, plays so heartily with the children, and makes fun with those who can receive it. He is brimful of humour.' He played croquet, helped the children catch crabs on the beach, and when they all went for a drive in the hills 'we had a delightful little time, race, scramble, lunch, fun'.

As to Emma, 'one day was enough to show what a source of strength and comfort she was to her husband. The more I saw of her afterwards, the more convinced I was that a great deal of his usefulness was owing to her, not only in the work she did for him, relieving him of all correspondence, but also from her character. Her independence of thought... her calmness, meeting so quietly his impulsiveness, her humility.' When telegrams poured in urging him to squeeze in a visit to yet another place and he said 'Which way should I go? I really don't know what to do,' Emma would not sway him. 'You decide, and tell me, and I'll write.' 'Dear, uncomplaining Mrs Moody,' – Jane had not adjectives enough – 'so patient, quiet, bright, humble; one rarely meets just so many qualities in one woman.' But Emma had the last word. That very week, from the Mackinnons' house, two days before leaving Scotland at the close of those formidable nine months, she wrote to her mother in Chicago: 'Mr Moody is nicer and kinder every day. He is a gem of a husband. I ought to be *very happy*.'

The Moodys crossed to Ireland for five weeks with Sankey in Belfast, where Glasgow scenes were repeated. The Belfast memories of the Moodys ranged from sublime to the ridiculous – from the immense audience on a Sunday afternoon in Templemore Park, where Moody preached downwind from a platform rigged on a couple of wagons, to the abominable pet monkey at their hosts' house which knew perfectly well Mrs Moody was scared. One evening it secreted itself in the chandelier above the dining-room table and leaped on to her head: 'One of the few times I ever heard her scream,' her daughter tells.

Moody snorted at a warning to avoid Dublin with its Roman Catholic majority, capital of the whole strife-infested island, and the first Dublin meeting drew great crowds. There followed the slowest grind since Edinburgh, to reach a climax that was reckoned to surpass any in Scotland. For the first time Moody and Sankey had broad support from Episcopalians, including several bishops of the recently disestablished Church of Ireland. Moody astounded the Irish by refusing to attack Roman Catholics, who therefore did not scruple to attend. The campaign became the talk of the town, Irish volubility giving Emma choice snippets: 'Shure and it's Mr Sankey I like best. And which would it be you prefer, ma'am?' At a music hall one comic turn said to the other:

'I am rather Moody to-night. How do you feel?'

'Sankeymonious!'

The gallery hissed. Someone started singing 'Hold the Fort', which the whole audience took up till the comedians fled to the wings.

The Dublin correspondent of *The Times,* bringing Moody and Sankey for the first time to London breakfast-tables in November 1874, commended the mission as 'the most remarkable ever witnessed in Ireland', adding that it had 'a character essentially different and seemed to possess elements of vitality which were wanting in others'. He noticed especially the 'absence of any effort at self-display but rather a sensitive avoidance of it', and the 'reverence and devotion' of the services. Among the thousands who heard the evangelist was a youth called George Bernard Shaw. Five months later, reading of the London campaign, he wrote a letter to *Public Opinion* ascribing it all to publicity, curiosity, novelty and excitement; as to converts, the effect was 'a tendency to make them highly objectionable members of society'. The editor printed the letter of April 3rd, 1875; thus, by a quirk of history, Moody was responsible for Bernard Shaw's first appearance in print.

The campaign closed with a great 'Christian Convention for Ireland'. Railway companies brought ministers and laity from every corner of the unpartitioned land at reduced fares to the Exhibition Palace, its 'long vista lined on both sides with festoons of climbing plants, with two beautiful fountains in the centre'. Once again the world wondered at the submerging of bitter sectarian feelings: 'It was the first time that all these ministers had met on a platform broader than their churches.' Moody's touch could be felt in the committee's arrangement that clergymen from a distance were lodged with clerical families of denominations other than their own.

Of the several thousand converts reported from Dublin, the most charming of stories comes through a young American visitor twenty-five years later, who on asking the Dublin YMCA to find him lodgings was escorted to a near-by house. The man who opened the door shook his head: they were no longer taking lodgers. The YMCA member said: 'The gentleman comes from America.' 'Oh, it's from America you are? Then come along in. You shall certainly stay.'

When at the end of a week the American asked for the bill, the landlady said there was none; pressed, she replied that the only payment could be another week free. He argued. She exclaimed, 'Our home was the home of a drunkard. Through the influence of one of your Americans, Mr D L Moody, my husband was converted and my home is now a Christian home. It is very little we can do to show our appreciation, but hospitality is one of the few things we can do and we hope you will not take that pleasure away from us.'

At the end of November the Americans crossed the Irish Sea, a 'very fine smooth passage, but there was a slight roll'. Jane Mackinnon saw Moody distinctly green. 'I was naughty enough to

enjoy his downcast look and to see him not master of the situation.'
Manchester, Sheffield, Birmingham; and over all the unspoken question, would Moody fail in London?

Manchester in the rain: the Albert Hall in the city where Moody
might have begun in '73 at some back-street chapel. Little 'Arry
Moorhouse, aiding his old friend, rejoiced that 'Success has not
made him proud. He uses his ten talents, I use my one and we both
together praise the Lord for using us at all.'

For Christmas, the North London suburb where Emma stayed
because Willie was unwell. She had written on December 22nd, 'I
think I am more of a baby than either of the children, for I had
really felt that I should have had hard work on Christmas not to be
homesick without him.' When he left again the family had 'an attack of influenza all around' and retreated to Bournemouth.

Sheffield over the New Year: 'There is a degree of religious
feeling in the town,' a Church of England newspaper, the *Record*,
reported, 'which has not been equalled for years.' Birmingham in
the icy January of 1875, where the effect may be gauged by doggerel sold on the kerbs and in the Bull Ring:

Oh, the town's upside down, everybody seems mad,
  When they come to their senses we all shall feel glad,
For the rich and the poor, and the good and the bad,
  Are gone mad over Moody and Sankey.

After service at Bingley Hall night after night, in the words of a
convert looking back after fifty-three years, 'groups of people would
be collected here and there, on gallery and floor, round some worker
in the mission, anxiously inquiring for the way of salvation, con-
fessing sin or doubt or difficulty'. An Anglican clergyman wrote,
'Such a chance of guiding souls comes only once in a life time.'

A few days' rest in Bournemouth, then Liverpool in February,
where the local committee had erected a monster auditorium of
timber. Liverpool in the snow. At Liverpool Moody had an awful
premonition of danger which drove him to take such precautions
that he began to wonder whether overwork had unhinged his mind
– until one evening the police told him they had just caught an

escaped lunatic whom Confederate ghosts were goading to murder the Yankee preacher.

When about to leave a city Moody would summon young Henry Drummond from the previous place, generally by telegram 'in a great hurry scurry', to work together the final days and continue on his own as Moody moved onward, each week bringing London nearer – vast, critical London, which he must face with his stock of sermons not only used again and again but now printed in newspapers and pirated by pamphleteers.

All Britain was singing. From Liverpool Moody scrawled a page to Whittle about Bliss: 'I am delighted with his music. I do not think he has got his equal on earth at this time & raised up of God to do the work that he is doing, his hymns are all ready sung around the world, we are using them to do a great work in this country. To let you know something of how they are liked we are selling of the penny book 250,000 per month they are going all over the United Kingdom & God is using them as much as he did Wesley's hymns in the days of the Wesleys. Tell Bliss to keep at it, God bless him is my earnest prayer.'

The august Dr Dale of Carr's Lane Congregational Church, Birmingham, theologian, preacher, politician, felt puzzled. He had been expecting a revival, for religious life had been touched with expectancy for two or three years, but 'I certainly did not suppose' it would come through 'two American strangers'. Watching the attentive faces of the great crowd at Bingley Hall, 'of all sorts, young and old, rich and poor, keen tradesmen, manufacturers and merchants and young ladies who had just left school, rough boys who knew more about dogs and pigeons than about books, and cultivated women... I could not understand it.'

He told Moody: 'The work is most plainly of God, for I can see no relation between yourself and what you have done.' Moody laughed and replied, 'I should be very sorry if it were otherwise.'

Many were puzzled. Even those who ascribed the movement's force to the tremendous wave of prayer it generated wondered why this particular man, an American at that, should be the focal point.

The secret was partly the way Moody preached. 'Perfect naturalness,' Dale described it. 'He talks in a perfectly unconstrained and straightforward way, just as he would talk to half a dozen old friends at his fireside.'

In an age of ponderous English sermons when Spurgeon, most popular of all preachers, mouthed rolling periods, piled metaphor upon metaphor, Moody merely chatted, 'to thirteen thousand as to thirteen', on what the Bible showed him. He made it alive in the context of every day. Daniel in the lions' den takes out his watch to check if it is the hour of prayer. Scoffers before the Flood 'talk it over in the corner groceries, evenings: "Not much sign of old Noah's rain-storm yet!"' Bartimeus, suddenly seeing ('the first object that met his gaze was the Son of God himself'), rushes into Jericho 'and he says, "I will go and see my wife and tell her about it" – a young convert always wants to talk to his friends about salvation – Away he goes down the street 'n he meets a man who passes him 'n goes on a few yards 'n then turns round 'n says, "Bartimeus, is that you?" "Yes." "Well, I thought it was, but I couldn't believe my eyes! How've you gotten your sight?" "Oh, I just met Jesus of Nazareth outside the city and asked him to have mercy on me." "Jesus of Nazareth! What! is he in this part of the country?" "Sure. Right here in Jericho." "I *should* like to see him!" and away he runs down the street...'

It's Zaccheus (or 'Zakkus' as Moody would say) soon in the sycamore tree. And thus the sermon leads to another scene of Christ meeting a man in his need. 'Sin, gloom and darkness flee away. Light, peace, joy burst into the soul.'

Moody had the gift of fading from his hearers' consciousness. 'Throughout his address you entirely forgot the man, so full was he of his message and so held were you by his earnestness, intensity and forceful appeal. He had many illustrations drawn from his personal experiences, but never did self appear prominent... He was completely absorbed in the message and in getting it over to the mind, heart and conscience of those listening.'

At one Liverpool meeting for men, a force of rationalists were reported present. In the speakers' room before the service F B Meyer was awed by Moody's prayer, his overpowering 'burden of heart'. Moody preached. Large numbers stayed for the after-meeting. Moody came down from the platform, stood on a chair 'and launched out in a wonderful discourse. His invectives against sin, and his lashings of the conscience, were awful. He seemed to be wrestling with an unseen power. Beneath those burning words men's faces grew pale under a conviction of the broken law of God. Then he began with the wooings of the Gospel, in a strain of tender and heart-breaking entreaty; and before he was through the whole audience seemed completely broken. One man arose and said, "Mr Moody, I want to be a Christian." It seemed but a moment when forty or fifty men were on their feet...'

Moody's message sprang on an England where basic thought-forms were strongly Christian, where only the lowest knew nothing of the Bible. He touched English religion at its points of sharpest need. As he said, 'The Church is dying of respectability' – smothered by its own success.

By the 1870s the Evangelical Revival had filtered into every nook and cranny to dominate much of the outlook even of those, whether Tractarians or new-fashioned agnostics, repudiating its tenets, with thousands upon thousands of the unthinking mass who obeyed Evangelicalism's dictates yet lived untouched by its heart. Beliefs and ethics revolutionary in the eighteenth century were now necessary for promotion or a good name. Sins of the flesh must be concealed behind a veneer of the spirit. The Golden Rule had changed: 'Thou shalt not be found out.' Moreover, reaction from past bawdiness had created prudery in the present, while inequality of the sexes never was more marked than in Victorian damnation of 'fallen women', whose seducers or patrons, if reasonably discreet, flourished unabashed, undamned.

Moody pierced this screen of hypocrisy.

More widespread lay the diluted Christianity which supposed heaven to be earned by goodness and hell by being wicked, used fear of hell as a sanction to protect the accepted code, and knew nothing of grace. Against this, Moody proclaimed eternal life as the gift of God to the undeserving. He did not deny eternal punishment for those who refused this gift, 'but I believe that the magnet that goes down to the bottom of the pit is the love of Jesus'. He repudiated the nicely calculated less or more of moralizers. 'When the prodigal came home, grace met him and embraced him. Law said, Stone him! – grace said Embrace him! Law said Smite him! – grace said, Kiss him! Law went after him and bound him. Grace said, Loose him and let him go! Law tells me how crooked I am; grace comes and makes me straight.'

Moody proclaimed that God wanted men more than they wanted Him, that salvation was not a grudged reward for a consistent climb into goodness, but the new birth of a repentant sinner into the life of Christ. '*Instant* salvation' he called it, again and again. 'He preached,' wrote Dale, 'in a manner that produced the sort of effect produced by Luther, and provoked similar criticism. He exulted in the free grace of God... His joy was contagious. Men leaped out of darkness into light, and lived a Christian life afterwards.'

It had been so in the days of Wesley and Whitefield, and in Ulster and parts of Scotland in 'fifty-nine, but during recent years only here and there among individuals, or in limited sectors such as that of the very poor who came to the appeal of General Booth and his new Salvation Army. Moody was bringing this joy to all classes. In each city these leaps out of darkness came first among the middle-class, then among the poor, then the rich and leisured. That was in the provinces; for the movement to become national, he must win London.

Dale saw this 'instant transition take place with nearly every person with whom I talked' at the close of after-meetings in Birmingham. 'They had come up into the gallery anxious, restless, feeling after God in the darkness,' and after a conversation of fifteen or twenty minutes 'their faces were filled with joy, and they left me not only at peace with God but filled with joy... These people carried their new joy with them to their homes and their workshops. It could not be hid.'

Nine years later Dale told a friend that of the two hundred who joined his own church through Moody, three-quarters 'have stood well'. And thirty-five years later, another Birmingham convert, one

Charles E Brown, described his own very typical experiences. 'A lonely and miserable lad... embittered,' he had followed the crowd to Bingley Hall, heard Moody and 'thought nothing of it. I was scornful in my spirit. But there was some fascination about the man that brought me there the next night. An address given that night on "Excuses" tore away from my heart every shred of excuse that stood between my soul and Jesus Christ. At the end of that address, in that great assembly of eighteen thousand people, I yielded up my life to Jesus Christ. I was one of the multitude who never gave in their names. I have lived an unworthy Christian life since that day, and of all men in the Christian ministry I am probably the most unworthy; but the last influence coming on top of a mother's prayers and a Sunday school teacher's letters, the last influence that led me to surrender my unworthy life to Jesus Christ came from the Spirit of God through the lips of D L Moody.'

18: Dockers and Duchesses

Police Constable George Ling of the A or Westminster Division, Metropolitan Police, aged twenty-three, thought it 'very remarkable' that he should be on duty at the preparatory reception to Moody and Sankey on March 8th, 1875, for his father in Norfolk had asked him to send newspaper reports of the coming campaign: not that the constable cared about that sort of thing.

His post in Exeter Hall was at the bottom of the wide stairs, and he heard Sankey's voice clearly through the doors. This 'gave me the desire to attend their meetings to hear the evangelists. The result was my conversion.' Becoming Queen Victoria's personal police-constable, in attendance for many years, he held evangelistic services at the Windsor YMCA, and, when the Queen was at Osborne, a men's Bible class at Cowes.

George Ling was one of thousands transformed during Moody and Sankey's London mission between March and July 1875.

A vigorous committee – clergy, Members of Parliament, high-ranking officers – had flooded London with notices, had organized a visitation of the entire capital and, for a start, had booked the Agricultural Hall in Islington – then north London's principal middle-class area – for ten weeks at a weekly rent of £50. This home of the annual prize cattle-show had been adapted by the contractor, Mr Sharman, to hold over fifteen thousand chairs.

When the crowds poured in two hours before the opening service on Tuesday, March 9th, they saw the west end arranged in rising steps which to the *Illustrated London News* gave the 'appearance of a gigantic infant school'. The red baize dais had seats on the left for participants and distinguished guests, in the centre 'a kind of railed pulpit or reading desk', to the right the voluntary choir of nearly two hundred. All round the hall red banners proclaimed texts such as: 'Repent ye and believe the gospel', 'The gift of God is eternal life', 'Ye must be born again', 'They shall sing in the ways of the Lord'. Gas jets hung in chandeliers and in three lines down the side and two or three semicircular arches over the centre, making the crowded building hot as well as light, and causing a mist which spoiled the view from the gallery. The enormous sounding-board over the dais proved ineffective, and after ten days a large quantity of thick galvanized wire was suspended from the roof, to be replaced later by a canvas awning.

At seven-thirty Moody and Sankey stepped on to the dais. Moody's opening words created a sensation: 'Let us rise and sing to the praise of God. Let us praise Him for what He is *going to do* in London.' The whole audience sang the doxology.

The service proceeded on the familiar plan described by the *Daily Telegraph* as 'the interchange of precept and song, the omission of anything that could tend to monotony, and a constant opportunity for all to take part in the service'. The *Daily Telegraph* correspondent – who must have had a bad place, for he described Moody as tall, if stout, with a 'not unintellectual cast of countenance' – was relieved to discover him 'altogether as unlike the conventional "ranter" as it is possible to conceive', and, with unconscious snobbery, assured readers that Moody had little American about him except a strange western twang, and that Sankey might be mistaken for an Englishman anywhere.

Apart from two isolated incidents, sixteen or seventeen thousand listened in perfect quiet 'except for the occasional coughing which always attends the gathering of a vast congregation in England'. Moody spoke in his usual style, polished a little since Edinburgh but very much his own, 'straightforward, racy', recorded *The Times* in a remarkably friendly article, 'full of American humour, often it must be owned, a little vulgar' because he described venerable Bible narratives 'as if they were good American stories picked up in Chicago'; but for all that a 'strong clear voice', showing his hearers the 'means of becoming better men and women, and of having a better hope in this world and the next'.

Thus, quietly, the evening moved towards its climax. Moody said: 'God has laid it upon the heart of the world to pray for London. It must be that God has something good in store for London; the Son of Man is coming to London to seek and to save that which was lost. And I pray that the Good Shepherd may enter this hall tonight and may come to many a heart and that you may hear the still small voice: "Behold, I stand at the door, and knock: if any man hear My voice, and open the door, I will come in to him, and will sup with him, and he with Me." O friends! open the door to-night and let the heavenly visitor in. Do not turn Him away any longer. Do not say with Felix, "Go thy way this time, and when I have a convenient season I will call for thee." Make this a convenient season. Make this the night of your Salvation. Receive the gift of God to-night and open the door of your heart and say: "Welcome, thrice welcome into this heart of mine!"'

Moody had warned his sympathizers: 'We must expect opposition. If you think a great work is to be done here without opposition you will be greatly mistaken. The opposition will be bitter... There will be many bitter things said, and many lies started, and as someone has said, a lie will get half round the world before the truth gets its boots on!'

Despite the friendly tone of *The Times* and several other papers, a shower of vituperative printers' ink splattered the evangelists.

High Church Tories in London clubs and prim maiden aunts

read in the *Morning Post:* 'their teaching is wild, baseless, and uncertain... Moody and Sankey will be a puff in the wind.' Coachmen
and bar-tenders thumbing through the *Morning Advertiser* were
told: 'there must have been thousands in that crowd of uplifted
faces who looked with horror and shame on the illiterate preacher
making little better than a travesty of all they held sacred.' Moody's
accent was 'broadly and vulgarly American'. 'Vulgar' was worked
hard in the London press, to deride Moody's accent and his preaching. The *Saturday Review* decided, from afar, that he was 'a ranter
of the most vulgar type' whose mission appeared to be 'to degrade
religion to the level of the "penny gaff",' an itinerant guttershow
such as Punch and Judy. 'Mr Sankey's singing is as vulgar as Mr
Moody's preaching' said *Vanity Fair,* publishing one of its famous
cartoons.

  Punch called them 'comic evangelists' and brought out a long
poem beginning:

> *At Islington Hall those Revivalists Yankee*
> *Pious pair D L Moody and Ira D Sankey,*
> *Are drawing, they tell us, immense congregations*
> *By eccentric devotions and droll ministrations.*
> *Their manner seems strangely at odds with their matter,*
> *The former grotesque and most serious the latter.*
> *They proclaim Gospel truths, in spite of grave prepossessions,*
> *In colloquial slang, and commercial expressions.*
> *State Scriptural facts in American phrases,*
> *And interpolate jokes 'twixt their prayers and their praises...*

Mr Punch meant no harm and next week apologized, rather lamely.

  Scurrilous libels circulated: 'Where the corpulent old expounder
is known he is regarded as a selfish, sensual, hypocritical variegator
of facts.' Sankey was said to have started as a nigger minstrel but
had found evangelism paid better, and both were amassing fortunes
from hymn-books, commission on sale of organs, the gifts of
admirers, and penny lives and pictures hawked in the streets. On
their return to the 'land of the everlasting dollar' they would 'gaze
upon their cosy homesteads purchased with good English gold, and

with a merry twinkle of the eye exclaim: "We have spoiled the Egyptians, *I guess*.'" Moody had done his utmost to suppress the 'lives', he refused to be photographed, rejecting lucrative offers and turning his back should an amateur set up his cumbrous camera on a tripod and dive under the black cloth. Unauthorized prints were so imaginative that an earnest sympathizer hastily issued a pamphlet: *Mr Moody not a Jew*. As to *Sacred Songs and Solos*, Moody and Sankey had been using the mounting royalties to defray personal and family expenses until, on January 1st, 1875, an enlarged edition was published, of which sales would be enormous. The evangelists already had sufficient for expenses until the end of their stay. The London committee refused to touch the money. Moody announced that Sankey and he had asked the publishers, as from January 1st, to 'hand over the royalty upon all our hymn books to one of your leading citizens, Mr Hugh Matheson, who will devote the same to such charitable objects as may be decided upon'.

Strict Baptists and High Calvinists wrote tracts ('This Goliath of Free Will... Mr Moody has *no* good seed to sow'). Even Spurgeon, commanding and supporting him publicly, was annoyed privately because Moody refused his 'very dictatorial' advice to attack the Church of England. In the East End Spurgeon 'scattered Baptist papers' before Moody's arrival, urging converts to be rebaptized. This, so Moody told Whittle in 1876, created resentment and 'few converts went into Baptist churches'.[1]

Despite libel and criticism, Agricultural Hall attendance, which had dropped slightly the second night, rose until reaching, after more space had been arranged, an estimated 20,000 nightly except Saturdays, the evangelists' day off; Sunday meetings were early morning and late evening to avoid interfering with churches. The figures probably exaggerated by several thousands, but for a nightly draw were unprecedented, to the England of 1875 fantastic.

The Lord Chancellor of Disraeli's new Conservative Government, Cairns, an Ulsterman, attended frequently: he was the sec-

---

1. This new sidelight on Spurgeon comes from the entry for May 3rd, 1876, in the unpublished diary of D W Whittle, recording a conversation with Moody that day at Augusta, Georgia.

ond of those two who in Moody's view helped most in Britain, 'for people said if the Lord Chancellor came to my services they had better come too'. Gladstone, lately fallen from power and now Leader of the Opposition, talked privately with Moody and once or twice sat on the platform among the lay and clerical supporters from every denomination. A High Churchman from an evangelical background, 'Gladstone, Moody says, is a converted man and a true and humble Christian'. A young Scotsman heard Gladstone exclaim: 'I thank God I have lived to see the day when He should bless His church on earth by the gift of a man able to preach the gospel of Christ as we have just heard it preached!' At which Matthew Arnold, standing beside him, said: 'Mr Gladstone, I would give all I have if only I could believe it.'

Gladstone envied the man whose voice night after night reached so far in an age without mechanical aids: 'I wish I had your chest, Mr Moody!'

'And I wish I had your head on top of it!'

The aged Lord Shaftesbury, to his surprise, had not been asked 'to join them on their committee or to give my name[1] [?] or to express any sympathy', merely for a subscription. He received no invitation to the preparatory reception at Exeter Hall. 'I shall wait to be called. I shall avoid intrusion, or obtrusion of any kind.'

From the distance of his house in Grosvenor Square he rejoiced at first reports, yet puzzled because 'from all I read and hear they "present the Gospel" but, I think, an imperfect Gospel – They preach Christ but not "Christ Crucified!" How then does the Divine Favour so rest upon them? It is almost impossible *now* to regard the power and influence, as not superhuman.' He was a little troubled lest they made the 'terms of life' too easy: 'Salvation is thrown broadcast; and almost at the heads of the Hearers.'

By March 25th he was writing: 'The success of Moody and Sankey not only unabated [?] but increased. It seems more and more a supernatural character. It comes at a time when the masses are lying in indifference, and are nevertheless impressible. They

---

1. Shaftesbury's handwriting in his Diary is very hard to decipher.

are sleepy, but have no objection to listen. They will not seek, but they may be found. It looks amazingly like the "right man, at the right hour".' Next day, Good Friday, Shaftesbury went for the first time and gladly admitted that they 'preach Christ Crucified'. 'Deeply impressed; the more impressed, because of the imperfection of the whole thing.' Down at his Dorset mansion the following week he stood at his tall desk and scrawled page after page of diary. How Sankey's song, so simple, went 'to the inmost soul, and seemed to empty it of everything, but thought of the good, tender, and lowly Shepherd'. Moody's voice was 'bad and ill managed', the language colloquial, and Shaftesbury a little scandalized that the anecdotes were 'oftentimes bordering on the "humorous", almost to the extent of provoking a laugh!' (This must have been a masterly understatement dictated by the earl's old-fashioned sense of propriety; unless Good Friday had muted Moody.) There was nothing externally to win, perhaps something to repel, 'and yet the result is striking, effective, touching and leading to much thought... the Holy Spirit can work out of feeble materials. Is it not so to-day?'

He launched into a meditation. How, when bishops were lecturing right and left 'upon Homiletics and the persuasion of the Masses – Here come two simple, unlettered men from the other side of the Atlantic...' Untrained, unskilled, having no denomination; on the other hand, not sinister: 'They are calm, without an approach to the Fanatical, or even the Eccentric. They seek neither to terrify, nor to puff up; eschew controversy and flatter no passions!' Yet thousands of all degrees, 'workpeople, shopkeepers, merchants and lawyers, clergy and laity alike confess the power and cannot explain it'. Shaftesbury repeated that there must be 'something in it superhuman'. God has chosen the foolish things of the world to confound the wise. Dipping his quill (they were going out but he used one still) and hovering over the top of the right-hand page, he thought of the greatest Tractarian preacher of the day; and scrawled, 'Moody will do more in an hour than Canon Liddon in a century!'[1]

Thenceforth Shaftesbury gave Moody the full weight of his pres-

---

1. Liddon of St Paul's might have been chagrined had he read this. A year later, on Whitsunday of 1876, in an Oxford University Sermon, he paid a glowing tribute to Moody

tige and wisdom. At a discussion of committee and sympathizers on the morning of April 7th, Shaftesbury more than anyone directed Moody to the scene of his most remarkable influence.

Shaftesbury pointed out that the Agricultural Hall had not attracted widely either 'the lowest grades of the people' or the upper classes. (The *Saturday Review* had jeered that it was filled 'by smug, self-satisfied, middle-class respectability, smirkingly confident of its own spiritual security'.) For the former a vast temporary structure was being hammered together in the East End on Bow Common. For the wealthy, afternoon Bible Readings would start the next week in the Queen's Opera House in the Haymarket, but Shaftesbury, the 'Poor Man's Earl', 'in a most earnest and powerful appeal to Mr M, which carried with it, as appeared from the cheering, the general sympathy of all present', urged evening meetings there too. 'In the Opera House your preaching will be heard by multitudes who will throng in of an evening from the university clubs, the naval and military and other clubs in the neighbourhood. There will be many of high intellectual and social position who will thus have the Gospel brought nearer to them, and not only these but many tradesmen and shopkeepers and their dependents who cannot or will not go to Islington.'

Moody disagreed. He wanted to extend the Islington mission beyond schedule to the end of May, when he was due to begin in South London. Why should he abandon a hall of twenty thousand for the five thousand of the Opera House? Privately, he did not relish being thrown to the lions of the aristocracy. He could just imagine them: 'Aw, my deah fellah, have you heard these – aw – vulgah Yankees, awfully funny, what?'

In the event, the impact of the West End Bible Readings caused him to hand the Agricultural Hall to an associate nine days early, on May 9th.

When he had to begin in East London Moody announced that for a while there would be *two* evangelistic services each evening: Bow, 7.30 pm, Haymarket, 9.0 pm. On Bow Common, in the new-

and Sankey, although to his mind 'they knew little or nothing of... sacramental channels whereby the life of grace is planted and maintained in the soul'.

rigged gas-lit monstrosity with galvanized iron roof and sawdust floor, he preached each evening to eight or nine thousand of the sort he loved most to be among; he might have been back in Illinois Street. At half-past eight he and Sankey jumped into a brougham, trotting as swiftly as traffic allowed up the Mile End Road and through the City, under shored-up Temple Bar, round Trafalgar Square to the Haymarket; from the East End to the West, from a world of slums and squalor to that of great mansions and the royal parks, from dockers to duchesses. Arthur Kinnaird (afterwards 11th Lord Kinnaird), then aged twenty-eight, told Will Moody in 1900: 'Nothing showed the wonderful adaptability of your father more... coming from Bow Road, the poorest part of the East End, to the very antipodes of it all in character and surroundings, and yet at once hitting on the right note of dealing with the new conditions.' St. James's, Mayfair and Westminster lay close, Belgravia a short carriage drive: the heart of fashionable London, proud, close-knit, still fairly exclusive, a society of privilege, pleasure and wealth. The stage of the Opera House (it replaced that burned in 1867, and was demolished in 1892 to be rebuilt as Her Majesty's Theatre) served as platform for committee and clergy, Moody's reading-desk in the centre, and the auditorium, except for the pit and the galleries high above, consisted of stalls and circles of boxes: an indignant boxrenter, Mr Leader, sought an injunction from the Court of Chancery to prevent the theatre's use for untheatrical purposes. Refused the injunction but awarded costs and nominal damages, Mr Leader and several others kept their private boxes locked and empty. [1]

'The scene in the Haymarket baffles description,' wrote an eye-witness. 'It was literally blocked with the carriages of the aristocratic and plutocratic of the land; and the struggle for admission was perhaps more severe in the West than in the East.' 'When we got to the Opera House,' wrote another, 'we found an immense crowd outside. We got a place at the very top of the highest gallery, and although at that distance Mr Moody seemed a tiny figure of a

1. The present writer regrets to state that the motion to stop Moody using the Opera House was put to the court by his great-uncle by marriage, J W Chitty, QC, afterwards a Lord Justice.

man, every word, even his whispered words, were heard... I was struck with the impression which Mr Sankey's singing made on the audience.' The Duchess of Sutherland 'insists upon going every day'. The Sutherlands had entertained Moody at Dunrobin Castle in the Highlands, the Duchess being a chieftain and a countess in her own right and lately Mistress of the Robes, the Duke the owner of more acres than any man in Europe. 'God bless you,' wrote the Duke to Moody, 'I shall never forget what I have heard from you. If you knew what a life mine is, in ways I was not able to tell you the other day, and what a terrible story mine has been, you would pray for me much.' In another note the Duke thanked the former farm-hand from Northfield 'for all the joy and strength our dear Lord has given me through you, and I pray that your wonderful work may be more and more blessed'.

The Duchess would collect bevies of friends and relations at palatial Stafford House (now Lancaster House) and whisk them in the ducal carriage along Pall Mall to the Haymarket. Some of them hated it: 'The mixture of religious fervour and the most intense toadyism of the Duchess,' a Lady Barker sourly told a dinner party, 'was horribly disgusting.'

'Moody's and Sankey's Meetings are quite noticeably one of the events of the Season,' a visitor to London noted. Nearly everybody who was anybody went once at least, from high motives or low; it was the talk of ballrooms and garden parties and rides in Rotten Row. Moody had an impact on the aristocratic because he was quite unaware when he rode roughshod over prejudices, privileges and attitudes. They took from him what they would have resented from an Englishman.

To one of the first Bible Readings came the Princess of Wales, the ravishingly beautiful thirty-year-old Alexandra, entering the royal box a few minutes before the service. Sankey burst into the backstage room, eyes popping, hands nervously straightening bow-tie and whiskers.

'Moody, the *Princess of Wales* has just arrived!'

Moody, talking to a young English helper, glanced up. 'May she be blessed. I'll be out in a minute. Now, Inglis, as I was saying...' Inglis 'thought to myself, "What a difference between the two men. There is Sankey, all in a flutter. Moody takes it as a matter of course." When we came out on the platform, I watched them. Mr Moody rolled into his chair like a New England farmer. There he stood with a tweed suit on, pockets full of papers and said, in his usual way, "Hymn number so-and-so, let's all rise and sing it." '

The Princess, who seemed to know the hymns already, attended on two or three occasions and told an evangelical peer, Lord Radstock, that Moody had been a definite help to her.[1]

One of the Ladies of the Bedchamber, the Dowager Countess of Gainsborough, decided to write to the Queen.

19: Climax in Britain

'17 Hyde Park Sq. April 26th 1875. Private.
'Madam – I have been thinking Your Majesty would like once to hear these American Evangelists, who are so occupying men's minds at this time – & drawing such crowds to hear them. It would interest Your Majesty I am sure, very much and if Your Majesty wished it, might it not be? – There is the Royal box, which Your Majesty could go to quite privately... I have the honour to be Your Majesty's devotedly attached and faithful old servant and Subject –

F Gainsborough.'

'Windsor Castle, 27th April 1875.
'Dear Fanny – I received your letter yesterday on the subject of Moody and Sankey, "the American Evangelists". It would never do for me to go to a public place to hear them, or anything of that sort, nor, as you know, do I go to *any large public places now.*

'But independently of that, though I am sure they are very good and sincere people, it is not the *sort* of religious performance which I like. This sensational style of excitement like the

---

1. His son, the late Lord Radstock, told me this in 1952.

Revivals is not the religion which *can last,* and is not, I think, wholesome for the mind or heart, though there may be instances where it does good.'

The Queen concluded her unconsciously ironical letter: 'Eloquent, simple preaching, with plain practical teaching, seem to me far more likely to do *real and permanent* good, and this can surely be heard in all Protestant Churches, whether in the Established Church or amongst Dissenters, if the Ministers are thoroughly earnest.'[1]

The only Moody to get near the Queen remained little Willie, who at York Station back in 'seventy-three had darted under a barrier when the Queen's train was in, and for his rapt stare received a royal smile.

Round the corner from Lady Gainsborough's was the London house of a rich, retired tea-planter in his fifties, with Franz-Josef whiskers, who regarded Moody not with the Queen's distaste so much as a blend of amusement and sporting adoration: 'There must be some good about the man, or he would never be abused so much by the papers.'

Edward Studd had made a fortune in North India. He owned a fine country house, Tedworth Hall in Wiltshire, was Master of Foxhounds, and had a passion for the Turf. He had lately bought the best horse ever to come his way, entered it in an important flat race and had sent a hot tip to another retired planter named Vincent, a keen racing man: 'Put every penny you can on my horse.' In a few days he accosted Vincent in London: 'How much money have you put on my horse?'

'Nothing!'

'You're the biggest fool I ever saw. Didn't I tell you what a good horse it was? But though you are a fool, come along and dine with me. My family are all in the country and you shall say where we shall go after dinner.'

Unknown to Studd, Vincent, in Dublin for the Punchestown Races the previous autumn, had annoyingly missed the steamer home. Wandering around to find a show he saw a theatre advertis-

---

1. Quoted by permission from the *Letters of Queen Victoria*, published by John Murray.

ing, as he supposed, a two-man American vaudeville, and went in...

Dinner at Studd's over and the port sipped, the host lit a cigar. 'Now where shall we go to amuse ourselves?'

'The Queen's Opera House.'

'What? Isn't that where these fellows Moody and Sankey are? Oh no, this isn't Sunday. We will go to the theatre or a concert.'

'No, you are a man of your word. You said you would go where I chose.'

Thoroughly grumpy when they reached the Haymarket, Studd was relieved to see they were too late, the place obviously full. Vincent pulled out his card-case, scribbled on a card: 'Come and get us in. I have a wealthy sporting gentleman with me but will never get him here again if we do not get a seat,' and sent it in to a committee man he knew. Studd found himself following Vincent through the greenroom door on to the stage and placed right under Moody's nose.

He never took his eyes off Moody until the end of the address. 'The fellow has just told me everything I've ever done!' he exclaimed. 'I'll come and hear him again,' and did so night after night until conversion.

Afterwards he asked Moody: 'I want to be straight with you. Now I am a Christian, shall I have to give up racing and shooting and hunting and theatres and balls?'

'Mr Studd, you've been straight with me, I will be straight with you. Racing means betting and betting means gambling. I don't see how a gambler is going to be a Christian. Do the other things as long as you like.'

Studd pressed the point. What did Moody really advise about the theatre and cards?

'Mr Studd, you have children and people you love. You're now a saved man, you want to get them saved. God will give you some souls, and as soon as ever you have won a soul, you won't care about any of the other things.'

Studd lived a bare two years, but it was said at his funeral that he did more in two years than most Christians do in twenty. He withdrew from the Turf, turned the great hall at Tedworth into a

meeting room, wrote to his friends about their souls and laughed
when they replied rudely, called on his tailor and his shirtmaker
and the man from whom he had bought his cigars, and spoke of
Christ. 'All I can say,' said his coachman, 'is that though there's the
same skin, there's a new man inside.'

Edward Studd's three eldest boys were at Eton. To that bastion
of privilege, nursery of statesmen, Moody and Sankey were invited. The resultant uproar disclosed the depth of their penetration
into British life.

It was not Edward Studd; the astonishing storm in a tea-cup began
on Saturday, June 12th, when Quintin Hogg and John Graham, MP,
both Old Etonians and the latter a parent, called on old Provost
Goodford with a formal introduction from Gladstone.

Several of the senior boys wanting to hear Moody and Sankey,
Graham wished to hire a tent to be erected in South Meadow, private land near the College, and to admit boys by free ticket for an
hour's service on Tuesday week, June 22nd. The Provost was understood to say he would not oppose the plan (afterwards he denied
it). The Head Master, Dr Hornby, said he could not give sanction or
connect himself or the school, but 'in the event of their coming to
preach once in our neighbourhood I should not feel bound to put
any special restriction upon our boys on the day selected'. In other
words, go ahead as a private arrangement.

Three days before the chosen Tuesday another parent, Edward
Knatchbull-Hugessen, MP, lately Under-Secretary for the Colonies,
a staunch High Churchman, came down to Eton. He saw the tent;
heard that a Revival Meeting would be 'held under the protection
of forty policemen', and stood aghast at the idea of Eton boys being subjected to the 'semi-dramatic performances which have lately
caused so much excitement in London'.

Knatchbull-Hugessen was a great-nephew of Jane Austen, and
a writer himself. *Whispers from Fairy Land* had come out the year
previous, *Higgledy-Piggledy* was published in 1875. He at once
resolved to slay the dreadful American dragon that threatened to
blow down the walls of Eton.

He attacked the Provost, Lord Lyttleton (the Chairman of the Governing Body), and the Head Master. He wrote to *The Times* and the *Morning Post*: 'I had always imagined that the religious instruction afforded at Eton was full and satisfactory'; the letters appeared on Monday, the 21st, and Eton authorities were deluged with telegrams for and against. The dragon-slayer secured seventy-four signatures from fellow-MPs, all Old Etonians or parents, to an urgent protest, to which the Head Master replied calmly: 'I have never heard this language used with reference to the Windsor Fair of old days, or the present Windsor Races and Steeplechases.'

Just after five o'clock that Monday evening the Marquess of Bath ('frozen down into the very exemplar of an immaculate, unemotional, self-possessed British aristocrat') rose in the House of Lords to ask Lord Lyttleton whether the Provost and Head Master had given sanction to the visit of Moody and Sankey, for 'Nothing', he declared, 'can be more fatal to the discipline of the school, nothing more calculated to interfere with good regulation in the management of the boys!' Lord Lyttleton made a rambling reply, two other Governors spoke, Lord Shaftesbury rebuked Bath, saying 'in a matter of such importance, and one in which the feelings of the country are excited, the House ought to have had full notice'. The Duke of Richmond, Leader of the House, moved that they proceed to business, the Poor Law (Paupers' Order of Removal) Bill.

Next morning the newspapers laughed – '...discussed with as much heat as if it had threatened the peace of Europe... Such a prodigious agitation... Now we really hope the Governing Body of our greatest Public School will not be induced to make itself ridiculous... Leave the preachers alone and the boys alone.'

Sankey put on his very best tie; Moody, saying the Eton affair was doing great good by making aristocrats show their colours, stuffed his pockets with papers and they caught the Windsor train.

Dispute had blown so hot in the school that the Buckinghamshire police said they would not be responsible for order in the tent, and Graham and Hogg had no option but to abandon plans for its use. The Mayor of Windsor agreed to lease Windsor Town Hall, and disappeared by the eleven o'clock train. He could not have gone far for at one o'clock the Superintendent of Police reached him to say, 'The Eton boys have purchased a large quantity of eggs! There will be a breach of the peace!' The Mayor wrote out a telegram. Shortly before three, when boys already were gathering, a policeman pinned a notice on the door: 'No Meeting To-day'.

A linen-draper offered his large garden opposite. And there, on that sunny June afternoon, standing on a chair in the shade of a chestnut tree before some hundred and fifty boys, four masters, and two or three hundred parents and Old Etonians and townsfolk, all listening quietly, Sankey sang and Moody preached. Attentive audience, decorous meeting, *The Times* said it was 'impossible to see' how Moody could have done the boys 'the slightest harm'.

Edward Studd was not singled out among those present. Nor were his sons Kynaston, George and Charlie. Because no one realized that these four were to be the link between Moody's work for a nation and his work for a world.

The Lord Chancellor, who was a Presbyterian, urged the Archbishop of Canterbury, A C Tait, to give Moody and Sankey 'some official countenance'. Churchmen and dissenters were learning love by working together in the campaign, yet numerous Anglican clergy stood aloof, while others pressed the Archbishop to come out for Moody. After 'communicating with parochial clergymen of various opinions', Tait wrote a long letter to Cairns for publication in the press.

The Archbishop, a Broad Churchman, expressed 'the deepest interest in a movement which... has been so wonderfully blessed in drawing together great masses to hear simple addresses on the great Gospel doctrines'. He prayed it might 'bring a blessing to many souls', and rejoiced that it was 'conducted on so great a scale and with such apparent success'. But he would not give 'any direct sanction'. His chief objection lay in the 'after meetings for confession of sin and guidance of the conscience', of which his minute and careful inquiries in all directions (as his biographers described them) had apparently provided a false picture. But he quoted Moses, 'Would God that all the Lord's people were prophets!' and ended with a broad hint to the clergy to 'assist all of their people who seem to be awakened by this preaching'.

Cairns was deeply disappointed, Dr Dale of Birmingham indignant. Yet it was truly said to be 'the first occasion on which an Archbishop has so courageously avowed his sympathy with the efforts of lay missionaries', and the most friendly official word to non-Churchmen since the Exclusion of 1662. Tait's attitude to Moody differed profoundly from that of his predecessors to Wesley and Whitefield, Anglicans though they were. The Archbishop's letter was a milestone on the long road towards Reunion.

Londoners had taken Moody and Sankey to their hearts. Errand-boys whistled, barrel-organs instead of 'Pop goes the Weasel' ground out 'Hold the Fort'; indeed, the common expression 'hold the fort' dates from this time.

In the last weeks great services were held simultaneously at different centres, each in charge of associates, with Moody and Sankey now here, now there. A plan for them to give a month to each quarter of the capital was abandoned because 'the people flock to whatever part the Americans are labouring in', one reason why Moody at the time doubted the value of the London campaign, a doubt he lived to discard.

Any attempt to interpret these four and a half months in terms of statistics is utterly misleading. The attendance figure calculated by enthusiasts, 2,530,000, is as meaningless as the announcement of the total cost : £28,396 19. 6d. The latter ignores the evangelists' services given free and the considerable outlay by helpers who met their own out-of-pocket expenses; the former ignores the enormous number of frequent attenders. Nevertheless, it cannot be doubted that Moody was heard and seen by at least a million and a half in London in 1875, long before radio and television made mass audiences usual.

Equally deceptive is any statistical assessment of conversions, a practice which Moody deplored. Every letter from clergy who denigrated the mission's lasting effect on church membership could be balanced by contrary, favourable evidence.[1] Much depended on whether a church encouraged or rebuffed converts, whose spiritual health in after years was not Moody's responsibility, although his contention that a man should give to new-found faith lips and legs and hands could bring rapid – sometimes over-rapid – progress.

The mission had plumbed the depths. 'Such tales of woe I've heard in Moody's inquiry room,' said Drummond, 'that I've felt I must go and change my very clothes after the contact.' The wider value lay in the atmosphere or spirit generated. It was not merely that dockers were said to swear less after the East End campaign, duchesses no longer ashamed to talk openly about God; after Moody English religion became warmer, more personal. When the full force of rationalism and extreme higher criticism and the battle between science and religion, all hitherto limited in impact, burst on the English educated classes in the late 'seventies, thousands throughout England who might have been swept from a cheerless, formal faith into agnosticism were secure in the friendship of Christ.

Moody caught up and pushed forward movements already active or stirring – Dr Barnardo's, the Shoe Black brigade, Ragged Schools, 'rescue' missions, temperance crusades, the YMCA, children's missions. He gave discriminating encouragement to the feeling after 'practical holiness' which had led in June 1875 to the first Keswick Convention. Church of England parish missions had been held for six years past; by persuading Hay Aitken to abandon his Liverpool living to be a full-time missioner, and by going down to the House of Commons, sending in his card to several wealthy allies and getting them to write cheques, Moody was virtual founder of the Church Parochial Mission Society which operated for decades.

At the farewell reception to Moody and Sankey Lord Shaftesbury, conspicuously absent at the welcome five months previously, said: 'I have been conversant for many years with the people of

---

1. Dr William G McLoughlin in his *Modern Revivalism* (1959) quotes an adverse comment by an East End minister in November 1875, of which he found a copy 'among the Moody Papers in the possession of Mrs Emma Moody Powell of East Northfield', but he quite omits the favourable comments of the same date by three other ministers, which are in Mrs Powell's Papers.

this metropolis, and I may tell you that wherever I go I find traces of these men, of the feeling they have produced, of the stamp that, I hope, will be indelible to many.' And thirty-four years later Eugene Stock, Lay Secretary of the Church Missionary Society, with a finger in most London pies for fifty years, wrote of 'that wonderful Mission' of 1875: 'The Church of England has little idea what she owes to it, both in the general standard it set of *reality* in religion, and in the men and women whom it influenced – scores and scores of now honoured clergymen and laymen and women, yes, even bishops.'

The closing service filled the great temporary building in South London on July 13th. After a short holiday, the Moodys in Wales, the Sankeys in Switzerland (where 'about 500 beautiful Swiss singers came and sang Hymns under my window'), they sailed from Liverpool on August 4th. 'Tears often come to my eyes as I think of you all,' Moody wrote to Hitchcock in Chicago. 'I shall be delighted to take you by the hand again. I do not think you know how much I have thought of you all in the last two years and now the time is so near for me to go to you I am just homesick to see you all again.'

The influence upon Moody of these two years was unfathomable. His physique had not bent under 'the terrible strain which he never seems to feel at all', so Drummond wrote from London. Charm and irrepressible gaiety had kept their bloom. He remained unspoiled. His intimate friend, D W Whittle, soon after the return to America marvelled that 'the only change I see in him now is a growth in conscious power, and a speaking with added weight and conviction. He is thoroughly and wholly conscious that it is all of God. Praying alone with him I found him humble as a child before God. Out in the work with him I found him bold as a lion before men. No hesitation. No shrinking. No timidity.' And instead of being emptied to the dregs he had more knowledge, sharper insight, for he was always like a sponge soaking up, consciously and unconsciously. A Scotswoman, Mrs Barbour, who had known him in Edinburgh right at the start in December 1873, watched him in

London in the summer of 1875. 'He has given up a great deal of those peculiar out-of-the-way things he was wont to say. He is much calmer and exceedingly self-possessed; he is what I would call "combed down" though not a whit less fervent and earnest.' Britain had brought Moody to maturity. It had given him international fame.

At the early age of thirty-eight he had reached a dangerous eminence. The world had yet to see whether he would slip or climb.

Part Three

REMAKING AMERICA
1875-81

20: Chickens at Northfield

Widow Moody's chickens at Northfield were for D L Moody as decisive as Mrs O'Leary's cow, popularly supposed to have caused the Chicago fire.

Moody and Sankey and their families entered New York harbour on August 14th, not knowing what would be the attitude of their countrymen. The *New York Times* still asserted they had been sent to England by Barnum the showman; thousands would have agreed with an elderly Episcopal clergyman in Philadelphia, a Mr Portal, who remarked at a London luncheon party, 'America had heard with amazement and *shock* how they were run after. They owed their success partly to their cheek, partly to their music.' Other ministers sent urgent invitations or pleaded for their cities through laymen such as Farwell, Wanamaker and Stuart, who had crossed the Atlantic to join the London campaign.

Moody and Sankey returned as international figures, distinguished Americans. A horde of reporters met the steamer *Spain,* and Moody would say nothing of the future except: 'I am going right up to Northfield, Massachusetts, to see my mother.'

The Moodys reached Northfield on August 16th, driven from South Vernon depot by George in an aged buggy drawn by a plodding farm-horse, Samuel in a wagon behind with their baggage: over the Connecticut by the railroad toll-bridge, up the hill into the avenue of elms in summer splendour, to Betsey's little home.

Betsey, seventy, venerable in her white widow's cap, had deep pride for her Dwight, of the crowds he had drawn, the fame he had won, even if he had hobnobbed with English dukes. She did not approve of what he preached. She would be 'a Unitarian till I die'.

They squeezed themselves into the small frame house that already contained Betsey and the unmarried brothers, Edwin and the beloved Samuel, red-bearded, short, epileptic and frail, the town tax-collector yet popular, a little amused in his intellectual way at Dwight's revivalism. Moody could not see too much of him. Together they drove about the lanes. Alone or with his children Moody climbed those glorious hills and valleys where once he had pastured cows and picked berries and gathered chestnuts, and from the bleakness of New York next winter he would often 'think of the pleasant hours we had at the old home last summer and the children will have it there's no place on earth like the old house at Northfield'. He called on his relations. 'One rainy day,' writes a Holton cousin who was Willie's age, 'a man with a full dark brown beard drove into our yard and talked with Father. He was in a covered carriage and had the storm apron buttoned up to his neck and drove with the lines through a slit in the apron made for that purpose. He seemed carefree and happy as a child.'

Moody intended these short weeks as recreation for body and soul: that body ('He weighs 220 pounds, hard, compact flesh,' D W Whittle noted nine months later) needing exercise and country air, that soul crying for study and quiet before bustling away to Chicago or wherever the future lay. Jabez Sunderland, the young minister of the First Parish Church which Betsey's family attended, who had been a Baptist in Chicago before turning Unitarian, presumed upon previous acquaintanceship in the west to invite this distinguished native son to occupy the pulpit on a Sunday – he was a liberal man, Jabez T: he allowed his wife to preach sometimes, in daring grassgreen gloves.

Moody refused. 'Those who believe in Unitarianism insult Christ, and whoever insults Christ insults me.' The invitation fired him. Family, cousins, neighbours, the whole countryside, 'cold unitarians... My heart burned to draw them to Christ.' The 'Orthodox' or Trinitarian minister, T J Clark, was in no hurry to see Moody disturb the placid moderation of Northfield religion, but grudgingly agreed to an extra service in the Second Parish Church, the old four-pointer, on Sunday afternoon, September 5th.

Betsey came from pride, determined not to budge from her convictions. Samuel came. Everybody. 'Early as we were the church was already half full,' found one family from across the river. 'The ushers had begun the farthest back and filled the seats solid as they went. Mr Moody was in the pulpit giving out hymns.' In a few minutes the place bulged – literally: the underpinning was giving way. George Moody walked swiftly up the aisle as they sang and murmured urgently in Moody's ear. At the end of the verse Moody lifted a hand. With that wonderful smile he said in his usual tone: 'The place is full. Many are still outside. I'll preach on the steps so all can hear. While we sing the next number all will go out beginning at the rear.' They sat around on the grass and the dusty street, a small boy up an apple tree, and when they saw the old white building spreading dangerously, perceptive townsfolk understood that Moody's skill in emptying the church swiftly had averted panic and disaster. Before the next meetings the deacons shored it up.

Sankey perched his little organ on the narrow covered platform designed for churchgoers to step off wagons without wetting their feet, and sang 'The Ninety and Nine'. On that still, summer afternoon, the words sung so distinctly were wafted by the water to be heard, amazedly, no less than a mile across the Connecticut, by a Mr Caldwell who had refused in anger to attend the service, as he sat in his porch: stirrings of conscience at the words of the distant song led to his conversion.

Moody's subject was Zaccheus. Northfield folk never forgot that 'quiet Sunday afternoon'. After seventy years W T Holton, son of Moody's first cousin Jonathan who farmed across the Connecticut River at Gill, could remember the details. 'The sun shining over the distant hills from the far side of the river; the air, so calm that not a leaf stirred; not a sound to disturb the quiet except the low murmur of voices from little groups as they discussed in subdued tones the meeting and sermon. The familiar surroundings of the town and the faces of the neighbours were only a little more real than the scenes that had been vividly portrayed by the speaker... With these scenes diverting us we were loth to do anything to break the spell, but the crowd gradually dispersed and we realized that evening chores must be done after driving several miles behind an old farm horse.'[1]

---

1. W T Holton ascribes the collapsing church incident to this service in the summer of 1875, but Eva Stebbins Callender, who also remembered it as a child, puts it on a warm summer day of some unspecified later year of this period. George Moody's son Ambert (aged twelve in 1875) gives no date. There is doubt also if Sankey is correct in assigning the song-across-the-river incident to the first Sunday.

Sankey, Whittle and Bliss having been sent for to confer about the future, Moody used them for two weeks of special services, and in other ways: one afternoon the four friends went over in the flatbottomed ferry to dine with Uncle Cyrus, and Moody told Bliss and Sankey to sing while he helped Stebbins the ferryman pull on the hawser. Whittle wrote in his diary, 'We all thought we crossed slowly. Sankey, after a third or fourth song, looked round and discovered Moody holding on to the wire and pulling back while the ferryman pulled forward.' Moody wanted Stebbins to hear soul-saving hymns, loved to hear Sankey and Bliss, and roared with laughter when found out. Bliss struck up his 'Pull for the shore, sailor', 'and by watching Moody [we] reached the land'.

Up and down Main Street wandered inquisitive strangers hoping for a glimpse of the great evangelists. By special trains from Brattleboro, by buggy and wagon and surrey the District converged upon the Orthodox Church. (But the town blacksmith 'hated me, spoke most bitterly against me. The smithy was the rendezvous of all the strong opposition men.') Betsey did not shirk, confident in convictions which had withstood her son since his crazy days. A Unitarian till she died. On the hills, alone or with his friends, Moody wrestled in prayer. Some song, some graphic Bible story pierced her shield of moral confidence, but she gave no sign until on one of the last evenings, when Moody invited those to rise in their places who wished to acknowledge Christ as Son of God and trust in Him as Saviour, 'that we might pray for you', Betsey rose. Moody was so overcome that he could barely ask one of the others to lead the prayer.

On the last night Samuel stood.

His was no passing emotion. Like a river suddenly undammed, love poured out. In the short remainder of his life 'my long sought brother ... took a leading part in religious meetings. He went and talked with weak brothers and set them on their feet. He searched for souls on both sides of the Connecticut River, in both sides of the valley.' When Northfield formed a YMCA they elected him president.

Now that Betsey and Samuel loved Moody for his work as well

as for his own sake, his roots thrust into Northfield. From being a centre of cold if unmilitant Unitarianism, it became a focus of 'the greatest revival ever known in that part of the state. By the following winter,' (the memory is W T Holton's) 'for miles around prayer meetings were held in most every schoolhouse and often in private homes; while active workers, speakers and singers alike would go round in crowds.' When Whittle stayed in Northfield the next summer he wrote: 'A wonderful work has gone on here in this community for the past year... Moody is loved by everybody high and low, and has the confidence of all. He greatly enjoys the results of his labors here in his native town. The testimony of the converts delights him, and their shrewd, pithy illustrations are treasured up by him for use in his work. He is a man among men and thoroughly at home with them.'

Moody needed roots in soil. He had been able to serve Chicago because beyond the acres of city slum he had seen in imagination the valley and the river and the hills, Northfield, not dryly Unitarian but a redeemed Northfield active in the cause of Christ. The dream would be fulfilled, Northfield would mean more to him and he to it than either could imagine in 1875.

Nevertheless, for all that wonderful homecoming, he would again have made his home in Chicago except for Betsey's chickens.

They were trespassing beyond Betsey's fence into a cornfield of Elisha Alexander, whose larger house stood to the north-west higher up the hill. Uncle 'Lisha, as everybody called him, a distant relation two years younger than Betsey, was deputy sheriff, shrewd trader, chief creditor of the townsfolk, an important man. He was annoyed. He would not have Widow Moody's hens stealing his corn, and he let her know it.

Moody, spanking down a lane in a buggy, pulled up sharp when he saw Uncle 'Lisha.

'I want to buy a strip of that field.'

'No. I don't care to sell unless it's the whole place.'

'How many acres?'

'Twelve.'

'How much?'

'Well,' said Alexander, relishing the prospect of a long hard dicker lasting months, and determined to start really high, 'I'll take thirty-five hundred dollars for the whole place with house and barns.'

'I'll take it!'

This leap into real estate was intended to be brief, the farm to be resold except for the chicken strip. On reflection Moody decided to keep the whole, at least for the next few years when they would be working in cities of the East, for it could be their base, their summer home. The Homestead stood on the high road with a magnificent view down to the river and away to Brattleboro Mountain; it was in typical New England style, substantial, not grandiose.

He had been able to buy because Edward Studd had pressed upon him a personal gift of £500, approximately $2,500. Twice Studd's cheque was returned, until he begged Farwell, 'How can I get it into Moody's hands without offending him?' They succeeded because at the third time Moody did not wish to hurt Studd's feelings. Thus Edward Studd, the Englishman from India, stands at the crossroads of Moody's life, by a cheque in 1875, by his sons in the next decade.

The source of the remaining $1,000 (and $2,500 spent on alterations) is not known, but since Moody had served two years without pay it could hardly be grudged.

Now came the Great Renunciation.

Royalties on sales in Britain of *Sacred Songs and Solos* for the first six months of 1875 totalled slightly over £5,600. The English trustee, Matheson, declined to give a British charity the earnings of Americans and after discussion with Moody, Farwell and Sankey in London, decided that the fund should help to complete the Chicago Avenue Church which had lost its leaders for two years. He sent the Church $27,000. Larger royalties would accrue from the most popular hymn-book in Britain, and already Morgan and Scott had issued a first slim volume of sermons (the vernacular Moody polished anonymously by Drummond). *Sacred Songs and Solos* could not be published in the United States because of copyrights, but an American counterpart was in preparation, *Gospel Songs*.

Moody said: 'I am not going to give any man ground for saying we're making a gain out of preaching the Gospel.' While Sankey, Bliss and Moody were at Northfield this September, 1875, they sent for William E Dodge, Jr, New York businessman and philanthropist, and made him draw up a trust to which all royalties would be paid. Not discerning yet this money's possibilities, the trustees at first distributed it to worthy but casual claims: 'If you can hold the Assn for a few months we can lift the debt,' Moody in October 1875 told Farwell who was helping the Chicago YMCA. 'I do not want you to say anything but I think we will make enough from the hymn books.'

More than $357,000 poured into the trust over the next ten years, in an age when one dollar went far, and at Moody's death an estimated million and a quarter had been earned by the hymns.

When he abandoned a business career he had discarded the means of a fortune. Riches came unasked. He refused them, a brave act because wealth was post-Civil War America's one gauge of success. He did not even retain an annual sum to keep his wife and family, but merely bought a life insurance of $1,500 a year for Emma on his death, and relied on occasional spontaneous gifts from wealthy friends, together with modest privately raised honoraria for American campaigns, and from the later 'eighties some income from books, which went direct to Mrs Moody, who kept the accounts and paid all family, household and farm bills. Moody maintained a reasonable standard, sent his sons to college, and showed constant generosity to his relatives; but from time to time, while vast sums flowed into the Hymn-Book Fund, he himself ran distinctly short.

Sankey's sacrifice, however, was sharper. Sankey, brought up in prosperity, had thrown off a good salary and pension rights, had refused large offers; and God had brought this unexpected wealth. Sankey loved money, loved to be smart and comfortable. Moody never noticed surroundings or clothes. Moody always would have work; Sankey's voice might fail. Yet he signed away his earnings.

The Trust lawyer told Paul Moody that his father 'did not seem to care what happened to the money provided he wasn't bothered with it'. Paul considered Moody was 'scared of money'. The memory never left him of the struggle to give up business, and if he loved to play the philanthropist he dared not face the temptations of a rich man; of Marshall Field, Leiter 'and other men of our age in Chicago who had succeeded in business and become wealthy', Moody said to Whittle (in 1884), 'Whenever I think of them and the worldly influences that surround them and their families, I feel so thankful to God for being right out of the whole of it. What should I want of their money? I have had more money to give away to the cause of Christ from the Hymn Book Fund than the wealthiest one of them.'

The streak of fear was weaker than the streak of indifference. Money was transient. At any moment Christ would return to reign in glory; Moody looked for Him every day. 'It's the truth of the Second Coming of Christ was used of God to get me out of "the world".' Deeper than these reasons lay Moody's utter scorn at trading in souls. It seemed to him intolerable that he should get rich because he was used in a particular line of Christian service. Introduced to a colourful elderly evangelist called 'Uncle Johnnie' Vasser, who exclaimed 'How glad I am to see the man that God has used to win so many souls to Christ', Moody replied: 'You say rightly, Uncle John, the man whom *God has used*'; and stooping to pick up a handful of earth he poured it through his fingers: 'There's nothing more than *that* to D L Moody, except as God uses him!'

During the first three decades of the twentieth century, when mass evangelism passed through a regrettably commercialized phase, men would look back wistfully on Moody's and Sankey's attitude to money.

They did not advertise what they had done. Seven years passed before Jane Mackinnon knew: 'I call it simply a magnificent fact, the relinquishing of a great fortune, as far as I can judge.' An eminent New York counsel was more blunt. The trustees, needing a legal opinion, selected Charles F Southmayd, not only for his reputation but because he hated Christians; and at mention of Moody and Sankey he gave them 'all sorts of bad names and stated they were making large money out of their meetings'.

After looking through the papers he sent for the trustees' lawyer: 'Mr Coffin,' Southmayd said, 'I withdraw the charge they are rascals but will say instead, they are damned fools to let such money slip through their hands!'

21: All America Stirred

'We will all go East in a week,' Sankey wrote to Hitchcock of Chicago from New Castle, Pennsylvania, on October 13th, 1875, 'and I cannot tell when we will be able to go to your city much as we love you.' He asks if his 'stoves, tables, sofa etc.' could be sold and the 'bedclothes, pictures, etc.' be sent to New Castle. 'The reason for this move is that we have become Religious *Tramps*, and in all human probability will never be long enough in one place to have a *home.*'

When Moody and Sankey were at Northfield much coming and going of church personages heralded four years of intense campaigning. 'Water runs down hill and the highest hills are the great cities,' said Moody. 'If we can stir them we shall stir the whole country.' Whether they would be effective in their own land was in doubt: most of the New York newspapers were sceptical.

America needed religious revival. The decade since the end of the Civil War had seen the North cankered by easy money and the pursuit of wealth. Political corruption strangled public and municipal life more tightly, each passing year of the Presidency of General Grant, who was personally incorruptible but too easygoing. Unceasing streams of immigrants altered the texture of the nation. Americans, new or long-established, strode towards some technological Utopia, old moralities discarded. The onward rush had braked sharply on the Wall Street Panic of 1873, and now in 1875 the trade depression might make men pause and listen.

Moody, having decided reluctantly not to begin in Chicago because 'I was rather afraid the ministers would not come together', accepted a united invitation for a month at Brooklyn. Pessimists

were at once confounded as Brooklyn pressed into and around the
Rink on Clermont Avenue, the *New York Herald* estimating that
'twelve – possibly twenty – thousand were unable to gain admit-
tance'. Streetcar companies had laid extra tracks to the building
and at the close of the service, 'though cars were run at intervals of
only one minute many thousands had to wend their ways homewards on foot'. 'All goes well here,' Moody wrote to Farwell. 'Pray
daily for me. I never needed the help of my friends as much as now.'

It was soon said that Moody 'has held in silent attention and
deeply moved, some of the largest assemblies that any speaker has
addressed in America, at least in our day'. Moody knew that many
in the crowd were drawn by curiosity, New Yorkers hurrying across
Brooklyn Bridge to look at the latest lion, that the 'selfishness of
excitement-seeking professed Christians' left no room for the great
unchurched whom he felt at the close he had failed to reach. But
Brooklyn launched him with a bang, had proved that clergy would
unite 'zealously and harmoniously and intelligently to carry on the
work'.

From late November 1875 until January 1876 the evangelists
campaigned in Philadelphia. One hundred and eighty ministers had
signed the invitation. The story again was of vast crowds and
reinvigorated churches, 'the greatest series of religious meetings
that Philadelphia witnessed during the 19th century', according to
a YMCA estimate of 1905; perhaps the convert who became best
known was S D Gordon, future writer of *Quiet Talks on Prayer* and
other best-sellers. 'Moody's meetings,' wrote a Philadelphian to an
English friend on January 18th, 1876, 'are within gunshot of my
home. The doors open about 1½ hours before the time and it takes
about 10 minutes to fill – 12,000 persons. Sometimes the seats
reserved for those who get tickets as the unsaved and the companies from the country by train fill the whole body of the house. It is
wonderful.'[1]

Moody held special meetings every Friday for alcoholics, of
the class all too widespread in American cities of the 'seventies. He

---

1. Robert Pearsall Smith to the Rt Hon William Cowper-Temple (*Broadlands Papers*).

had women's meetings. And he gloried in the special meetings for young men. On December 4th Moody scrawled to Henry Drummond in Scotland: 'The work among young men in this country is growing splendidly. I am glad I went to England to learn how to reach young men. Could you come over and help us? We want you so much and will see that all expenses are paid, I think you would get a few thousand souls on these shores if you should come. I miss you more than I can tell, you do not know how much I want you with me, come if you possibly can.' Drummond wisely declined to interrupt his college studies again.

By special request Moody went for a day to Princeton. Of his reception by the students he confessed 'that I have not seen anything in America that pleased me like what I have seen in Princeton. They have got a Holy Ghost revival there. The President of the college told me he had never seen anything like it in Princeton ...'

In Philadelphia Moody showed the same unaffected, integrated personality known to his friends in Britain. In work, utterly absorbed. One of his church officers from Chicago came to the platform at the close of an evening service as the inquiry meeting began. 'I touched Mr Sankey on the shoulder, and he did the undignified thing of embracing me. After a little conversation with him I went where Moody was, and touched him on the shoulder also, when he turned and quickly and earnestly said, "Talk to that woman!"' President Grant and several of his cabinet, visiting the preparations for the Centennial Exhibition, sat on the platform on Sunday, January 19th. Moody made no attempt to be introduced afterwards; he had a bad cold and a hoarse voice, but even if well would not have sought out the President.

In play, utterly absorbed. Back at the Wanamakers' mansion, where Emma and the children stayed too (Willie's and Emma's education was peripatetic throughout these years), Moody could relax in a moment. 'The thing I remember most,' wrote one of the Wanamakers, 'was Mr Moody and father playing bears with us children. Such wild exciting times as we had. They would get down on all fours and chase us. We would shriek and scream and run. It was pandemonium.'

The New York campaign, February 7th until April 19th, 1876, had been prepared as carefully as that of Philadelphia. At the end it could be said that Moody's 'position today, whether at home or abroad, is unrivalled'.

He reached New York only a day before the opening, but had let the Committee of laymen and ministers know precisely what should be done, and they had organized the campaign with true New York business skill. They leased Barnum's 'Great Roman Hippodrome' which stood on Madison Avenue, future site of Madison Square Garden. 'On one side of it,' runs a contemporary description, 'lie the homes of wealth, the avenues of fashion, and the great hotels, on the other the masses of the middle class and, a little beyond, the crowded abodes of the poor and the dens of wretchedness and vice.' The Hippodrome was thought too large for the whole to be addressed at once. 'We are fitting up 2 large halls opening into each other,' the Chairman, William E Dodge, had told a friend, 'one holding about 8 or 9 thousand and the other about six thousand.' Inquiry rooms were arranged, and an up-to-date touch was an internal electric telegraph whereby orders could be sent to regulate lighting, heating and ventilation.

A choir of a thousand led a song service for half an hour before the little door opened at the back of the wide platform and D L Moody stepped in. '*Stepped* in, did I say?' recalled James M Gray thirty years after. 'Yes, literally, for he seemed to cover the space between the door and the pulpit in one step! Mr Sankey was more deliberate, and tried our patience before he settled at the keyboard and touched the keys to melt our hearts, but Mr Moody was a meteor. He was at the little railing in front, his hand raised, our heads bowed in prayer and we all saying "Amen" almost before we knew it... How lithe, springy and buoyant he was. How full of life and spirit!'

His weight was still primarily muscle and bone, not fat. He used a 'health lift' every day, since New York gave no time for open air exercise. The press described him as 'short, stout-built, square shouldered with bullet-shaped head set close on the shoulders, black eyes that twinkle merrily at times, and a full but not heavy beard and moustache'. Few observers correctly noted the grey of Moody's eyes; most remembered them as brown, even some who worked closely with him: the grey of the eyes reflected the light and shade of his surroundings.[1]

Day after day New York responded. 'The tone and character of the services here has disarmed all prejudice,' wrote William E Dodge from his Madison Avenue home on March 3rd to an English acquaintance, 'and nothing is wanted to prove to all fair thinking men that they are of God. Nothing has ever reached our great masses of non-church going people as these meetings have. Our ministers have been warmed and helped, cold Christians [?] won over, and very many careless brought to Christ. I do not think the work has been truer or larger in any place Mr Moody has visited. He is staying with me and I find his cheery whole-souled humble consecration a great spur and help.'

The message was the same as in Britain – Moody said his creed was printed in the fifty-third chapter of Isaiah – the method brisker to American tempo. Yards of newsprint recording daily incidents blend into a haze – crowds converging nightly on the Hippodrome, thousands of voices lifted in chorus, Sankey's songs, Moody's torrent of words.

It was the individual hearer who gripped Moody's imagination. As he faced the serried rows his mind and prayers and words focused on the inquiry room to follow, for he never forgot that long before becoming a mass evangelist he had relished what he called 'personal work', and he could not bear that any man or woman should lack or spurn Christ's friendship. Moody had outgrown the habit of throwing texts: 'His questionings speedily determined whether an inquirer was sincere and genuine, or hypocritical and evasive. With astonishing rapidity he could turn a man mentally and morally inside out, expose his fallacies, moral inconsistencies, perversions, wilfulness and alienation from God.' 'Mr Moody evidently prefers the inquiry meeting as his place,' wrote J E Rankin (the author of 'God be with you till we meet again'). 'And what does he find most lacking? Competent men and women to guide

---

1. The fact that his eyes were grey is put beyond dispute not only by Mrs W R Moody's memory, but by a passport application filled in by Moody in his own hand in 1891.

inquirers.' Moody taught New York what Rankin called 'the laymen's opportunity... Let men and women learn the act of personally winning souls.'

As in Great Britain the value of a campaign could not be gauged
by numbers who professed conversion but by skills imparted to lay
people, encouragements to ministers, the impact not of evangelism
only but of a 'Christian Convention' held towards the end, and the
promotion of Christian unity. Moody did not need to bring forward
the idea of unity when Beecher and others had preached and striven
for it, but Moody proved that unity will not be found in a vacuum,
is not an end in itself. It grows in the midst of mission.

At the close of the campaign the *New York Times,* so long an
opponent, conceded that 'the work accomplished this winter by Mr
Moody in this city for private and public morals will live. The
drunken have become sober, the vicious virtuous, the worldly and
self-seeking unselfish, the ignoble noble, the impure pure, the youth
have started with more generous aims, the old have been stirred
from grossness. A new hope has lifted up hundreds of human be-
ings, a new consolation has come to the sorrowful, and a better
principle has entered the sordid life of the day, through the labours
of these plain men.' For the rest of his life Moody on his travels
met men and women converted in Philadelphia and New York in
1875-6, and when in December 1896 there was talk that 'little permanent good resulted', the pastor of Faith Presbyterian Church in
West 46th Street, James H Hoadley, wrote to Moody that 'looking
over the statistics of my own church the other day I noticed that in
the year 1876 there were received into the church 139 persons. Of
the number 121 were received on confession of faith in Christ. The
large part of these brought to Christ under the influence of your
great revival meetings. Only a very small per cent have fallen away
so far. Never since that day have we received so large a number
into the church in any one year.'

At the end of the New York campaign Moody went to the south,
where Emma had already taken the children because New York
weather had nearly killed Willie, and on April 22nd brought them

to Augusta, Georgia. Here D W Whittle was in the midst of a mission. Whittle - 'stalwart and austere, but there was in him the sweetness and gentleness of John Alden and of Whittier' – had his wife and six-year-old daughter, May, a year younger than Willie: they had been babies in Chicago, now they became playmates. Moody was supposed to be resting, but at once took part in the mission, inevitably overshadowing Whittle, who rebuked himself for a slight temptation to resent the intrusion: 'I have considered that Moody is a mighty man of God, the Whitefield of this century, owned and honoured of God, and if he has been led of God to come here and speak it is a very petty spirit that would think of self in connection with the work.'

To Whittle, as they walked on the banks of the Savannah River in the sunshine of a Southern spring, Moody revealed that all was not well. 'I don't know that I will ever go to England again. I am entirely bankrupt as to sermons and material – have used up everything. I'm going to study and make new sermons but I think it will be three or four years before I shall go – if I ever go. You and Bliss had better wait until next year before going, and you must study all you can.'

'Bankrupt' – that was Moody's inner feeling. At the moment of reaching a height of influence in the United States he stood in danger of spiritual insolvency.

He continued to rise early to study his Bible and pray, for he could work on a minimum of sleep and drop off any time of day or night. He had evolved a filing system, using for each sermon a large envelope into which he slipped a scrawled sheet of headings, and 'notes and stories clipped from papers or jotted on paper' for illustrations. On the envelope he listed the place and date of each delivery. As Jane Mackinnon wrote in Britain, 'the peculiarity of his preaching was that although one heard the same address several times it always came quite fresh home to the heart and conscience'.

Nevertheless he was nibbling into his spiritual and intellectual capital. It was not his only danger. Whittle put his finger on another. Moody had spoken of his passionate desire for unity 'in getting the Gospel before the people'. Whittle noted: 'I think M in having before him just the one thing of the success of his immediate work, may be in danger of sacrificing principle and that he magnifies those things that have immediate effect... His heart is in the triumph of Christ's cause. Divisions, jealousies, everything that hinders success he wants out of sight, and the army to move on with united front.' Whittle was shocked when Moody said, discussing that long-drawn out scandal, Henry Ward Beecher's alleged adultery with Mrs Tilton, 'I hope if he is guilty, it will never be known, it would have an awful effect.' Whittle was, however, sure that 'if M. knew he *were* guilty and the responsibility rested upon him of delivering him to justice, he would do his duty unswervingly.'

One other danger Whittle did not note: that Moody had no anchor. He had bought the Northfield homestead merely as a summer home. He had his own church in Chicago, but could not bring himself to settle there again. If he did not anchor he would burn out in a few years of wandering ministry. Where he anchored, Northfield or Chicago, would shape the remainder of his life.

His present influence was enormous. A small but significant indication lies in Farwell's advice in June 1876 to McCormick, who toyed with running for the vice-presidential nomination, that $5,000 given to Moody's cause in Chicago and widely advertised would do more 'than all the money you could put into the hands of political wire-pullers'.

Moody, who told reporters 'I am the most over-estimated man in America,' considered himself 'only the mouthpiece and expression of a deep and mysterious wave of religious feeling now passing over the nation. The disasters and disappointments of the year, the reaction against the scepticism and selfish greed of the day, the deep religious sentiment lying at the bottom of the American character, and the eternal wants of the human heart have prepared the minds of the people for a profound religious transformation or impulse.' By newspapers, which often reported his sermons in full, by volumes of collected sermons which enterprising publishers issued without permission or royalty, by 'Lives', to which he objected on principle and tried to suppress, although at least one was fair and honourable if inaccurate, the message of Moody penetrated the length and breadth of the nation. In log cabins of the Appalachians, in frontier wagons drawn up fearfully in some remote valley of Montana Territory this summer of Custer's Last Stand; in Texan ranches where men and women lived hard and lusty and a clergyman might be seen twice a year; in the soot and grime of Detroit or Pittsburgh or Cleveland, shadowed by unemployment; in Atlantic fishing villages, Southern plantations, in skid rows and millionaire avenues, Moody and Sankey were read and sung, bringing comfort, inspiration, rebuke, a breath of heaven to an all too earthy grind.

Imitators were inevitable. 'The would-be Moodys abide and abound,' complained a Methodist minister of New York in September 1876. 'Moody and Sankey meetings are advertised, at which Moody's sermons will be read, Moody and Sankey hymn book used, etc., then somebody dashes out like Bro Moody, or tries to sing a solo like Bro Sankey – perfect copyist, and always more or less a failure.'

Exploiters were worse. 'Perhaps you noticed,' Moody told one audience, 'that there is someone at the door selling photographs of Mr Sankey and myself. I want to say that this is one of the thorns we have in the flesh. Those are no more photographs of Mr Sankey and myself than they are of you or anyone else.' With press photography in its infancy only those who had attended their meetings knew their likeness; no one could photograph them unless they consented and sat still. Moody had tried to stop the fakes by law, 'and we can't do it. And now we ask you, if you have any regard for us, not to patronize them... I hope I will never have to refer to it again, for I always feel like a fool when I have to talk about myself.'[1]

From Augusta the Moodys and Whittles travelled overnight to Atlanta, and next day, reversing Sherman's march (Whittle excitedly pointing out battlefields and fortifications), came to Chattanooga, where the landlady nearly gave them hysterics by begging Moody to sing 'The Ninety and Nine'. After a picnic of strawberries and

---

1. After a year or two Moody appointed his brother-in-law, Fleming H Revell, as publisher of his sermons, which were the basis of Revell's rise to being, by 1890, one of the largest publishers in the United States. The early American Moody collections were all pirated.

milk on Lookout Mountain they returned to find 'a large number
of ministers and Christians who prevail upon M to speak at Presbyterian Church'.

The last half of May was no holiday. Northward, westward:
Nashville, St Louis, Kansas, Omaha and Council Bluffs, into Iowa;
a sort of whistle-stop tour which laid a trail of illuminated lives
across the Middle West. Thus James G Butler, a man of Moody's
age, a stranger to St Louis, wandered complacently into an after-
meeting there. Moody 'came down where I was sitting, and said:
"Are you a Christian?"

'"Yes sir!" I replied, rather expecting he would say something
courteous and cordial. But, no. He only said, pointing to another
man just across: "Talk to that man about his soul." I did. There was
just nothing else for me to do. If the man was blessed as I was, he is
a happy man to-day.'

At Des Moines the ministers determined to cancel all Sunday
services and concentrate their congregations on Moody at the local
Rink. Moody refused. 'I can't do it! You will have to have your
church services. You must have your church services, and then at
2.30 so as not to interfere with the services we have the meeting in
the Rink.'

It was an example of Moody's brisk treatment of committees. 'I
have often to do a shabby thing,' he confided to a friend. 'A committee takes a great deal of trouble about something, I see it will
not suit, so I cut discussion short by saying I am going to do it
another way. It is very mean of me, but would take a tremendous
time in committee and I have to do it.' His briskness could cause
offence. Whittle described Moody receiving a deputation: 'Some
of the committee have been grieved because M has ignored them
and gone ahead with meetings as he pleased. Some fifteen are
present. Moody keeps quiet and draws out in full all the complaints
and injured feeling and then explains and makes right everything,
and suggesting what he thinks best draws out the ministers to adopt
it as from themselves.'

And so the Mid-west tour continued, until on May 27th, after
nearly three years, Moody, with Sankey, came at last to Chicago.

22: Moody's Dilemma

Farwell had half wondered whether Moody was losing interest. 'If you can give a poor sinner a little advice, if he does hail from Chicago ...' he had written in jocular vein the previous March. At heart he knew that Moody's 'own church has been second only to the all absorbing idea of making the world feel the power of Christian union in active work for the masses'.

Moody called that church his 'first love. For years I seldom get on my knees in private but I think and pray for the dear church in Chicago,' and when one of his deacons had come to Philadelphia Moody took him to the Wanamaker mansion 'where for more than two hours he went over the membership of the church, calling each one by name and inquiring minutely how they were getting on'. At the site on Chicago Avenue he had secured before leaving for Europe stood the new building, still with a debt despite the hymnbook royalties, but one that Moody wiped out by a few masterly begs and some indifferent giving by the regular congregation. On June 1st, 1876, an evening of pouring rain, the church was opened, Moody preaching, and formally dedicated on July 16th.

The old haunts – changed beyond recognition by rebuilding, yet smoky still and impregnated with that evocative stockyard stench; crowded and bustling and cosmopolitan, where ragged children yelled and thieved and the booze ruined more lives than Chicago bothered to count – drew out Moody's suppressed longing. As if to indicate that Chicago might anchor him after all, he decided to postpone a promised campaign in Boston in order to accept Chicago's invitation first. Farwell let the committee erect, on his company's property at the corner of Monroe and Franklin, a 'tabernacle' which he would buy at the campaign's end for conversion to a wholesale store.

The Moodys returned to Northfield for two summer months, and Emma was 'a very busy woman', as she wrote to Jane Mackinnon on September 11th. 'We are in our own home, as you have probably heard, and though in a most delightful spot with such beautiful scenery it is a place where it is very difficult to get servants, and I have had to act in all sorts of capacities. We have had company every day since we came into our house, and [it] has been a pleasure to my husband and myself, but I found my husband's urgent letters took most all of my spare time.' The holiday was slightly spoiled by reports in the British papers which brought letters from England asking if Moody and Sankey really had quarrelled over money in New York. 'The whole thing is a wicked fabrication,' wrote Emma, 'Mr Sankey and Mr Moody have never quarrelled about anything ... I have not seen anything from the newspapers trouble Mr Moody as this has done.'

Moody delighted in the Homestead and in driving around with Sam, who for all his weak, epileptic constitution, bubbled with plans for the welfare, spiritual and temporal, of Northfield. Once again Moody's anchor seemed cast here, not in Chicago. The drama of these critical years 1875-6, first flush of fame in his own land, lies partly in Moody's indecision as to where should be his base – an indecision scarcely conscious, absorbed as he was in his immediate surroundings and opportunities. He was even less aware of the consequences if he cast his anchor in the wrong place.

The Moodys reached Chicago on Saturday, September 30th, and stayed with Emma's sister and her husband, the Holdens. Moody was 'in peace as to the work and has faith that God will bless us'.

Six thousand Sunday school teachers and the like, five hundred singers, a hundred ministers, filled the Tabernacle at 8 am on Sunday. Moody took his seat 'and spends a half a minute in prayer'. After hymns and prayer and reading and Sankey's solos, Moody 'rises and commences very abruptly his sermon on "Rolling away the Stone". His talk,' thought Whittle, 'is as earnest, plain, simple and practical and as absent from all self-consciousness as if delivered to his own Sunday school teachers. You are interested and inspired, and think he has just begun when he stops as abruptly as he began, offers prayer, pronounces the benediction and the meeting is over.'

Chicago had forgotten 'Crazy Moody' days. Chicago raved over its own great evangelist. This campaign, it seemed, would proceed like any other: the first Sunday afternoon service packed out, the new Farwell Hall overflowing too, thousands turned away; the opening evangelistic service on the Monday filled, and the Chicago Omnibus Company running special buses, the horses kept at it every three-quarters of a minute to connect with the tram cars; a learned theological professor writing, 'It is perfectly astounding to me that a man with so little training should have come to understand the public so well. He cannot read the Greek Testament; indeed he has difficulty with parts of it in the English version, but he excels any man I ever heard in making his hearers see the point of a text of Scripture.'

Whittle dined with Moody on the first Thursday afternoon and found him 'unusually solemn'. Moody said, 'I could pray to-day, "O God search me", but when it comes to asking God to "try me" it's a solemn thing. I don't know as I could stand *trying*. Am I ready to be laid aside from my work, to be tried? Am I ready to meet affliction?'

The following day, Friday, October 6th, Moody at dinner was again 'very solemn with the thought of praying God to try him'. That evening he invited the officers of the Chicago Avenue Church to take tea at Brevoort House before the meeting. Whittle arrived a little late carrying Moody's mail collected at the YMCA, a pile of letters and one telegram. He handed it all to Moody. 'While sitting at the table he opened the telegram and upon reading it made an ejaculation of pain, stood upon his feet and said "Sam is dead" and sat down with his head buried in his hands to cry. In a few minutes he said, "Whittle, you will have to take the meeting tonight. I cannot be with you longer," and went out.'

Whittle tremblingly reached the Tabernacle to find Moody in the ante-room surrounded by ministers; he was going east to bury his brother. Whittle was invited unanimously to lead the meetings 'and push right on'.

Moody was away a week. During travel to and fro he wrote letters which seem to epitomize two loyalties, to Chicago, to Northfield, which each dragged softly against the other.

He wrote to the Chicago Avenue Church from a hotel where he, who never would travel by hired or public transport on 'the sabbath', had broken his journey: 'Of late you have been on my mind and heart far more than usual... The only way any Church can get a blessing is to lay aside all difference, all criticism, all coldness and party feeling, and come to the Lord as one man; and when the Church lives in the power of the 13th chapter of First Corinthians I am sure that many will be added daily to the flock of God.' To his mother he wrote after the funeral, waiting for a connection at Springfield: 'A strange and lonely feeling comes over me tonight as I am here for 3 hours. But *dear* mother I know you will miss him far more than any of us who are away... You and Edwin will be lonely I am sure but we will all pray for you that God may give you strength and hold you both up... I must say goodbye now & hope the death of Samuel will draw us all much nearer to Christ than we have ever been before I feel as if it had drawn me much nearer to Christ than I ever have been before – give my *love* to all & tell them it seems as if God had enlarged my heart to love you all much more.'

Samuel's death made him want to do all that Samuel had longed for Northfield. Yet Moody must give himself to Chicago. He loved both. To the pastor of Chicago Avenue he wrote: 'I do hope you will hold the people to the thought of love. I am sure that is where the churches have all gone astray. We must have it above all things.'

The Chicago campaign bowled on through the bitter, long-drawn-out presidential campaign of 'seventy-six, over Christmas and into 1877.

A Presbyterian minister, looking back after twenty-four years, wrote of 'That wonderful revival... That tremendous audience, and its voice in song like the voice of the ocean... The mighty faith and courage of the undertaking. Think what it required to prepare for an audience of ten thousand people, and what failure, in the presence of such vast preparation, would mean!' The campaign reached its closing weeks. It had been a strange time for Moody: Samuel's death; a dangerous attack of scarlet fever for twelve-year-old Emma; Mrs Moody (but she did not reveal this to Moody) had been told by her doctor that her heart was diseased, in critical condition, 'she might at any time be taken'. And on a wild night, December 29th, Philip Bliss who, Moody said, was like his hymns, 'full of faith and cheer – in all the years I have known and worked with him I have never seen him cast down', was in the Pacific Express near Ashtabula, Ohio, when an iron bridge gave way in a snow-storm, the train plunged seventy feet on to a frozen creek and caught fire with the loss of over a hundred dead. Bliss managed to crawl out but went back to free his wife. Not a button or a bone of them could be identified.

These afflictions made Moody, in Whittle's words, 'very kind and tender'. But when the campaign ended on January 16th, 1877, he lay no nearer the answer to the unspoken inner question: where would he anchor and what would follow? Even more pressing: would he burn out in a few more years?

On January 28th, a week before Moody's fortieth birthday, the Boston campaign began. Failure at Boston could kill Moody's influence in America. Instead, when he finished there on May 1st he had received a new vision.

Unitarians, liberal intellectuals, snobs and Irish Catholics battled against him. Of his friends, led by A J Gordon, the saintly Baptist pastor of Clarendon Street, a large stocky man whose clean-shaven face stood out among Boston's bewhiskered divines, few boyhood figures remained, for Kimball had long moved, and lived in San Francisco, Kirk had died nearly three years before, Moody's Holton uncles were retired. Ninety churches cooperated to fill the specially built Tabernacle for which not all the money had been raised when the campaign opened, 'the smallest, though one of the pleasantest, of the series of great buildings erected for the Moody and Sankey revival meetings'.

'Boston's a peculiar place,' Moody was warned. 'You can't expect to do the same as elsewhere.' Moody scorned such advice.

'Christianity,' cried Moody the first night, 'has been on the defensive long enough, specially here in New England. The time's come for us to open a war of aggression. Remember during the

War of the Rebellion some of the generals kept their armies on the defensive until they got confusticated? I guess a good many Christians here in New England have just got into their cushioned pews and gone to sleep – *Now* is the time to wake up and move forward in solid columns – We want not to be on the defensive but to begin a war of aggression. These drinking shops 'n billiard halls 'n gambling dens should be visited 'n told of Christ 'n heaven 'n if they wont come to the Tabernacle 'n hear the Gospel let us go to their houses 'n preach the Gospel to them 'n it wont be long before hundreds are reached.' It was not long before the *Sunday Times* ('the spiciest paper in New England') complained that 'the masses in Boston are undoubtedly becoming permeated with piety'. The weekday papers 'ran the revival' strongly, the *Globe* even recovered from financial disaster by printing so-called verbatim reports. 'We never sold 25,000 copies quicker than we did yesterday.'

Everybody sang. The street urchins had their own version of 'Hold the Fort':

> Hold the forks, the knives are coming,
>   The plates are on the way,
> Shout the chorus to your neighbour,
>   Sling the hash this way.

Photograph-hawkers did their usual roaring trade (at five cents), and somebody heard a toy pedlar in Tremont Street shouting 'Here's yer Moody and Sankey spiders! Two cents each.'

The *Sunday Times* sneered weekly in a ribald column by a former Sunday school teacher who hid under the pseudonym 'I A M Cumming' and said he believed 'Man is his own saviour'. Some of his jokes and insinuations were clever and amusing, others obscene. Or he would write loftily of Moody's 'cant blasphemous phrase', or assure Boston that Moody, having read Barnum's *Humbugs of the World,* 'found out that the public was an ass, and should be fed with thistles'. 'Moody is not only a mesmeric but a muscular Christian. And, verily, he is not to be bulldozed by the weak and watery sinners.' I A M Cumming professed amazement that 'Boston humanity, most musical of all humanity', should 'sit and be tortured with this astounding discord' which was the 'weird and majestic voice' of Sankey, who, said I A M Cumming, had discovered his vocation chasing off a charge of Apache by singing 'What Shall the Harvest Be'.

Walt Whitman the immortal poet, whose humanism and tendency to homosexuality scarcely preconditioned him to Moody, came up in his grey suit from Camden, New Jersey:

After all, not to be converted only,
But to see for myself what sort of a man this Moody is,
Moody, who has on several previous occasions, innumerable and often, set the people of other cities religiously crazy,

Moody, the magnet of religion, inventor of legends miraculous and mythical, the boss story-teller of this year 101 of the States.
Also to listen to the singing of Sankey, the vociferous and voiceless, to see him demolish cabinet organs, to hear his ear-piercing but holy howls.
Wonderful singer, wonderful destroyer of cabinet organs!
I sing the praise of Sankey, sweet singer of Israel,
And what I sing others shall sing and be Sankeyfied and happy.

O Sankey I love thee, my camerado, for voice which you have not and care not for, you have substituted volume, you sing on tremendously, incessantly and noisily, paying no heed to time or tune, but in a large, bold, rugged, unmusical and unfathomable way, deafening men's ears and singing sinful souls to eternal bliss.
So not because I lack religion, but for these reasons, do I go to the Tabernacle.

Whitman scribbled six stanzas in parody of his *Passage to India:*

Wait a moment, O Moody, delay the Chicago man a brief and ephemeral minute,
Hold the Fort O Sankey, for I Walt am coming...

In the last stanza he bares his teeth and tries to forget:

Having heard Moody I am satisfied
But I shall not come to him to be saved.
He is not my idea of a Saviour.

I do not believe in him
Nor his God
Nor his method of swaying sinners nor his stories which sound like
   lies.
I Walt tell him he is an ignorant charlatan, a mistaken enthusiast, and
   that Boston will ere long desire him to *git*.

Boston did not desire him to git. Not even cultured Boston. When
the famous Thomas Orchestra gave a benefit for the 'Old South'
Fund, the hall was reported half empty while six thousand heard
Moody and Sankey.

One of the evangelical clergy claimed that privately Moody and
Sankey ranked the Boston campaign with Edinburgh's. Moody made
new friends, such as the six foot three and a half inches of Phillips
Brooks, the famous Episcopalian, author of 'O Little town of Beth-
lehem', who preached on Moody's behalf in his absence one night.
Moody, as usual, held a great two-day Christian Convention. He
tried, and failed, to get an entrance to Harvard students, and he
pushed temperance hard.

For Moody's future the decisive factor was not to be reckoned
by sinners saved or drunks redeemed. His host throughout the campaign was Henry Fowle Durant. Durant had founded Wellesley
College for girls. Durant talked. Moody listened. It seemed almost
as if the dead beloved Samuel was there too.

23: The School on the Hill

One day of Sam's last summer, 1876, the two brothers had driven
by buggy to look at cattle near Warwick. Returning over the mountain lane the brothers saw a cripple in a cabin doorway and stopped
to pass the time of day. They found him reading aloud the Greek
New Testament to his young daughters as they braided straw hats
for a livelihood. Horace Parmelee Sikes lay on his couch, a pile
beside him: Thomas à Kempis, Madame Guyon, *Pilgrim's Progress*
and 'other similar well worn books'. He had been at college and
taught at a select school but, paralysed, was reduced to dependence

on the meagre earnings of his daughters Jennie and Julia, to whom he could not hope to give an education such as he had enjoyed.

Moody said: 'How do you get along?'

Sikes smiled. 'We don't have much roast turkey or plum pudding, but we get along!'

'We just have to take things right out of the hand of God,' said Mrs Sikes, appearing from indoors wiping soap suds from her hands.

'But we have a *real* home,' added one of the daughters.

Moody and Sam drove home deep in discussion. That old cripple taught those girls Greek, yet what could be their future with no education beyond that and the little district school in the hills? A life of married drudgery on a mountain farm or of dreariness as a factory hand was the most they could expect. A girls' school at Northfield had been Sam's dream; he had talked of it to D L already. Now he pressed.

Sam died. The dream became a sacred trust. Yet Moody never might have moved to its fulfilment – nor to all that followed – had he not been guest of Henry Fowle Durant at Boston in those early months of 1877.

Durant, a prominent, wealthy Boston lawyer who retired from the bar to devote himself to Christian service after the death of his only son, was one of Moody's 'old friends and one that stood by me in days before I was much known'. Recently he had opened at Wellesley, his fine estate on the north-western outskirts of Boston, a first-class college where girls of moderate means might receive 'opportunities for education equivalent to those provided at Harvard'. From Mary Lyon's famous Mount Holyoke Seminary he had adapted the idea that every girl should do a regular share of domestic service, saying he did not want 'velvet girls' but 'calico girls'. The fees were set at $250 a year, half of the cost, the other half being made up by the college. Every teacher was to possess not only academic skill but 'vital Christianity'.

Durant and his college for higher education crystallized Moody's determination to organize a preparatory seminary 'for young women in the humbler walks of life who would never get a Christian education but for a school like this'.

Contrary to one of his favourite proverbs, 'Don't wait for something to turn up. Go and turn up something', Moody did not transfer dream to reality with his usual impulsiveness. The Boston campaign ended in the spring of 1877. First moves at Northfield waited until the following year, partly because Moody was uncertain whether sufficient money would come, partly because of pressure of work.

In the autumn, winter and spring of 1877-8 Moody and Sankey held shorter missions in New England cities. The Moodys placed thirteen-year-old Emma (whose hair cut off in scarlet fever 'has now grown in again *curly'*) at a 'little family school at Amherst'. 'We left Emma Tuesday morning seeming quite happy,' Mrs Moody wrote to her mother-in-law from Manchester in New Hampshire on November 9th, 1877. 'I think I miss her more than she misses me. Mrs Stearns spoke of her very nicely, and said Emma made her no trouble and was so conscientious in studying. I have put Willie into school here in Manchester. I found there was no private school in the place, so I put him into the public school under a very nice teacher... The meetings have commenced well here, more encouragingly than they did in Burlington, and D L is much pleased and especially so with the ministers here who seem very earnest.'

The tide had not turned against the evangelists. 'The wave of sympathy with them,' ran an article in the *Hartford Religious Herald* during the campaign there, 'has been so strong that it seems to have flowed out and covered everything... We have come to a time when, for a season at least, Religion has come to the front.' They ended with a powerful fortnight in New Haven, 'town of grand old elm trees' and of Yale. What Harvard had scorned, Yale's eleven hundred students heard with respect. Mrs Moody wrote from a hired house on April 1st, 1878, to Mrs Mackinnon in Scotland, 'A building has been built specially for the meetings which will contain about six thousand, and the first week of meetings has just passed with marks of success that we thank God for. I am sure Mr Moody would be glad of you and your husband in the inquiry room, or any Christian "Scotch man with a Bible under his arm". My work is still the *waiting at* home and writing and *little* things.'

Early next autumn, 1878, a close friend of Durant, H F N Marshall, a retired merchant who had helped to organize the Boston campaign, arrived in Northfield to aid Moody's plans for a school.

On the high road below Betsey Moody's cottage the two men poked around a dilapidated house which had once been a tavern and now, with a shed, a pond, Parson Doolittle's grave and fifteen and three-quarter acres adjoining Moody's land, belonged to the town tinsmith, who came by just as they decided that this could make the site of the school. They asked if he would sell, closed at $2,500, took him into the Homestead, made out the papers, wrote a cheque and completed the sale before the tinsmith recovered breath. In succeeding months Marshall quietly bought barren, sandy, hilly land above the valley, until he had formed an estate of one hundred acres.

Moody by then was away again, making a flying visit in mid-October to Chicago before settling at Baltimore, where the family took a house for the winter.

That winter of 1878-9 was a crisis in the careers of Moody and Sankey.

They never referred publicly to this crisis, which has not been mentioned in any biography and would have remained unknown had not Moody told Whittle in London in 1884.

Plans for the school had brought forward Moody's deepening sense that if he were not to burn out he must study. During the past two summers he had stayed part of each morning in his library, but not until the autumn of 1878, the school emerging towards reality, did he take himself fully in hand: Northfield Seminary, yet unborn, saved its founder from premature decline. Moody thought that Sankey and he should find some city where they could try a mission of less intensity which would enable him to study at the same time. Sankey, however, according to a letter from Mrs Moody to Mrs Mackinnon, 'urged Mr Moody to go to Europe somewhere and study instead of staying here'. Moody gave a confidential, exciting reason why they could not travel: 'We are expecting a new arrival in our family next spring.' Moreover, he was not ready to face Europe again until he had burrowed into books and more deeply into his Bible.

Sankey itched to be back among England's notables. If Moody would not come he would go alone and have a singing campaign. Moody dissuaded. Sankey insisted. And they parted.

Sankey crossed the Atlantic in high expectation, Moody made a sudden decision to start at Baltimore to the delight of its ministers, who presumed Sankey's absence to be temporary. But Sankey had walked out of the partnership.

It was the end of Moody and Sankey. It was the end of the school project except as a small affair with day girls of Northfield; Moody would not be able to afford a boarders' dormitory, for although Sankey had shown no desire whatever to bespeak any hymn-book money for his own interests – finance had nothing to do with their parting – the trustees obviously could not make disproportionate grants to Moody's pet schemes. Already they had disbursed $5,000 to found a Wellesley scholarship for which preference was to be given to girls from the proposed Northfield seminary, and a substantial grant towards the purchase of property. (Marshall paid for most of the land, holding it until the school could buy from him at cost.)

Sankey failed in England. 'He wrote to me,' Moody told Whittle, 'that if I would take him back, the money might be disposed of as I pleased. With this settled I went ahead with the Schools.'

Moody and Sankey reunited. Sankey bought a house in Northfield for the summers and became a hearty backer of the Schools – and an enthusiastic if rather improbable countryman: he went riding in the rain and 'was thrown off with his umbrella raised up and left sitting in the road'. He fell into a brook 'while crossing on a tree bridge in the Catskill Mountains', to Moody's glee. Moody 'enjoys having a laugh at Sankey's expense. Sankey reciprocates.'

Baltimore in all respects was a campaign with a difference: not 'in any way a prearranged matter', without Sankey, and to an entirely new design. Moody felt that the enormous interest generated in the past by mass meetings in ice-rink or hippodrome or converted depot had not been ploughed back fully into churches because the public, for all the arrays of ministers on platforms, tended to treat a revival as detached. Therefore at Baltimore he held few meetings in large public halls in the city centre. Most were in church buildings, Moody working district by district in close association with each church selected.

It took strict self-discipline to keep hours of study in the midst of a campaign. 'We have been here in our home for the winter just two months,' wrote Mrs Moody, who except for asthma and her 'little difficulty in the heart' enjoyed excellent health, to Mrs Mackinnon early in December, 'and are quite settled, Mr Moody at study and work in the meetings, the children in school, and I in all sorts of work, writing for my husband, attending to some of his calls, and helping him where I can, besides a variety of other things that don't seem to amount to much and yet make me tired by night. Mr Moody has made quite a *rigid* rule where by he takes six hours each day for study. Besides this he has daily except Mondays and Saturdays a Bible Reading in the afternoons, and preaching services in the evening with their inquiry meetings. Sundays he preaches four times besides inquiry meetings, so you see he did not come here to Baltimore for *rest,* as some say, but for *study.*'

During these Baltimore months Moody's anchor dropped firmly, daily more deeply, at Northfield. Chicago meant much: 'I wish you would write me often and let me know how you are getting on and all about the church,' Moody scrawled to a young helper, Robert Aitchison, on arrival at Baltimore. 'I do want to see that church made a power in Chicago for good.' To Chicago Avenue went regular, long letters; but the breathless, unpunctuated scribbles hastening northwards to George Moody, acting as farm-manager for Homestead and school lands, revealed where home lay: '...Did you send a turkey to the Sykes [*sic*] family I wish you would have some of the snow forks in the cellar (small ones) given to Joseph Lyman I promised him some seed but forgot it before I left how about Willie's heifer is there any hope have you got any snow did the grass come up north of the house & has rye got up in the school house lot how many turkies did you kill on Thanksgiving write us all the news tell us what you said at the south church & what they said & what they are doing this season give love to all we are well very well your brother D L M.'

Willie's very own heifer hoofs into letter after letter: 'Is there hope for Willie's heifer or shall we have to kill her for beef?'...p.s. you did not tell me about Willie's heifer'... On February 15th Moody detailed his plans for the year: 'I want the corn planted this year up in the dalton corner & the oats between the corn & garden... you did not write me about Willie's heifer...' 'Willie is anxious about his goose,' the long-suffering George was told a month later, 'he wants it to have a good place to lay its eggs so it can have some little ones this spring.'

Farm affairs did not fill the letters. George had at last left the Unitarians, but reported resentment over his nomination for president of the Northfield YMCA. Moody urged him not to 'let any strife get in among the people, you had better get John Fisher to take the Presidency if there is any feeling against the Moodys, do not let the church get down on us take a back seat & it will come all right in the course of time but you see what a fearful thing it would be to have a division just at this time & we must do all we can to keep peace, if there is any trouble in the church let it come from others & not us...'

Baltimore felt Moody. Between October 28th, 1878, and May 25th, 1879, he preached two hundred and seventy sermons.

One evening at the Maryland Institute as Moody addressed a mass meeting, a criminal or suspect on the run slipped into the anonymity of the crowd. Detective Todd B Hall, to avoid a disturbance, would have abandoned the chase had not the doorman, an ex-saloon keeper who knew them both, said, 'If you will wait until the service is over I will help you to get him.'

The detective was gripped by Moody's sermon and, the criminal forgotten, went straight to the City Hall 'and told the Chief of Detectives and the men what I had made up my mind to do and live the life of a Christian, and asked them for sympathy as I had enough of the tough worldly life I was living'. When he got home to his wife he confessed unfaithfulness and begged her to forgive. 'We then kneeled down and asked God to help me live the Christian life and be true. When I arose to my feet, to my surprise my wife ran up to me, throwing both her arms round my neck and kissing me said, "Nothing shall separate us. If you have made up your mind to live as a Christian I will live it with you and take Christ as my Saviour."'

'Oh what a happy family ours has been,' Todd B Hall wrote in 1900, 'and what comfort has come to our lives... For twenty years by the grace of God I have been kept in that sweet life being still in the detectives' office and have been a blessing to many poor fellows who have been arrested by me, telling them what Mr Moody told me.'

It would be interesting to know if Detective Hall was shown a scrap of paper found wrapped round a gold watch in a box tied to the parsonage door bell of the Broadway Methodist Episcopal Church on the first Wednesday in March, after a Mr Brown had reported losing his watch at Moody's service in the Church the previous Friday.

Headed 'Mr D L Moody' and addressed to Mr Stitt, the minister, it ran: 'dear Sir, please send this watch to the owner I stold it from him in your church ask him to forgive a pour thief Jesus has forgiven me of my sins and I dont want nothing that is stolen Jesus Christ clenseth from all sins he pardoned the thief on the cros and he pardons me glory be to his name his blood clenseth me from all sin. A Christian.'

The family descended on Northfield in late spring complete with the infant Paul Dwight Moody, born on April 11th, 1879, ten years younger than Will.

Moody hustled the building of the Recitation Hall on the site of the tinsmith's demolished dwelling, and on August 21st before a large company he laid the corner-stone, not with a proffered silver trowel but with his father's old working trowel.

Moody reckoned that if Wellesley College could fix its annual fee at $250, his secondary school need ask no more than $100, half the estimate for keeping and educating. As he begged around for the considerable sums required above the hymn-book money, Moody stressed to his friends the school's threefold basis: the Bible a vital part of the curriculum; every girl to take a regular share in domestic duties, thus inculcating a right sense of proportion while keeping down costs; thirdly, the low charge.

On Durant's advice he appointed as Principal a young Wellesley woman, Harriet Tuttle. When she arrived at Northfield the Recitation Hall was rising slowly ('Looks like a jail,' said a visitor. 'Oh no, you are mistaken,' replied one of Moody's friends, 'It is an institution gotten up on purpose so to educate the people that they shall be sure to keep out of jail!'), but foundations had not even been excavated for a boarders' dormitory. Moody could not bear to wait until it should be built; he adapted the part of the Homestead above the coach-house to form a set of cubicles.

The summer sped by, the maples turned red and gold and the Moodys had left for the winter's work in the Mid-west. On November 3rd the first pupils arrived in a record blizzard which laid snow sixteen inches deep, according to George Moody's son Ambert, who next morning coasted down the hill on a sled to stoke the two large boilers. Jennie Sikes from the mountain passed top of the entrance examination.

'Has the children got into new school building yet,' Moody wrote to his mother from St Louis on November 24th, 'and how do they like it and how do they like the teachers etc etc etc.' All through the Moody and Sankey winter campaign at St Louis (on the Baltimore pattern), Moody's imagination roved to Northfield, especially during the first weeks when he was without his family, left at Mrs Revell's. 'I find I cannot get on well without them and then they have been sick in Chicago and I think it will do them good to come down here for the winter.' He was no less devoted to mass evangelism, but those girls at Northfield... 'Mr Marshall came here on Saturday, and of course we had a great deal to ask him about Northfield,' wrote Mrs Moody in January 1880. 'The children have been homesick to get there... D L is well and very busy.' And Moody to his brother Edwin: 'Do you think Willie's calf will ever come to a cow is there any signs he is most anxious to know.'

At last, with the spring of 1880, Moody could see his school in action. A hundred girls were on the roll. Despite setbacks the dream took shape.

Moody spoke of that dream at the formal dedication of the first dormitory during the summer vacation. After remarking that 'my lack of education has always been a great disadvantage to me. I shall suffer from it as long as I live,' he continued: 'I hope after all of us who are here to-day are dead and gone this school may live and be a blessing to the world, and that missionaries may go out from here and preach the gospel to the heathen, and it may be recognized as a power in bringing souls to Christ.' Then he prayed.

'The words of that prayer,' said a Boston man, 'burned into our souls.' Moody thanked God for the urge to found the school, for the friends whose gifts had raised it ... 'O Lord, we pray that no teachers may ever come within its walls except as they have been taught by the Holy Spirit; that no scholars may ever come here except as the Spirit of God shall touch their hearts. O God, we are Thine, this building is Thine! We give it over to Thee. Take it and keep it and bless it, with Thy keeping power!'

24: Both Sides of the River

Moody never had forgotten how nearly he degenerated into a harassed organizer of institutions. 'The Chicago Fire was the turning point of my life. I had become so mixed up with building Farwell Hall and was on committees for every kind of work, and in my ambition to make my enterprises succeed because they were mine I had taken my eyes off from the Lord and had been burdened in soul and unfruitful in my work. When the Fire came, as a revelation, I took my hat and walked out!'

And now again, eight years after the fire and the epochal experience that ensued, he was immersing himself in institutions. Would they throttle again his 'preaching of Christ and working for souls'?

Conscious of this grave danger, yet assured that in founding the school he had not mistaken divine guidance, Moody on his way to Chicago and St Louis undertook a brief campaign and convention in Cleveland, Ohio.[1] One morning, the very week the first girls

---

1. Henry Drummond, having a few days to spare before sailing back to Scotland following a geological expedition, refused the chance of dining with Longfellow and Oliver Wendell

were starting at Northfield, he entered a Cleveland church for the prayer meeting. Proceedings opened with a brief address by a local Methodist editor whom Moody had not previously known, Henry Burns Hartzler, on 'Prayer for the Church'. Moody sat exactly opposite in a characteristic posture, head bowed as if too heavy for the short neck, beard nestling on chest. Hartzler was dilating 'upon the absolute necessity of the Holy Spirit, in order to succeed in the church, etc.' 'Suddenly,' Hartzler noticed, Moody 'lifted his head, flashed a glance at me as though struck with a bolt, and then resumed his former position. After the meeting he rushed by, catching me by the arm and taking me into the pastor's study. Abruptly he said "I want you to come to Northfield next summer. Will you? Want to have a meeting to wait on God. Want you."'

In that flash Moody had lost his fears. How had he doubted that the Lord had an answer? The school, instead of dragging his eyes off God, would be a place of greater blessing, deeper joy, for himself, for hundreds, perhaps thousands; the round-topped hill should be a mount of transfiguration where they would see Jesus. He had given Bible Readings for his Northfield neighbours, sitting on the porch during long summer evenings; in cities had regularly held Christian Conventions; this should be different.

Immersed in the winter campaign he did little about it until back at Northfield and summer had come. As late as July 2nd, 1880, he mentioned the idea only casually in a letter of thanks for a cheque, 'I should have said I am in hopes to have a Christian conference here sometime at the close of August & the first of September I would like much to have you come up to be at it.' 'I do wish,' he wrote to Farwell, 'you would come and let us wait on God together for a few days... Do come and bring all the hungry Christians with you that you can.'

In the first days of August he scattered broadcast a circular calling a 'Convocation for Prayer' from September 1st to 10th, 'the object of which is not so much to study the Bible (though the Scrip-

---

Holmes at Boston in order to dash to Cleveland, where he found his friends the same as ever, 'Mr Sankey down to the faultless set of his black neck-tie, Mr Moody to the chronic crush of his collar'.

tures will be searched daily for instruction and promises) as for solemn self-consecration, for pleading God's promises, and waiting upon Him for a fresh anointment of power from on high'. The invitation was to 'all Christians who are hungering for intimate fellowship with God and for power to do His work'. To Hartzler he wrote: 'Now will you come? I WANT you above any other man in this *nation do* not say me NAY but come & let us wait on God together.'

Moody pitched a large hired tent on the hill soon to be known as Round Top. For accommodation he offered the newly completed dormitory, East Hall, put beds in the Recitation Hall, filled the Homestead, booked lodgings in the town. Others camped in shady corners. Scores of day-visitors from the neighbouring counties made up the full attendance of men and women at the main meetings to about three hundred. All thirty-seven states were represented; Moody had collected Canadians, Britishers, and others from overseas who happened to be in America. (It is almost certain that no visitors crossed the seas specially, as they did to later conferences.) 'He sought,' wrote one of those there, S F Hancock of Cleveland, in a letter of 1896, 'to concentrate all Christendom, so far as he could reach it, in one earnest cry to God for the recovery of Pentecostal power. For this the Convocation was to wait prostrate before God... The first convocation, "The Northfield Convocation" *par excellence,* met the longing of my heart.'

'Don't,' Moody pleaded, 'think of your homes, your work or your churches now. Don't pray for anything or anybody but yourself. Attend now to your own heart only.' He had no formal programme, and urged Hartzler to conduct the conference 'but I declined, saying he was the predestined leader. He insisted I repeat the lecture given in Cleveland...' Day by day the sense of God's presence grew until at one smaller meeting all those present, twenty-six men sitting on the straw in the tent (there were no chairs) rose, clasped hands in a circle and solemnly pledged 'a covenant of consecration with God and with one another'. In the emotion of the moment one man suggested they swear to pray for each other every day till death. 'No,' said Moody, 'pray but don't pledge or you'll make an irksome duty out of a delightful privilege.'

Moody was adept at keeping the conference steady, pricking any bubble of emotional excess. 'Oh!' sighed one man, 'I hope to get enough out of this to last me all my life!'

'Might as well try to eat enough breakfast to last you all your life!'

'I have lived,' claimed another, 'five years on the Mount of Transfiguration.'

'How many souls did you lead to Christ last year, eh?'

At the man's confusion Moody said: 'We don't want *that* kind of mountain-top experience. When a man gets up so high he can't reach down to save poor sinners, something's wrong.'

During a conversation hour in the big tent, its flaps upturned to admit the faint breeze of a warm September noon, Moody sat plump against the pole. An Episcopal minister ('presuming and officious') in the front row facing him had aired his opinions for the second or third time that morning.

Moody, abruptly: 'Brethren' (he pronounced it 'Brearth'n'), 'Brearth'n, how many of you have so grown in grace you can bear to have your faults told?'

Up shot hands.

Moody looked straight at the Episcopalian, whose hand waggled high. 'Brother, you've spoken thirteen times in three days. P'r'aps shut out twelve other good men.'

The young man hotly defended himself. Then a 'real old Yankee vinegar face on the outer rim of the circle turned loose and sharply rated Moody for his bluntness'.

Moody blushed. Demurely he listened out the tirade, then covered his face with his hands. Speaking through his fingers: 'Brearth'n, I admit all the fault my friend charges on me. But brearth'n, I *didn't hold up my hand*!'

One evening in the orthodox church occurred a famous incident which E S Millains, writing in 1907, called 'the greatest thing I ever saw D L Moody do'.

Moody on the platform had begun to speak on the high standards required 'of a true minister of Jesus Christ'. He castigated failures, etching a picture of unfaithful clergy in blistering words that 'searched us all keenly'. Suddenly a handsome student from Newton Theological Seminary blurted out from the front seat ('frank and outspoken but not rude'): 'Mr Moody, I don't see any such ministers as you describe!'

Moody snapped: 'You will, young man, if you live long. Tarry in Jericho till your beard be grown!' And continued his address.

The retort, recalled Millains, 'was not said savagely but it was said keenly. I think everyone in the chapel sorrowed and the young man wilted. But too good a man was speaking, and there was too much love and prayer in the consecrated room for the meeting to be spoiled.' The uncomfortable atmosphere slowly dispersed as Moody unfolded his theme. He reached his close. He paused. Then he said: 'Friends, I want to confess before you all that I made a great mistake at the beginning of this meeting. I answered my young brother down there foolishly. I ask God to forgive me. I ask him to forgive me.' And before anyone realized what was happening the world's most famous evangelist had stepped off the platform, dashed across to the insignificant anonymous youth and taken him by the hand. As another present said, 'The man of iron will proved that he had mastered the hardest words of all earth's languages, "I am sorry".'

Throughout this first Northfield Conference – which determined those present to set aside, next year, the entire month of August – letters and telegrams cascaded through Northfield post office in response to Moody's request that those in sympathy who could not come should send 'salutation & greeting that there may be concert of prayer'.

Moody held back these communications until by the ninth day, according to Hartzler, 'there were more than three thousand requests for prayers piled up on Moody's desk', and presumably all over several chairs. On the two final days as fitting climax he read them out at memorable prayer meetings that shrivelled distances right across the United States and over the sea.

For Moody there was one very special subject for prayer. On the last day he announced that Northfield, in addition to the Seminary, would have a school for boys.

Some months earlier an elderly gentleman of peculiar appearance had called on Moody at the Homestead.

Hiram Camp was seventy and dressed (so Will Moody remembered) in 'black broadcloth frock coat, trousers of curious cut, old fashioned top boots worn beneath the trousers, a soft bosomed white shirt with collar of antique style and conventional black tie, a black velvet waistcoat against which was displayed a gold watch chain which twice encircled his neck, and a broad brimmed black felt hat surmounting a shock of snow white hair'. He had a white beard too. Hiram Camp had founded the New Haven Watch Company which produced most of the millions of 'dollar watches', cheap clocks, nickel alarms, which ticked on American waists, stood on parlour mantleshelves, shrilled Americans awake from California to Cape Cod. It could really claim to be 'the world's greatest clock manufacturing organization'. Hiram Camp was a merry old soul, skilled story-teller, judge of good horses, a benevolent paternalist who, though company president, paid the wages with his own hands every Saturday. The New Haven campaign of 1878 had made him the warmest admirer of D L Moody. And now he had come all the way up the Connecticut Valley to take counsel.

They sat in the library. Camp said he had provided amply for his family and wanted to decide on charitable bequests. What, he asked in his slow Yankee drawl, did Mr Moody advise?

'I'm the wrong man to come to. I couldn't counsel in making a will. Why don't you have the fun of being your own executor and see your money do good? You've had the fun of making it. Now try giving it.'

The memorable conversation continued between Camp's New England drawl, and Moody's equally Yankee gallop.

'What shall I give to?' drawled Camp.

'What's y'r denom'nation?' rapped Moody.

'Con-greg-ation-al.'

'Why-don't-y'r-give-y'r-money-t'y'r-own-denom'nation? Look at the ABCFM, Home Board, Ministerial Relief, all the others. Well manned, efficiently run.'

'But I would like to give to something specific.'

'Well, here's something. I'm being hounded to take boys in the school I've started. I don't want to add to my troubles by going into co-education. Now you start a school for boys on the lines that I've started this school for girls. There is something specific and you can see it and watch it grow.'

Camp laughed his infectious laugh. 'I'm too old. I've lost touch with youth. But I'll tell you what I'll do. If *you* start such a school I will give you twenty-five thousand dollars for that purpose.'

'*What?*'

Moody was trapped. He had not meant to start a boys' school just then. Yet some such possibility must have been in mind, for the previous November when a fine farm beyond the river had been auctioned, H F N Marshall bought it as an investment giving Moody a year's option at the same price. This farm had belonged to the late Ezra Purple, Jr, none other than the son of Betsey's creditor of 1841 who had forced a way into her bedroom after the birth of the post-humous twins and tried to turn her out. Moody as a lad, vowing revenge, said he would one day own 'the Old Bear's' farm. On the Old Bear's death the place had been divided. Moody now had the northern half. The smaller, southern farm had been sold by the younger of the Old Bear's sons to his cousin, John Purple, and the proposed school must lack room for expansion unless he was bought out to give possession of the whole Purple place, some two hundred and seventy-five acres.

Hiram Camp attended the Northfield Conference and heard Moody's announcement on the last morning, Monday, September 10th, 1880, that an anonymous donor had given $25,000 to start a boys' school. Very early next morning at about a quarter past four Moody crept down to his stables, harnessed Nellie Gray to the buggy and disappeared in a flurry of dust at his usual pace (local riddle: 'Why is D L so good? Because he drives so fast the Devil can't catch him.').[1]

Before five he was banging on the door of his first cousin,

1. Moody once drove P P Bliss so fast to a meeting at Greenfield that 'when they arrived Mr Bliss was actually sick, and had to lie down for a time before he was able to sing' (W T Holton MS).

Jonathan Holton, whose farm bordered the Purple place. He found him in the barn milking, asked him to arrange to buy out John Purple instantly before he got wind of the school announcement and put two and two together about Marshall's farm, pulled from his pocket two prepared forfeit bonds of $1,000 for the vendor and purchaser to sign, mounted the buggy and was away.

By noon a price was settled, the bonds signed, and in ten days the sale to the school completed, and Moody took Hiram Camp and three other friends to explore. They looked over the buildings, walked to the height of land where they could gaze down the property to the river and across north-eastwards to Northfield marked by its elms and Northfield Mountain beyond, then northwards to the green hills of New Hampshire. They tramped the fields and climbed over a fence into a woodland where, as they rested on the moss in the shade of a great tree, Moody told them of 'Old Bear' Purple, and 'spoke most reverently', one of them wrote, 'of the way God had ordered events, and said that he regarded the securing of the farm as "poetic justice".' In the quiet of the woodland 'each of us in turn besought God to accept and bless the new enterprise'.

Back in Northfield they fell to discussing possible names, and Camp, on his way to New Haven, hit upon Mount Hermon: the Biblical Mount Hermon was on the far side of the river; it 'shall rejoice in thy name'; and in the great, short psalm of unity, Psalm 133, 'there the Lord commanded the blessing, even life for evermore'.

Mount Hermon, like the Northfield Seminary, had to be made ready in Moody's absence. In October the family disappeared for the winter, going this year – more distantly from Northfield than when in Britain – to the Pacific Coast.

Moody had come primarily to rescue the debt-ridden, aimless, spiritually decadent YMCA of San Francisco. With his usual sense of values he set about reviving the church life of 'the Wicked West'. By February 9th, 1881, he could write to Cyrus H McCormick in Chicago: 'You will be glad to know that our work on the Pacific coast has been owned of God.' Several churches had received 'large accessions' to membership. 'The work is going very well. But I am troubled about its continuance after I leave here...', and since 'few of the business men and still fewer of the young men are Christians', and McCormick, with his reapers, was 'well known all over the coast', he must please send $10,000 at once to launch a fund to secure a YMCA building. McCormick wired back: 'Too many undertakings here to meet your wishes,' but relented and helped to raise $82,000. At Moody's departure in late March the YMCA had 'a building for saving young men', new officers, new zeal.

As soon as the spring of 1881 made the railway through the mountains no longer dangerous, merely rough, Moody and his family and team travelled east. In Chicago a conversation with his old friend B F Jacobs, the Sunday school leader, showed the direction in which Moody's mind was working: 'Jacobs, I sometimes wonder if you will not get more out of your life than I will out of mine... I work for the salvation of men who have grown up to years of maturity in sin, in evil habits, in evil surroundings. I perhaps reach one out of ten that I try to reach. And then I am not sure that the one out of ten I think I have reached will stick. I am not sure after all they have gone through, whether it is a real surrender and a real victory. Jacobs, you work with them when they are young, before these habits are formed. You are sowing the seed in that most precious soil. Oh, do not let go! It will last there, and it will spring up. Of those I bring in, I do not know whether one out of ten will ever amount to anything in Christian work, but you can help them not only to Jesus Christ, but to see the blessedness of His service. Nine out of ten that you reach will stand fast and be true to God and Jesus Christ.'

The Seminary with its more than hundred girls was proving itself. At Mount Hermon the north farmhouse had been enlarged and a matron engaged, the widow of a missionary to Turkey. The school at that time being intended for small boys between eight and fifteen he appointed as teacher a woman, Mary Louise Hammond.

Applications had piled up, a hundred or more. Mary Hammond

recalled answering them at Moody's direction, 'with dear Mrs Moody sitting by (in his library), and helping in her quiet way. You know she was always a "balance wheel". I remember so well reading aloud one from a mother who expatiated, quite at length, on the waywardness of her son, etc. etc., and that she wanted him to be under Mr Moody's own roof, etc.... He despatched that in a few words by saying "Tell her it is not a Reform School". Another wrote in such a way as to make it quite evident that her boy was not of special promise but she wanted to send him there because she did not know what else to do with him, and did not even enclose a stamp, so he said "Throw it into the waste basket", looking at his wife as he would dispose of *such*, in like manner. I can see her now, as she sat there, looking as if she would make sure that it was the wisest thing to do, and now and then suggest a reply which might lead the mother to some other recourse, even if it were not best for her son to go to Mount Hermon.'

The first boy arrived on May 1st. Symbolically of a school for boys of small means, his name was Tommy Tomkins. On May 12th Moody wrote to his nephew Ambert, now nearly eighteen, whom he had sent on a short business course in Boston to prepare him as quarter-master of the schools, 'Your father got his sheep to pasture yesterday I bought 25 old ones & 25 lambs for the boys school of him & we turned the cows over to them today from the South barn & from mine so we have 8 cows over there now & will have 75 hens there when yours get there. One of the turkeys that you bought is setting I am going to have some geese over there to make things lively. We have or will tomorrow night seven boys... expecting more next week.'

Lessons began on June 1st, when thirteen boys had arrived. The basis was similar to the Seminary, the boys doing most of their manual work on the farm and clearing the land. Miss Hammond deep in her heart thought this hard: 'knowing that the most of them were from the city and not accustomed to exposure in sun, heat and cold, I used to fear the consequences often times'. Moody had no such fear. He drove Nellie Gray there frequently and the boys 'would rush down the hill and shout to see him coming. Any one of us would run across a ten-acre plowed field to unbar a gate for him, if his gray mare started that way.' Plough, pasture or road was one to Moody in his buggy. Sometimes he disrupted work-hours by taking them for a swim in the river, his passion for cold water being unsated, whether to splash in or to drink almost by the bucketful – four or five glasses during a meal. He watched their lessons, set them competitions, brought scores of visitors from the second Northfield Conference to see them in the new frame school-house between two hickory trees on the hillside.

The boys, the girls, were as sons and daughters, and Moody, far in advance of the whitewashed walls, plain deal tables and poor food of most contemporary schools – especially those that did not ask high fees – created a homelike atmosphere.

To Hiram Camp he wrote on July 12th, 1881, 'If you... could see the boys as they are at their studies, work and play I am sure you would feel well paid for all your trouble & you would see it is much better to give than to receive it does not cause any sleepless nights to give to the Lord but think of the pain, troubles etc in making $25,000.'

As Moody and Nellie Gray sped back and forth between the Seminary and Mount Hermon he had only one sense of unfulfilment: Chicago had dropped to second place. During the 1876 campaign he had talked about founding 'a school for training evangelists, pastoral helpers etc'; nothing had been done.

But the Northfield schools were established. Moody now could respond to insistent invitations to revisit Great Britain, and on September 22nd, 1881, the Moodys and the Sankeys sailed from New York.

The founding of the schools and what they had wrought in their founder ensured that the ultimate outcome of Moody's second British visit, 1881-84, would be more than a national mission.

Part Four

'THE POWER OF CHRISTIAN UNION'
1882-99

25: Dan'l at Cambridge

John Edward Kynaston Studd of Trinity College, Cambridge, eldest son of the late Edward Studd of Tedworth Hall, sat writing in the Pitt Club at Cambridge on February 2nd, 1882, while outside down Jesus Lane the wind blew raw from the fens.

Kynaston Studd was twenty-four. He was a cricket blue. His younger brother George ('G B') was Captain of Cricket; their next brother Charlie ('C T'), though only twenty-one, was an All-England cricketer who would have the highest batting average that summer of 1882 and be reckoned by the mighty W G Grace 'the most brilliant member' of the family. C T would be Cambridge Captain next year, and J E K, though eldest (he had come up late), would succeed him in 1884 – a family record never since broken. To be a Cambridge cricketer in the eighteen eighties carried great glamour and prestige, and despite their father's death the Studds also were wealthy.

Kynaston Studd's pen scratched away: '...We have already (in October last) asked Mr Moody to come here in March and he replied that it was uncertain if he would be in England then or rather if he would have come south by that time. Last time he was in England a petition signed by three hundred undergraduates was presented to him asking him to come & if he should require such a thing now we could easily get that number of members of the university and probably a great many more to sign the petition. We fear that it would not be of very much use Mr Moody's coming up next term as the men are all very busy with reading and athletics...' Studd was President of the Cambridge Inter-Collegiate Christian Union which had been formed a few years earlier, and remembering how his father had become 'a real live play-the-game Christian', as Charlie put it, was determined to bring Moody to Cambridge.

On February 13th Moody replied from Glasgow to the friend acting as go-between: 'Your kind letters with others from London and Cambridge enclosed came to me a few days ago. Thank you very much for sending them. I feel much interested and gratified with the invitation to visit Cambridge and especially so from the fact that one of the letters comes from a son of my friend from a former visit, Mr Studd.' After further correspondence Moody and Sankey accepted an invitation, to visit Cambridge for eight days of November 1882, signed by undergraduates, town clergymen and dons.

One who signed, signed reluctantly. Handley Moule, future Bishop of Durham, saintly and learned Principal of Ridley Hall, the new theological college, leader of Cambridge's numerous evangelicals, admired Moody warmly but feared that the most intolerant and difficult audience in the world 'would not be reached'. Cambridge in 1882 numbered about 3,500 undergraduates, nearly all from homes of real or comparative affluence and bred in the arid religion of the British public school. Many had no need to study hard for they would not have to earn a living. Despite the strong force of 'pi' undergraduates inheriting the tradition of a Daily Prayer Meeting unbroken in term-time for twenty years, and the CICCU, what would be Moody's treatment by arrogant intellectuals or the breezily intolerant 'fast set'?

On the afternoon of Saturday, November 4th, a beautiful autumn day, Moody and Sankey boarded the Cambridge train at St Pancras station, with Mrs Moody and Paul (little Paul taken round King's College Chapel that week asked, 'Where's the 'quiry room?'').

'There never was a place,' Moody said afterwards, 'that I approached with greater anxiety than Cambridge. Never having had the privilege of a university education I was nervous about meeting university men.'

A year had passed since Moody and Sankey and their families had landed at Liverpool, where 'even the custom house officers', Mrs Moody had written, 'came and shook hands with D L as soon as he got off the boat and told him they were glad to see him back again in this country. At the railway station officials came and welcomed him and told him that they had received good when he was in Liverpool... We have been having quantities of letters of welcome.'

The evangelists began in Newcastle followed by six weeks in

Edinburgh ('The meetings here are being much blessed and D L is very much encouraged') and, early in 1882, the start of five months in Glasgow.

This time they did not normally stay as guests in private houses but took lodgings. Young Emma at seventeen was still having lessons from her cousin, Fanny Holton, who acted also as Paul's nurse, while Willie, 'a fine tall lad devoted to his father', was put to day school. Paul, not yet three, fell seriously ill in Edinburgh: 'dear little fellow has been real sick,' Moody told his brother George, 'I was afraid for a few days that I could not keep him, that he must sink, we could not get any doctor that could reach his case but he is now on the upgrade.' Paul's illness caused Moody to begin Glasgow without his family. This deepened homesickness. 'I like America so much better than this land,' he wrote on a bleak January day, 'we seldom see the sun in this country & it is so cloudy & dark most of the time but the days are getting longer now & I am not so lonely as I was.' He corresponded regularly with Northfield, where though keeping down expenses they had already installed a telephone, an instrument barely known to Glasgow, and busy as he was he answered letters from the girls and boys. 'I wish you would tell the boys I would be glad to hear from them at any time,' he wrote to Master George Cragin.

Jane Mackinnon, in raptures at having her old friends again in Scotland, found Moody, his beard trimmed a little shorter, his hair a little thinner but with barely a trace of grey, 'the same, simple straightforward and affectionate man... His style is also the same but quieter. We think he is quieter altogether – probably the difference between thirty-seven and forty-five. But... there has been a mellowing power at work, not all of nature. One feels that he has grown more heavenward.'

She continues: 'I have missed much, this time, those little peculiarities – partly American, partly personal – which used to attract and amuse us so much. I dare say it is all in the way of improvement, but it has carried away some of the uniqueness and piquancy that we loved so well.' She noticed that Moody 'seems to carry about with him now a little library; how he can have time to read, I

cannot think'. She thought also that he 'is not quite so frolicsome
as he was previously': she should have seen Moody, Sankey and
Whittle chasing a rat (and each other) with a poker in an Irish hotel
in 1883!

Return to Glasgow after eight years produced an outburst of
popularity. The *Christian* reported that the crowd 'blocked the streets
for hours and the excitement penetrated the meeting to such an
extent that an inquiry meeting was not even attempted... other revival movements seem to have flourished on excitement, but this is
at once killed by it; and instead of taking advantage of heated occasions, Mr Moody waits for the night of quiet power and the whis-
per of the still small voice.' During the months of widespread
campaigning with united churches Moody did not attempt to carry
a load as crushing as that of 1874. 'D L,' Mrs Moody wrote to
Edwin in Northfield on April 19th, 'though working very hard is
very well and having much less headache than usual. He has been
very much less in the work here in Glasgow. He is now preaching
in the very poor district of Glasgow and among people such as you
have never seen. It would make your heart bleed to see the wretchedness here and it is most of it caused by drink... People living in
Northfield would hardly imagine such wretchedness as is to be
met with here in the poor parts of the large cities. Fanny and Emma
have gone to the coast for a breath of fresh air and they will get it
pretty direct from the North Pole I imagine...'

The Scottish mission was less spectacular than that of 1873-4.
'There weren't such outward and visible results,' John McNeill
wrote. For one reason evangelistic emphasis, startlingly fresh in
1874, had been accepted as a regular winter feature in many parishes. And much energy that might have been brought to evangelism was absorbed in increasingly bitter wrangles over higher
criticism, then in a strident over-confident phase.

The early summer of 1882 they spent in northern Scotland.
Moody had received invitations from all over Great Britain 'to last
a lifetime' and agreed to give, after a fortnight's holiday in Switzerland, a series of shorter missions from September until April
1883 in Welsh and English provincial centres. His trail is marked

by YMCAs or mission halls raised as thank-offerings in almost every city he visited.

Down the corridor of time the most significant event, both for Moody and for the world, is seen to be the week's adventure in Cambridge.[1]

The Cambridge visit was planned for town and gown.

On Sunday morning, November 5th, at a mass prayer meeting of church folk sprinkled with university men who were staunch Christians, Moody delivered what to Handley Moule seemed 'a very admirable and searching address on the Spirit's power for service', but a row or two behind Moody sat J E K Studd whose 'heart sank when I heard him, for his way of speech was not our way of speech, his accent was not our accent, and I feared what undergraduates, full of spirits and ready to make fun of anything, would do'. To make matters worse, November 5th was Guy Fawkes Day, and though the annual rag with its fireworks and bonfires, its fights with town lads and police would take place on the Monday, the Gunpowder spirit was abroad.

As the Cambridge night filled with a symphony of chimes from the clocks of colleges and churches, striking eight, the new, ugly, cavernous Corn Exchange which had been the scene of packed, decorous meetings for the town began to fill with rowdy undergraduates. 'In they came, laughing and talking and rushing for seats near their friends.' Seventy who had braved sneers to form a choir

---

1. He took a fortnight's mission in Paris in October. British cities included Swansea, Cardiff, Plymouth, Bristol, Portsmouth, Brighton, Liverpool, Birmingham. Interesting unpublished evidence from Plymouth is the letter of fourteen-year-old Tommy Bewes, youngest of the twelve children of a solicitor, to his sister Evy, September 29th, 1882: 'I am writing to tell you some good news which you will be glad to hear. I went to one of Moody's and Sankey's meetings on Tuesday and there *I was saved*. He spoke from the 9th verse of the 3rd of Genesis. It is where art thou? He said that that was the 1st question that God ever asked man in the Bible, and that it was the first question that people ought to ask themselves and he said that there were two more he was going to speak about and they were, Where are you going? And How are you going to spend eternity? I don't think he could have chosen better ones. Thank you very much for praying for me...' Tommy became the Rev Canon T C Bewes (1868-1949). (Letter in the possession of his son, the Rev Canon T C F Bewes.)

('I wouldn't join that lot for £200' said a new arrival to another), sang hymns which were countered by music-hall songs. Several light-hearted men tried to build a pyramid of chairs. A fire-cracker from outside exploded against a window. Seventeen hundred undergraduates in cap and gown, about half the junior members of the University, had been counted entering.

The choir stopped. A door opened. Handley Moule, John Barton, Vicar of Holy Trinity in the centre of the town and university, Professor Babington (Professor of Botany; he caught a severe cold because of Moody's passion for fresh air) and other dons and clergy led Moody and Sankey to the platform. Hoots and cheers. After 'Jesus lover of my soul', Barton offered prayer. Some 'ill-mannered youths', as Mrs Barton called them when she heard about it, responded with 'Hear! Hear!'

Sankey began 'The Ninety and Nine' which had never failed to quieten and move an audience; 'the students', he says, 'listened to the first verse in perfect silence, but at its conclusion they vigorously beat the floor with canes and umbrellas, and cried "Hear, hear!" ' Each verse produced cries of 'encore!' When they ruined 'Man of sorrows' Sankey came near to tears. Two or three dons quietly warned the worst offenders off the premises and stayed at the back to keep order, while Moody courteously pointed out that this was not a political meeting. 'The service is God's and such proceedings are irreverent.'

He preached on a favourite and suitable opening subject, Daniel in the lions' den, with its theme of faith and manly courage. His monosyllabic Dan'l was 'too much', wrote young Barclay Buxton of Trinity, 'for the disorderly spirits who had come for fun, and they called out "Dan'l, Dan'l" whenever that unfortunate name appeared'. Scattered guffaws greeted Americanisms or unbritish intonations; the 'unconscious click in his throat before saying certain pithy remarks' induced imitation. There were bursts of loud laughter, pert shouts of 'Well done!'

The university's weekly journal, the *Cambridge Review*, reported that 'the majority paid every attention to the service, and marked their displeasure of the minority in no uncertain manner'. The rowdies stayed unabashed: 'We went meaning to have some fun and, by jove, we had it!' Moody fixed his eye on a particularly elegant young man in the front row fooling hard, who evidently led the others. To a generation less colourful, more indifferent, whose reaction would be to stay away in lazy scorn, the full-blooded hounding of Moody by the undergraduates of 1882 must seem astonishing. Had he lost his temper the history of that week and of all that flowed from it would have been different. Moule's young nephew thought 'Moody was visibly affected', but anecdote and teaching flowed on, somewhat smothered by the Corn Exchange acoustics which even his voice could not defeat.

Moody would have closed the meeting immediately after Sankey's final solo. John Barren whispered: 'Call a prayer meeting. Ask any who wish to pray to stay behind a few minutes.'

Four hundred stayed, many from a sense of sportsmanship and fair play: among them some of the rowdiest, by now 'quiet, impressed and apparently ashamed of their recent behaviour'. Moody spoke again briefly, still in good humour and still on Dan'l.

Christian Union men returned to their colleges 'with heavy hearts'. Their opponents laughed. 'If uneducated men *will* come to teach the Varsity they deserve to be snubbed,' said the elegant youth from the front row, Gerald Lander, as he entered the Great Gate of Trinity. Moody and Sankey accompanied by Studd returned to the hotel. 'Well, Sankey,' said Moody cheerfully as he removed his sweat-saturated collar, 'I guess I've no hankering after that crowd again.' Studd says that 'Mr Sankey was greatly upset at the reception his singing had received. What Mr Moody's feelings were I do not know, but he was a man of great courage and determination.' Studd joined the evangelists as they prayed with fervour and in faith for days ahead.

During Monday morning a bell-boy knocked on Moody's door and handed in a card: 'Mr Gerald Lander. Trinity College.'

'Show him up,' said Moody.

'I want to apologize, sir. And – I've brought a letter of apology from the men.'

'Come right in!' Moody warmly shook his hand.

Mrs John Barton says that some of the 'more gentlemanly (though not yet at all of Mr Moody's way of thinking) were so indignant at their companions' rude behaviour that they got up a memorial to apologize to Mr Moody'. They prevailed on Gerald Lander to present it. He went simply as an English gentleman who on reflection realized he had overstepped the bounds of decency.

They had a long talk. Lander agreed that to prove his apology sincere he must attend the next meeting. Could Moody have peered into the future he would have seen this young man, now interested in little but racing and cards, striding through South China as a missionary bishop.

In Market Passage, close under Great St Mary's Church, a gymnasium had been adapted to hold five hundred for the week-night university meetings. Monday night was wet. When 'we assembled in the Gymnasium', writes W H Stone, an undergraduate who had been converted during Moody's Swansea campaign two months before, 'the sight was enough to depress the spirits of the most sanguine'. The bare hundred included most of the seventy men of the choir. But Lander, subdued and attentive, kept his promise. And the sparse attendance enabled Moody afterwards to move round the hall to every man in turn. Moule noted in his diary next day: 'Last night it is said 5 men were brought to Christ at the University meeting. Lord make it *stand* and carry it on.'

On Tuesday town and country folk packed the Corn Exchange an hour before the start, but at the gymnasium Moody felt 'we've come up against a brick wall'. An old lady staying at Professor Babington's for the mission suggested: 'Why do you not call a prayer meeting of mothers?' It was a regular dodge of Moody's to invite mothers to unite in prayer for their sons. He had never attempted to ask them to pray for other mothers' sons.

Wednesday afternoon, when college men were digesting a restrained and well expressed letter of protest from Studd in the *Cambridge Review,* saw Moody at the close of the town meeting, 'with infinite tact and feeling', collect some hundred and fifty mothers. He would recall that prayer meeting as unique in his experience:

'mother after mother, amidst her tears, pleaded for the young men of the University'. And Wednesday night, wrote G E Morgan, the undergraduate son of one of Moody's earliest British friends, 'exceeded our strongest faith and showed us how little we really had'.

The gymnasium was fuller. Moody spoke, in Moule's opinion, 'with great power – a remarkable difference from the very discouraging occasion on Sunday night'. Moody sensed that the mothers' prayers were being answered. He determined to prove it. 'I have not yet,' he said, 'held an inquiry meeting for you gentlemen, but I feel sure many of you are ready and yearning to know Christ. When you are in difficulties over mathematics or classics you do not hesitate to consult your tutors. Would it be unreasonable for you to bring your soul-trouble to those who may be able to help you? Mr Sankey and I will converse with any who will go up to the empty gallery yonder. Let us have silent prayer.'

The gallery – the gymnasium fencing-room – was up a clattering iron staircase 'in the centre of the hall in full view of all'. No man would reach this impromptu inquiry room without a deliberate noisy movement before friends. In a Varsity quick to ridicule eccentricity, where men hated to show their feelings, it could hardly have been chosen better to prevent shallow decisions.

Not a man moved. Moody repeated the appeal. 'There was no response,' Studd writes, 'till the third or fourth appeal,' and then a young Trinity man, 'amidst an awful stillness', left his place, and 'half hiding his face in his gown, bounded up the stairs two at a time'. Another followed. Soon the gymnasium reverberated with clatter, man after man. The choir sang again. Moody said, 'I never saw the gowns look so well before,' and led Sankey up the stairs. Of fifty-two men counted in the gallery, one was Gerald Lander.

'*Cambridge. Nov. 9. 82...* When you get the cattle out of quarantine will you let me know how much it cost I have three more to send but I do not want to send them until I hear how much it will cost. How much did you get for your wool & have you sold the sheep that belong to the boys school... Will it be so Paul's heifer can have another calf by spring I think it would please him much & Willie's pony if it could have a colt it would please Willie but I do not know but it is too late now... I hope you will keep your eye on Ambert & see that he makes a good deal of manure...' Moody's letter to George on Thursday made no mention of the sudden change in Cambridge's spiritual weather. 'Never,' a local newspaper affirmed, 'within the recollection of the oldest inhabitant have there been such immense gatherings in Cambridge for religion.' Moody drew every rank and age to Corn Exchange or gymnasium. All over the university, in rooms or strolling along the Backs or coming up from river or field the most unlikely men – heavy smokers, racing enthusiasts, idlers – were talking and thinking. Those who resisted, respected. They recognized 'a true tinge of manliness' in Moody's preaching.

Arthur Benson of King's, whose father became Archbishop of Canterbury a few weeks later, went to the gymnasium on Thursday 'led by sociable curiosity'. To him Sankey seemed 'an immense bilious[1] man, with black hair and eyes surrounded by flaccid, pendent, baggy wrinkles – who came forward with an unctuous gesture and took his place at a small harmonium, placed so near the front of the platform that it looked as if both player and instrument must inevitably topple over; it was inexpressibly ludicrous to behold. Rolling his eyes in an affected manner, he touched a few simple chords, and then a marvellous transformation came over the room. In a sweet powerful voice, with an exquisite simplicity combined with irresistible emotion, he sang "There were Ninety and Nine". The man was transfigured. A deathly hush came over the room, and I felt my eyes fill with tears; his physical repulsiveness slipped from him, and left a sincere impulsive Christian, whose simple music spoke straight to the heart.'

Moody's address that night, on 'Sowing and Reaping', Moule called 'a noble masterpiece of Christian faithfulness, courage and wisdom; I take it to have been the most solid contribution to moral

---

1. Sankey had certainly put on fat but no other observer suggested that he had lost his good looks. Benson was writing twenty-two years later, and in a semi-fictional context. Neither Sankey's nor Moody's name is mentioned. The account appeared in A C Benson's book of Essays, *The House of Quiet*, which was published in 1904 anonymously, under his own name later. In the original edition, Benson pretends to have found the story in a manuscript of 'a distant cousin'. Afterwards he acknowledged it to be based on his own experience.

influence that has been made, by way of public appeal, for many a day'. Moody 'had not spoken half a dozen words', Arthur Benson writes, 'before I felt as though he and I were alone in the world... After a scathing and indignant invective on sin, he turned to draw a picture of the hollow, drifting life with feeble, mundane ambitions – utterly selfish, giving no service, making no sacrifice, tasting the moment, gliding feebly down the stream of time to the roaring cataract of death. Every word he said burned into my soul. He seemed to me to probe the secrets of my innermost heart; to be analysing, as it were, before the Judge of the world, the arid and pitiful constituents of my most secret thought. I did not think I could have heard him out – his words fell on me like the stabs of a knife. Then he made a sudden pause, and in a peroration of incredible dignity and pathos he drew us to the feet of a crucified Saviour, showed us the bleeding hand and the dimmed eye, and the infinite heart behind. "Just *accept* Him," he cried; "in a moment, in the twinkling of an eye you may be His – nestling in His arms – with the burden of sin and selfishness resting at His feet."'

Benson did not go up the iron staircase but 'into the night, like one dizzied with a sudden blow... my only idea was to escape and be alone'. He did not seek out Moody or speak to anyone of the spiritual conflict and 'intolerable depression' that led him through weeks of misery, never, in a long and honourable career at Eton and Cambridge of teaching, writing, editing, and holding the Mastership of Magdalene, to find the peace of heart offered that November night.

Others, like Arthur Polhill-Turner, a gay spark of Trinity Hall, crept away to face the fact that life would have 'to be a good deal adjusted'. Thirty mounted the staircase, including several who had been 'cynical and careless'.

On Friday and Saturday Moody had a stream of callers, and each night Christian Union men were amazed and humbled to see the iron staircase draw outstanding intellectuals and athletes, admired or popular, of whom most had given little previous thought to religion: and that those who clattered up one night would show by their company on the next that they had followed Moody's advice: 'No one can have really received Christ in his heart if he does not confess Him to his friends.'

The final university meeting filled the Corn Exchange on Sunday night.

Of that frosty, murky November 12th, 1882, a newspaper reported 'four such meetings as have never before been witnessed in this town'. Yet for all the massive impression on town and country-side 'success has been greater, and as far as can be judged, more real amongst the students of the University than amongst the general public'.

Moule called it a 'strange and unprecedented phenomenon in Cambridge life'. Studd, the following week, 'sent out a notice to say that any one who had reason to be thankful for the visit of Mr Moody might have the opportunity of writing their names in a book which would be on the table in my room at a certain date and hour, when I myself would not be there'. Among the signatures were 'the names of many men who made their mark in the world afterwards'. Moody, in 1884 at the close of his second British Mission, said: 'We have experienced the advantage of the Cambridge visit through the whole of our London Campaign,' and Moule that same year remarked to a friend as they breakfasted with the Ridley Hall theological students, 'I think there is not one man here whose life was not influenced more or less by Moody's Cambridge mission.' In 1906 Bishop Moule could state: '...and among the scores of true, deep lasting conversions were not a few men well known and of powerful influence. I could name more than one College whose morale was lastingly raised after Moody's week.'

The comment which, if extravagant, points to the wider consequences that were to involve Moody, comes from a distinguished New Testament scholar, a freshman at King's in 1882, James Hope Moulton, who in 1914, a year or two before his death in the First World War, wrote to Will Moody: 'I regard that week as the most momentous week in the religious history of this country during my lifetime, for it is certain that it was then the Student Christian Movement was born.'

All this the future shrouded as Moody, on Sunday night, November 12th, before nearly two thousand Cambridge University men, preached from the text in St Luke, 'Good tidings of great joy... a Saviour'. His address was heard without a 'shadow of opposition, interruption or inattention'. At the end he said: 'One last word. I shall never forget this week though you may forget me. I thank God I ever came to Cambridge, but I should like to give you one text before closing. "Seek ye *first* the kingdom of God."' He finished with the words: 'Believe the Gospel and make room for God in your hearts.'

The choir sang 'Just as I am, without one plea'. Moody prayed. Every head bowed. Then he asked that all who had received blessing should rise quietly in their places, silent prayer continuing.

Two hundred rose. Moody, looking up, murmured: 'My God, this is enough to live for.'

26: Seed-bed of a World Movement

Moody was now mountainous. 'Nothing will fit him he is so broad of back, so large of paunch and so destitute of neck,' wrote Whittle after he had gone with Moody and Sankey shopping for an overcoat. 'We tell him it would take a land surveyor to lay out a coat for him his back is so broad!' He did not look obese, for the massive flesh lay hard. His step was springy, his strength bull-like as his neck. He could not, however, be quite as prodigal of energy and had he not returned for the summer of 1883 to Northfield he would have collapsed during the following eight months in London.

And Northfield needed him. Miss Tuttle had left for an administrative post, the next principal married the minister, and Moody referred back to Wellesley to discover Evelyn Hall, very young but very able, principal from 1883 until her death in 1911, and reputed the only woman other than his wife who could manage Moody: he was even slightly in awe of her. Mount Hermon had new cottages, and Moody arranged for twelve boys from Manchester to join the growing number of Americans. He appointed a somewhat elderly

gentleman as principal and would have ordered the building of a
Recitation Hall if money had not been short.

Both schools were hindered by the lack. The Hymn-Book Fund
grew but during this summer of 1883, in Moody's words privately
to Whittle next winter, 'Sankey's relatives in New Castle got around
him and persuaded him that he should be allowed to have some of
the money to do something for his town and not let it all go to
Northfield. So we met the Trustees and $20,000 was voted to him.
I could not oppose it, nor did I wish to – I have always wanted him
to do something for his town, but he never seemed to care to do
so... In the meantime, I am pressed for means to carry on my
Schools. I am praying for money and believe it will come soon.'
Sankey gave New Castle a library, a Methodist church and, to
Moody's satisfaction, a YMCA building.

Work for the schools made the holiday the more invigorating.
Lapping up Northfield air, Northfield scenes, Northfield friends,
Moody saw to it that the family enjoyed themselves. Paul's earliest
distinct memories of his father were from this summer, 'as a nearly
ideal companion for a very small boy... He had a most engaging
way of treating a child, at least he always did me, as if I were more
or less his equal in years. He never talked down to me, but flattered
me with the constant assumption that my opinion was sought and
that he was interested in what I thought or had to say.'

They reached London in November 1883, after a short mission in
Southern Ireland.

The eight months' London campaign of 1883-4 Moody rated
'better, better in every way' than that of 1875; an immediate verdict substantiated by long-term effects. He had revised his opinion
that London 'seventy-five had not been 'of much value' when all
over the south and west of England in the early 'eighties, and in
London, 'I found so many of the best workers to be the fruit of
these labours', but he saw more brotherly feeling in 1883-4, and
increased spiritual life in the churches: 'the Church of England
especially is more alive than it used to be. The number of ministers, Established and non-Established that co-operated with us all

through has been much greater... less newspaper sensation, more meetings, better meetings, and the work has been of a more satisfactory character every way.'

Thousands of words were written about this London campaign. Archives and books teem with records and anecdotes. From the perspective of more than two generations its importance is as a seedbed for the movement growing out of the Cambridge mission.

The London Committee under its secretary, Robert Paton – 'an invaluable man but a little stubborn in his opinion: he and Mr Moody occasionally clash but Moody has a wonderful control of himself and so controls others' – had hit upon a novel plan. Two portable corrugated-iron buildings, 'tin tabernacles' they were dubbed, were specially constructed. The first was erected in open ground among the small terraces of middle-class houses, each with its little garden, in Islington. After three weeks Moody and Sankey and their helpers ('the caravan') moved south of the river to find the second tabernacle waiting on private land in the working-class area of Wandsworth. The first was dismantled and re-erected – it took about three weeks in the East End, 'the midst of awful poverty' in Stepney, – for the mission of December. Each tin tabernacle, which seated an audience of 5,180, with more seats on the platform and a spacious inquiry room beyond, appeared to Whittle, who served overflow and follow-up services, 'like three long cattle sheds placed side by side with no partition. Inside it has three separate roofs supported by pillars.' Each piece of timber and iron was marked and went back to the same place.

Eleven sites were used in the eight months, most of them in the outer ring of London. The only site in the City, at Temple Gardens between Fleet Street and the Embankment, had least success though crowded nearly every night. In some districts the crush to hear Moody taxed the resources of the committee to the utmost, and the *Pall Mall Gazette* reckoned that in the entire mission Moody had addressed 2,200,000 souls.

Within a few weeks of opening the London campaign Moody suffered a severe blow. Willie, now nearly fifteen, had bad lungs. Any illness among his children made Moody 'dreadfully concerned'

and Paul remembers how his father constantly placed a sympathetic hand on the tiny forehead, a hand 'little lighter than a dictionary but... all you felt was the weight of affection'. ('Once he
perched on the side of a sick bed and broke it down.') Money was
short, but the Moodys settled that Emma must take the children to
the mountain air of Zermatt in Switzerland. 'I am dreading the
going away from England very much,' she wrote on November 9th
to Mrs Mackinnon, who a few days after they had gone abroad saw
Moody at Islington 'looking so tired... [he] said to me that this
parting was the worst "pull" on him he had ever had'. He was 'rather
downcast at the prospect of having to go through the whole Mission without her help and the comfort that there is to him in her
presence'.[1]

He accepted an invitation to stay indefinitely with the Quintin
Hoggs who now lived off Cavendish Square, near Hogg's Polytechnic Institute, 'in fine style in a house built by an English Duke. The
rooms are very fine with exceedingly high ceilings', Whittle noted,
'with stone stairways connecting. Moody has a parlor and bedroom, a servant set apart for his use, and a carriage to take him
anywhere and at any time he wishes.' Hogg brought politicians and
public men 'for private interviews about their souls', among them
the great Liberal statesman, John Bright, whom Moody found 'nothing less than a Unitarian'.

Whittle, dearest, most perceptive of friends, rejoiced at Moody's
influence 'among this class of people... If I were asked as to the
direction in which his greatest danger lay, I should say that it would
come from his Ambition to lead and influence Rich Men.' So far
this had not led him 'to compromise his convictions'. Whittle praised
God 'every time I think of it that He keeps Moody so level-headed'.

Despite this plutocratic base Moody effectively reached the lowest
classes.

Some of the most interesting evidence comes from difficulties
in follow-up. At Wandsworth two thousand names were taken in

---

1. The Moodys reunited briefly in Belgium for Christmas.

the inquiry room. In the month after the meetings regular visitors reported that 'the conversions were *real* and the people rejoicing in Christ and turned from sin'. Why, then, for all this success did the local churches each receive a mere handful? Many of the two thousand were scattered widely around the district and beyond, but it was discovered that 'the large proportion of the converts are from the working-class, and that they are attending services in mission halls where they feel more at home than in the churches'. The Scripture reader who looked after the mission halls of the parish church found 'most satisfactory evidence of the reality of the work'. Moody himself had 'launched the project of a Gospel Hall to be erected on the site of the Iron Building', as a union endeavour. It continued in service for a century.

The London working-man was much exposed to noisy rationalists or 'free-thinkers'. At Stratford in the East End, where the destitution and overcrowding of Stepney had given way to acres of factories and cheerless streets of workers' dwellings, Moody waded into the thick of this militant atheism which thrived on Bradlaugh and gin and gloried in endless debate, in pelting bricks and stones at Salvation Army processions, but had no foundation of intelligence: 'they don't know what they do believe or what they don't believe'. Moody had been introduced to the president of a local atheist club, who 'snarled and growled at me as I spoke to him, and wanted to fight'. The man sent a note daring Moody to preach a sermon to atheists. The resulting famous incident of Thursday, January 31st, 1884, has been blown up into the legend of an entire hall of atheists, five hundred of whom leap to their feet in instant confession of Christian faith; a legend still produced in biographies of Moody. The facts, recounted by him four days later at luncheon with George Williams of the YMCA, Professor Simpson, Robert Paton and Whittle, who recorded it the same night in his diary, are less sensational.

The front seats were reserved for the atheists and 'hundreds came'. Moody preached his sermon on 'Their rock is not our rock', which focused on the emptiness of the atheists' hope, and by a succession of death-bed scenes caught them on their soft spot: the mockery of family love if there be no immortality, a theme to which, that night, his own family's absence abroad gave special tenderness. 'One man arose to interrupt but I held the audience and invited them all to remain to the second meeting, not to run away. I have something you all need and all could have. Many of them remained.' To the after-meeting Moody explained four words: *'Receive* Him, *believe* Him, *trust* Him, *take* Him.' 'Who will take Him?' he cried. 'Who will say "I will"?' Several responded among the general audience. An atheist shouted 'I won't.' Moody, compassionate almost to tears, sobbed: 'It's "I will" or "I won't" for every man in this hall to-night.' He spoke of the Prodigal Son's decision: 'I *will* arise and go to my father...' 'The battle is on the *will,* men,' he said, 'and only there. When the young man said "I will arise" the battle was won, for he had yielded his will, and on that point all hangs to-night. Men, you have your champion there who said "I won't!" I want every man who believes that man is right to rise and say: "I won't take Him."'

Not a man moved. Moody continued: 'Thank God! No man says "I won't." Now who'll say "I will", who will take Christ as Saviour, who will take Him?'

A long pause. Then: 'One of the atheists,' said Moody telling the story, 'called out "I will take Him!" It was a bombshell in their midst. Some were violent in anger as the meeting closed. But the backbone of atheism in the club received a terrible twist. I met the man who decided to Christ and found him an intelligent mechanic, and fully turned to God.'

Ten days later Moody accepted an invitation to family tea with the president of the atheist club, 'the street quite stirred and people at their doors to see if I was really coming'. In the course of the tea Moody said: 'If I lived in Stratford I should not try by argument to win you over, but I should try by kindness to win your affection and make you respect me.'

'You have done that already.'

The man came on with Moody to the tabernacle 'as mild as a lamb'. Moody sat him on the platform and during the sermon aimed several hard hits.

Unfortunately, as is often the way with facts, the rest of the man's story is lost.

At New Cross in south-east London in late February the crowds were almost unmanageable. One night a milling flow sought to press into the hall at the end of the meeting as the audience of five thousand were leaving, until the police inspector wanted to send for a mounted section. Moody jumped over a hedge, ran across a field to an omnibus on the edge of the crowd, climbed to the top and whispered to the driver, who gave a shake of the reins. A moment, and people heard Moody's voice boom. They converged on the omnibus which moved away at a walking pace, Moody using it as a pulpit, until the crush eased.

With triumphs New Cross brought trials. The Plymouth Brethren pitched a tent upon one side of the tin tabernacle to catch the overflow, the parish church arranged a 'ritualistic service' on the other, and both asked Moody to boost them. 'The Holiness people have been pulling strong to get my presence for five minutes at one of their meetings as a testimony I'm not antagonistic to them, and the friends of General Booth have been urging for some expression of endorsement of Salvation Army... And so I have had a time of it this week driving the coach through without upsetting!'

Sankey collapsed the first day, and for a week Moody had to depend on his American assistants, George C Stebbins and James McGranahan and his wife ('Mack' and 'Addy' to their friends). When Sankey came back he was 'crotchety' and would not take second place and sing at the overflow meetings. The local choirmaster hashed the hymns, some gunners from Woolwich Depot volunteered as a male choir for the men's meetings 'and it was the most miserable failure I ever saw. They broke down and had to commence over again three times on the same piece. Some of the audience hung their heads in shame for them, and others laughed at them. If you ever saw a man whistling through a graveyard, I was that man as I got up after that singing.'

By the closing Sunday at New Cross, March 2nd, Moody was visibly tired, and at the start at St Pancras, where the tabernacle had been erected close to the Midland Railway terminus on land cleared for a widening scheme, the noise from trains and the heat caused by high walls which blocked ventilation gave Moody such headaches that he drank gallons of tea and then suffered a rare bout of sleeplessness. Strain increased as the campaign lengthened – St Pancras, Kensington (the site where Olympia was to be built), Hampstead. He found relief in romping with the Hogg children, or in jokes and stories with his cronies. Laughter was always his safety-valve. During the Irish campaign the previous autumn when he, Sankey and Whittle were staying, grass widowers, in hotels, 'most every night before going to bed M would, as he sat at supper, have his laugh, shaking all over and holding his side and entering most heartily into anything funny. He is as natural as a child in this.' He knew how far to go, never joked about sacred things, and if an inquirer called could turn instantly to serious talk 'with perfect naturalness'.

Though tired Moody was a contrast to Spurgeon, a mere three years his senior, whom he found 'broken from overwork' and prematurely old. Spurgeon undoubtedly carried a heavier intellectual load, preparing and preaching fresh full length sermons to six thousand twice every Sunday and to three thousand every Thursday; he wrote books, he lectured in his college. But Spurgeon, unlike Moody, engaged in heated controversy. 'Spurgeon writes *Reformer and Preacher*. I am simply a preacher. I have nothing to do with reforms. I take things as I find them and simply work for a united work in getting the Gospel before the people.' A further strain on Spurgeon's physique was his very heavy smoking.[1]

Moody's level-headedness was part of the secret of his strength: 'If I were to get into such a state of nervous excitement as General Booth I should have been dead ages ago.' Yet he admitted that he had 'so many things on hand that I used to let little things annoy me', and was abashed when told by a prominent London clergyman with several curates and a large parish, that 'no man ought to undertake so much Christian work that it wears him out and makes

---

1. Moody said to a man who sought his approval of smoking: 'The Bible tells you to carry on.' 'What?' 'Yes. "He which is filthy, let him be filthy still"!'

him irritable'. Moody would confess, 'I know you men are way beyond me in the sweetness and peace of your daily lives and I wish I were more like you,' but he preserved a healthy scepticism about perfectionist claims and answered someone's boast of sinlessness with the blunt comment: 'I would like to meet your wife!'

By April his daughter was with him. Good news of Willie's health ensured that the whole family would be back with the sun, and in May the last district site but one opened in Croydon, close to the Crystal Palace.

Lady Ashburton, the banker's wife, put at Moody's disposal her near-by mansion in its park of one hundred and eighty acres, complete with servants and supplies. It was from this stately home that, on May 10th he wrote to Willie on the Continent:[1] 'You will see by the heading of this note ⅓ of May has all ready gone & the days will soon pass a way that seperate us from our dear home

'I have writen to have them get your garden ready & I think we Will find it all ready when we get home I bought some Bowls so we can have some games when we get back – as spring comes on I long to get home & to get into the green fields & see what is goin on there will be a good many changes in our end of the town Mr Marshall is goin to build two buildings so we will have a grate change & a number of things to intrest us I have some cooing doves & a butiful Peacock to take back with me & I am in hopes we will be enabled to keep this one

'You must take good care of Ma Ma & not let her loose to much sleep with Paul Can you not take care of him nights if she gets him to sleep & he wakes up mornings early & she does not get enough sleep it will give her a head ache I am afraid you must not let Ma Ma overwork see that she is not weary robbed of her sleep if she does not get enough night times let her go to sleep in the day & you take Paul out walking...'

Eleven days later he met them in London, 'one of the happiest days of my life'. The unlucky family brought Paul back with whooping cough.

---

1. Original spelling given as a later example of Moody's family scrawl. The letter is unpunctuated throughout.

Sankey sailed home sick, leaving Stebbins and the McGranahans to sing in his place. The London campaign had brought Sankey two bereavements: his delicate eldest son lies buried in Marylebone cemetery, and his father died far away in Pennsylvania. 'The reality of Sankey's consecration to the Lord,' Whittle had written, 'is impressed upon me in my intercourse with him this winter. His father's death has been blessed in bringing him nearer to God, and Christ and the Gospel are dearer to him than ever. His prayer with us this morning was *very* real and blessed.'

No assistant could fully take Sankey's place. Moody would miss him at Temple Gardens. From the Kinnairds' Mayfair home, where they moved from Croydon, Mrs Moody wrote on May 27th: 'My husband began his last district here. He keeps remarkably well, but I do think he has had a very long continuous strain on him and will be so glad when he has finished this district, though he does look well.' And all this time the London campaign nourished the remarkable movement among young men that would have such consequences for the world.

27: Student Volunteers

In November 1882 when Moody had left Cambridge for Oxford, where again disaster ended in triumph though the consequences were less, several of the Cambridge converts showed immediate awareness of the call of overseas. Moody had said little if anything about the 'foreign field', as the phrase was, at Cambridge or elsewhere. Yet within a week or two Hooper of Trinity thought about Africa, Tyndale-Biscoe of Jesus about India, and Arthur Polhill-Turner of Trinity Hall about China.

Shortly after the end of the Cambridge term Moody held a mission in the mosque-like Dome of the exotically oriental Pavilion at Brighton, where lived a retired major-general called Hoste who had one son, William, on vacation from theological studies at Moule's Ridley Hall, and another, Dixon Edward, on leave from the gunners, a subaltern of soldierly bearing and utter lack of interest in religion. William dragged Dixon to the Dome where, Dixon wrote, 'As Mr Moody, with intense earnestness and directness preached the solemn truths concerning God's judgment of the impenitent and ungodly... a deep sense of my sinful and perilous state laid hold of my soul with great power.'

Dixon frequented subsequent meetings in agonized indecision, fearing the cost of becoming a Christian, until on the last night, slipping into the back of the Dome, he yielded, sensed a flooding peace and assurance of forgiveness, and at Moody's call for inquirers went forward radiant. Within a fortnight he wanted to resign his commission to be a missionary. His father dissuaded him. By the spring of 1883 he was reading literature sent by William from Cambridge about the China Inland Mission, then an obscure but valiant pioneering band; and during the summer, when Moody was in Northfield, Hoste applied to its founder, James Hudson Taylor, a little man of acute perception and extraordinary courage, only to be advised to wait.

Moody's mind also worked towards overseas missions. At the Chicago Convention in September 1883 he had drawn attention to the appalling discrepancy between the world's millions of 'Christless souls' and the sprinkling of Western Christians who served overseas, backed by a trickle of money.

The London campaign saw Cambridge to the fore. 'Women had a way of fainting,' Jane Mackinnon recorded, 'and the young gentlemen stewards – some of them athletes from Cambridge and Oxford – got opportunities of showing their prowess!' At Wandsworth a Cambridge student who felt unfitted for service in the inquiry room told a London cabby that he would 'pay your regular fee by the hour if you will go in and hear Mr Moody preach. I will take care of your horse.' For two hours, in Moody's words, 'on that cold, bleak night that London gentleman stood by the cabman's horse and let that cabman go and hear the Gospel'.

In the Clapham mission served two slightly older Cambridge men, William Cassels, a curate, and Stanley Smith, a schoolmaster who stroked the university boat in 1882; his conversion as a boy during the 'seventy-five campaign caused him, when up for a long week-end during the Cambridge mission and introduced to 'dear old Moody' to give him 'such a shake of the hand!' Cassels and Smith had met little since Varsity but found a strong bond: 'after the meetings,' Smith wrote years later, 'we had some arm-in-arm walks and heart-to-heart talks about the Lord and China.' Smith spent his free time at the campaign. Moody noticed his skill and invited him to tea during the Kensington mission to put a proposition: he was taking, he said, several young working-class men who had asked if he would train them for home or foreign missions since they knew of no means in Britain, to Mount Hermon to form a specialist class. Stanley Smith must run it. Smith's heart lay in China. The very same evening Hudson Taylor dined with Stanley and his parents in their Mayfair home and that night Stanley Smith wrote in his diary: 'Decided to go to China with Hudson Taylor as a missionary, and to go, DV via America so as to see Moody's training home.'

Smith never saw Mount Hermon. His indirect influence there would be strong, and through Mount Hermon would have significance for the whole world.

No man under thirty lay more in Moody's affection than J E K Studd, now Captain of the Cambridge Eleven, 'of fine ability and promise, and very popular with the gentry, an out-and-out Christian'.

The next Studd, G B, was of J E K's stamp, but C T, now at the height of fame as a cricketer, had been spineless and effete as a Christian when the campaign began. In December G B fell desperately ill, and by his bedside in the small hours C T saw the emptiness of his own existence, living only for games, popularity and pleasure. When his brother was out of danger C T Studd hurried to Moody's meetings, then at Stratford: 'There the Lord met me again and restored to me the joy of my salvation.'

C T became a strong worker, his fame and charm and forthright, single-track enthusiasm combining to give his words punch. At a subsidiary meeting of the campaign he and J E K were heard by a young medical student, Wilfred Grenfell. Grenfell previously had wandered into one of Moody's Stepney services, where on the platform stood an elderly man coagulating a prayer of such long wind that the huge audience was suffocating and Grenfell, bored, tiptoed towards the door. An American voice broke in across the English. Moody 'kindly but ever so cleverly' called out: 'Let us sing a hymn while our brother finishes his prayer.' This announcement, Moody's usual gambit in the circumstances, stopped Grenfell in his tracks: 'his practicality interested me.'

After the singing the address 'moved me... It was a personal conversation with my heart... It was the real thing,' and a few weeks later at the close of the Studd meeting one of the brothers – probably J E K – asked those who intended following Christ to stand up. To Grenfell 'it appeared a very sensible question but I was amazed how hard I found it to stand up. At last one boy out of a hundred or more, in sailor rig, from an Industrial or Reformatory ship on the Thames, suddenly rose. It seemed to me such a wonderfully courageous act for I knew perfectly what it would mean to him, that I immediately found myself on my feet...' Twenty years after, in a letter to Moody's son-in-law, Grenfell of Labrador wrote: 'Anything with the name of "Moody" to it has a great call on my affections. You know I attribute my conversion to his work in Stepney years ago.' 'He started me working for all I was worth,' Grenfell wrote in one of his books, 'and made religion real fun – a new field brimming with opportunities.'

With summer C T Studd felt he 'must go into the cricket field and get the men there to know the Lord Jesus... My heart was no longer in the game. I wanted to win souls for the Lord.' Under his wing members of the MCC Test team heard Moody, and several whose names were household words told Studd, one by one, that they had accepted Christ. These young athletes would be invited to Moody's Saturday holidays in the spacious grounds of wealthy homes on London's outskirts where Moody, in Lord Kinnaird's words, 'would throw himself into games with as much zest as he took up all his other work and you can imagine that he did not like to be on the losing side, but generally secured one of the brothers Studd or Mr Steel[1] to play on his side! I shall never forget his portly

1. Allan Gibson Steel, the slow bowler (1858-1914).

form running in the game of rounders in which he used to take great delight.'

The campaign ended. While Moody picked up threads at Northfield and Chicago and immersed himself in a fresh round of American campaigns for autumn and winter, in Britain, one by one, Stanley Smith, Charlie Studd, D E Hoste, Arthur Polhill-Turner and his brother Cecil, Montagu Beauchamp and William Cassels, all converts or helpers under Moody, offered themselves for China. When it was known that men of wealth, birth and athletic prowess were to become missionaries the sensation was tremendous. 'The Cambridge Seven' swept across the universities of England and Scotland stirring students to faith and dedication, especially for service overseas. Where Moody had ploughed and sown, they reaped, and the climax came with a great meeting in London on February 4th, 1885, the day before the Cambridge Seven sailed. The missionary call sounded louder than ever before.

The story caught the imagination of America. And it was in the afterglow of the Cambridge Seven that the third Northfield Conference gathered in August 1885.

Moody allotted August 11th, half-way through the Conference, to 'prayer for world-wide missions'. The main address was delivered to about one thousand people by Arthur T. Pierson of Philadelphia, a recognized authority whose book *The Crisis of Missions* appeared next year.

Pierson urged that this was the hour for advance. An Appeal should be sent to the entire Church: 'Let us have an ecumenical council, representing all evangelical churches, solely to plan [a] world-wide campaign and proclaim the good tidings to every living soul in the shortest time! Let the field be divided and distributed with as little waste of men and means as may be. Let there be a universal appeal for workers and money, and a systematic gathering of offerings that shall organize the mites into millions.'

Moody jumped to his feet. With force and enthusiasm he called the Conference to vote their approval by acclamation. Then he appointed a small committee of six and himself to draw up 'An Appeal to Disciples Everywhere'. Three days later this was read out, endorsed by the Conference and signed by the committee.

'The whole world' the Appeal proclaimed, 'is now accessible, the last of the hermit nations welcomes the missionary.' And so it seemed, with little exaggeration, in 1885. Swift steamships took men across the oceans, the white man's flag had been carried into recesses of Africa, India was at peace under the imperial crown of Victoria, treaties promised free movement in China – the world was destined to peace and progress under Western leadership. If Tibet's gates were fast shut, New Guinea almost unexplored, Uganda, that very year, the scene of massacre of missionary and convert, what were these to determined men? 'And yet the Church of God is slow to move in response to the providence of God. Nearly a thousand millions of the human race are yet without the Gospel; vast districts are wholly unoccupied.'

Northfield appealed for 'the immediate occupation and evangelization of every destitute district', for 'a new effusion of the Spirit in answer to prayer... If but ten million out of the four hundred millions of nominal Christians would undertake such systematic labour as that each one of that number should in the course of the next fifteen years reach one hundred souls with the Gospel message, the whole present population of the globe would have heard the glad tidings by 1900.' They called for an ecumenical conference (which met three years later in London) in words that bear the Moody stamp: 'What a spectacle it would present both to angels and men, could believers of every name, forgetting all those things in which they differ, meet by chosen representatives to enter systematically and harmoniously upon the work of sending forth labourers into every part of the world field.'

The Appeal had been drafted in the Homestead partly bought with Edward Studd's gift. One of the seven who signed it was J E K Studd. One who acclaimed it as a member of the Conference was a thirty-one-year-old graduate of Princeton called Luther T. Wishard.

Luther Wishard, founder of the Inter-Collegiate YMCA, had twice failed to persuade Moody before 1882 to preach in colleges.

Moody 'almost took my head off... if he had a weak point it was an unnecessary abruptness in declining invitations'. Despite his impact on Edinburgh students in 1873, his day at Princeton in 1876, and the number of Yale men who came to the New Haven meetings, Moody's lack of higher education inhibited him. During December 1884 Wishard 'again tackled him' during the Cincinnati campaign. 'While he was still modest, and shrinking, and distrustful of himself, he intimated that if he could be assured that the students themselves wanted to hear him – not simply that somebody interested in students wanted them to hear him – he would seriously consider such invitations. It did not take long to secure invitations from students. They prepared petitions in Princeton, Harvard, Yale and Dartmouth... Thousands and thousands of signatures were obtained.'

Moody stopped short of Harvard. Princeton, Dartmouth and Yale heard him in 1885. At Yale in Battell Chapel 'he seemed rather ill at ease and not at all at home being introduced in a regular service and obliged to fit into the regular order', wrote a Yale man, Cornelius H Patton, to Will (in 1925). 'In the evening it was far different. Battell Chapel was packed and your Father in full control. He preached his famous sermon on "Whatsoever a man soweth, that shall he also reap",' the sermon which had overturned A C Benson at Cambridge and never failed in its freshness and reality; thousands who heard it could echo Sam Higginbotham's verdict: 'I never knew any preacher to reveal *sin* as such a hateful thing, and yet that was the undertone. The overtone was that in God's love there was grace enough to cover all my sin.' The Yale men listened in utmost silence and the scene afterwards was reminiscent of the iron gallery at Cambridge.

At best Moody's college sermons could be few. He wrote of his admiration for Wishard's lonely labours 'among our 1,200 American colleges, professional and preparatory schools', and in the summer of 1885 Moody induced J E K Studd to cross the Atlantic for the college year of 1885-6.[1] Aided by the glamour of his athletic

---

1. In 1927 Sir Kynaston Studd told Will that he joined Moody at Bridgeport, Conn. 'Your Father was in difficulty that morning because he had to take a meeting but had also to

renown and as brother of C T Studd of the Cambridge Seven, J E K exerted wide influence. At Cornell an able law student called John R Mott attended his address, 'an unbeliever... I listened to him and was converted' after a sharp spiritual struggle, 'with the help of comprehending and faithful counsel from the English visitor'.

The Northfield Conference brought Wishard, Studd and Moody together. One day Moody drove them to Mount Hermon, which now had settled towards its final form as a secondary school for older boys; the Training School for young men was then a part of it. Proper buildings, with more at Northfield were now being built, for the British had forwarded no less than £20,000 in hymn-book royalties: 'Look at that,' Moody would point, 'Sankey sang it up.' As they drove around the campus Moody suggested: 'Wishard, wouldn't this be a good place for a conference of the general secretaries of the city YMCAs?'

'Yes, it would be ideal.'

'Well, how would you like to bring fifty or a hundred of them up here next summer, and let them live in those little houses where the workmen are living? I will give them a Bible reading every day, and we will have a Bible conference.' Wishard did not encourage him 'because I had larger game to kill'.

In Atlanta that winter Wishard met Moody who again offered to entertain city YMCA secretaries at Mount Hermon, as many as two hundred. Wishard said: 'Mr Moody, if you are willing to do that for a couple of hundred general secretaries, why won't you do it for a couple of hundred students from the colleges throughout the country and Canada?'

But 'the old spirit of distrust', says Wishard, 'took possession of him again... It might be a good idea... he did not know... would think about it.' Moody seemed determined to miss this date with destiny.

Within ten days young Wishard rejoined Moody at the Univer-

receive a large St Bernard puppy. As he had no one to meet the puppy I was told off to do so. While he was taking his meeting I was walking the puppy, who was not at all anxious to come with me, through the streets of the town. I think he caught sight of me somewhere, and you can imagine the amusement that he got out of the incident and the fun he made of this Cambridge graduate leading a dog about the town.'

sity of Virginia to aid him in evangelistic meetings, and cannily
kept silent on the subject until about to leave for the train. Moody
replied in the negative. 'I'm afraid we cannot make a success of a
conference of college students in the summer time. They will want
to go home for recreation.'

'Let them have their recreation on Mount Hermon and in the
Connecticut.'

Moody said he would have to get strong speakers to attract the
students.

Wishard brushed the objection aside: 'The man who will draw
students is yourself. They know you. You underrate your intellectual qualifications. You have a message to the college boys of this
country...'

Moody surrendered. Wishard rushed to his train and immediately sent out invitations from New York.

Two hundred and fifty delegates from a hundred colleges came
for a full month of glorious July and early August weather. On the
first morning, July 7th, Moody mounted the platform 'with busi-
nesslike step, portly form and slightly graying hair and beard' and
had one hymn sung after another: 'I want to make as much of music as possible here. Music and the Bible are the two important
agencies with which to reach the world, and I've made as much of
singing as I have of preaching. I've been asked for programmes. I
hate programmes, and I don't have any. Then I can't break over
'em. If you want to know what is ahead, we don't know, except that
we will have a good time. We want to stir you up and get you in
love with the Bible, and those of you with a voice, in love with
music. If I find you getting drowsy in hot weather, I'll just ask the
speaker to stop and we will sing... Our talks are going to be conver-
sational. If you want to ask a question, speak out: that's what we're
here for, to get all the cobwebs swept away, and go back to our
college mates inspired with the truth.'

Moody had brought several eminent lecturers but, as Wishard
had foreseen, the students wanted Moody most. One of them wrote,
'Mr Moody's rugged, cheerful, transparent personality gave a great
thrill to me, and I am sure to other delegates,' and John R Mott said

it was the 'note of reality' in Moody's preaching that 'appealed
strongly to college men. They were impressed by his downright
honesty and transparent sincerity,' and his 'lack of sham', his frankness and directness. 'He brought religion out of the clouds and
made it a present day and every day personal and practical relationship and experience.'

Moody's enjoyment of the Conference grew daily: the long hours
devoted to baseball and swimming, the visits to the Homestead
where he could display his ducks and geese and chickens and the
peacocks and the ponies and the absurd barn built out of packing
boxes and boards by little Paul. Moody would challenge college
boys to race him carrying enough ballast to equal his weight – and
beat them over twenty-five or thirty yards.

The Conference took on an importance far beyond the expectation of Moody or Wishard, and brought to a climax the movement
first stirred in Cambridge nearly four years before.

One of the delegates, son of a distinguished retired missionary,
was Robert Wilder who in 1883 had formed a Princeton Foreign
Missionary Society, its five student members signing a Declaration: 'We are willing and desirous, God permitting, to become Foreign Missionaries.' He and his family prayed that a thousand
missionary volunteers should be secured from American universities. At the start of the Mount Hermon Conference only twenty-
three of those attending were committed. Wilder, sensitive, quiet,
sought out and gathered them each evening under the trees to pray
for more volunteers.

To every other he came across he put the claim of missions and
John R Mott's experience was typical: 'My first meeting with Robert
Wilder was when swimming in the Connecticut River... Before the
interview was over, which began in the water and continued as we
tramped back to the school campus, he had appealed to me to become a missionary.' Memory of the Cambridge Seven lay close to
the surface, the time was ripe. Wilder went to Dr Pierson and begged
him for a missionary address. Moody allotted a special evening
session, when Pierson illustrated his theme from a rough sketch on
the blackboard and, wrote his son, 'voiced the Macedonian call to

young men of the Church to give their lives for "the evangelization of the world in this generation".'

'Quietly and without forcing as I can see,' a journalist at the Conference reported a few days later, 'the mission spirit has spread. Each man has settled the question "Shall I go?" by himself with his Bible and his God.' In the third week Wilder asked Moody if nine students from overseas, and a North American Indian, might address the Conference. Moody consulted Wishard, who approved enthusiastically.

The 'Meeting of the Ten Nations' was the birthplace of the Student Volunteers. 'The delegates,' Wilder wrote, 'withdrew to their rooms or went out under the great trees to wait on God for guidance.' One hundred signed a declaration of willingness to serve overseas.

From Mount Hermon the Volunteer movement blazed across America.

Following the Cambridge Seven pattern, Wilder and John Forman toured universities. 'The missionary spirit is rampant among the students now, the interest is strong, vigorous and healthful,' a newspaper wrote next year. The summer of 1887 brought four hundred young men to Northfield. 'We have more people in town now than ever before at any time,' Moody wrote to his daughter who was in Europe. 'All the street is full, some sleeping in barns, and tents on the river bank, in the woods and no less than six tents on the round hill back of our house... We are hearing some fine speakers. Drummond is liked best of all... We had in front of the house fireworks like what we had at Denny's in 84... Last night the Harvard and Yale and Princeton boys had a fire down on the bank of the river in front of our house and Willie and myself were invited down. They sang songs, told stories, and they did have a time.' Thereafter men students came for ten days every year in the month before Moody's Northfield general conference, and at May Whittle's suggestion, he added later a women's college conference.

Moody never attempted to lead the Student Volunteers. 'It's my job to get things going.' Once again his genius had touched into life a latent movement which other men could carry forward.

The Volunteers girdled the globe, their watchword 'The Evangelization of the World in This Generation'. In 1891 Wilder carried the idea to Britain to blend with the movement begotten directly by the Cambridge Seven. Robert E Speer and John R Mott followed Wilder, and in universities throughout America and Europe the missionary roll lengthened, whereby the Christian Gospel went to untold thousands in Africa, Asia, South America who had remained unreached. If the evangelization of the world by 1900, the date suggested in the Northfield Appeal, slipped from the Church's grasp, the volunteers of the 'nineties believed it to be truly possible in their generation, that when they were old in the nineteen forties or early 'fifties, the Gospel should have been presented to every soul in the world, by westerners to nationals and nationals to their own folk, in such manner that, in Wilder's words, 'the responsibility for what is done with it shall no longer rest upon the Christian church, or any individual Christian, but shall rest on each man's head for himself'.

From the Student Volunteers developed the Student Christian Movement and, in its time, the Inter-Varsity Fellowship. John R Mott, after decades of service for students, said that Mount Hermon was 'the fountain head of a stream which has brought more blessings to the universities and colleges of the world than any which has gushed out in any nation under the life-giving influence of the Spirit of God'.

Moody had since early days pressed his 'all absorbing idea of making the world feel the power of Christian union in active work for the masses'. He had now an ecumenical vision. The target of call and dedication had enlarged first from city to nation, from Chicago to Britain and the United States; and from a nation to the 'whole present population of the globe'. The city, the nation, the world.

The far outcome was the Ecumenical Movement of which the chief springs, however many its sources, were Northfield, through the Appeal of 1885, and the ecumenical missionary conferences of 1888 in London and 1900 in New York, and Mount Hermon through the Volunteers. The streams flowed together at Edinburgh in 1910 under the chairmanship of Mott.

Whatever channels the Ecumenical Movement may have carved in later decades, its grandfather was D L Moody with his passion, echoed by the Northfield Appeal, 'to further the glorious object of a world's evangelization'.

28: Slow Birth of The Bible Institute

The women's side of Moody's Church was organized by Miss Emma Dryer. Whenever she could pin him in Chicago she asked him to found a 'Bible Institute' for training those who had never been to college, and as a centre for evangelistic activity in the surrounding slums, claiming that Moody had uprooted her from state schools after the Fire for this purpose yet had run off to Europe and forgotten. In 1876 and again during a lightning visit in 1883 Moody had indeed talked publicly of the schemes, but nothing had emerged beyond a handful of young women selected by Miss Dryer, who housed them at Mrs Cyrus McCormick's expense in a house on Warren Avenue.

Several Chicago residents who sympathized with Miss Dryer – though undecided whether the institute should be an 'order of deaconesses' for city work or a school 'for the preparation of workers for world-wide Missions' – met weekly to pray 'for Mr Moody to come and plan something commensurate with the needs'. The clergyman temporarily filling the pulpit of the Chicago Avenue Church, Charles A Blanchard, at Miss Dryer's behest organized free evening classes to prove to Moody 'that the thing would go', and at last, on January 22nd, 1886, Moody took the matter in hand.

He told a public meeting that to evangelize Chicago's masses they ought to raise $250,000, spending $50,000 on a building and with the remainder endowing a training school for workers 'who would serve to act between the preachers and the people. They should be taught the Word of God so they could answer every question put to them.' He pictured need and possibilities in his inimitable way until the meeting caught his enthusiasm and when he finished his address demanded more.

'What would you have me to say? For twenty-five years I have made this question of what shall be done for the working-man my study. It has been my very life. People ask me why I do not come back here and stay. Well, it seems I can't. I have a roving commission which takes me all over the world, nearly. O,' he exclaimed, his beloved Northfield forgotten in the emotion of the moment, 'I should like to come back and live here. I love Chicago. I love its people, but I must keep at work. But I will promise this: If this work is taken up as I want it done I will come back every year and help it along all I can.'

Young Cyrus H McCormick, son of Moody's deceased old friend, leaped to his feet. 'I will give fifty thousand dollars.'

'Better make it a hundred!'

'That will require some consideration,' McCormick laughed. Within a few hours he promised the hundred thousand. Moody told the assembled company, 'Let others raise the money and I will furnish my experience and labour.'

Nothing happened. The year 1886, dark with industrial strife and bloodshed, McCormick's own factory being the centre of the Haymarket Riots in May, brought the absent Moody's Bible Institute no nearer.

Moody returned for a four-months' Chicago campaign from January to April 1887 on the lines proved at Baltimore and St Louis: working district by district through the churches.

In the thick of it he brought together Farwell, McCormick and four others on his 50th birthday (he felt what he wrote on his 51st: 'It seems strange for me to be so old, I feel as young as I did at 30'), and as fitting jubilee they founded the Chicago Evangelization Society 'to educate, direct and maintain Christian workers'. This new society should build and administer a Bible Institute. A letter was on its way from China to forward Moody's ambition, nursed by the rise of the Student Volunteers, that the Institute should train not only for cities of America but for overseas. C T Studd had inherited on his twenty-fifth birthday a share of his father's fortune, which he promptly gave away. He sent £5,000 of it to Moody, ex-

pressing the hope that he would start Gospel work at Tirhoot in
North India, where the fortune had been made. Moody wasted no
time wondering how to do that but wrote, with the classic American touch which left Studd believing the inception was entirely
from his gift, 'I will do the next best thing and open a Training
School with it, from which men and women will go to all parts of
the world to evangelize.'

Once more the project stuck.

The Chicago Evangelization Society began operations in the
city, acquiring a tent for summers, visiting saloons and prisons and
slums. One night when the congregation of Chicago Avenue was
gathering to hear Moody, a helper found him outside the north-
west corner of the building. 'Is that you, Morrison? Do you see
that lot? Let us pray to the Lord to give it to us for a school.' Moody
prayed one of his brief, practical, childlike prayers and went inside
again. The lot stayed unoccupied. Once more there were difficulties and delays, centring on Miss Dryer, who seemed to block every
practical move for reasons unknown, until in July Moody resigned
as President of the CES: 'I have never had my heart so set on anything as on this society, but for six months I have had to oppose
some of the dearest friends I have ever had & I am tired & sick of
it. I now take it that God is closing the door to me in Chicago &
will open some other & will in his own way overrule it all & mag-
nify his grace.'

Moody's resignation caused consternation in Chicago, but Mrs
McCormick thought he wanted absolute control for its own sake.
Mrs Moody reassured her in nineteen half-quarto sheets and Moody
telegraphed withdrawing his resignation: 'Tell the trustees to do as
they please about the construction and push the building and I will
come as soon as it is ready.' On October 15th, 1887, he wrote from
Montreal: 'I find the committee just discouraged & do not know
what to do & they think I am standing in the way & if I am I want
to get out of the road. I am willing to work at the front or behind or
outside or inside & will go where they say only for the sake of the
Master let us get the work pushed this season.'

Nearly a year later the site had not even been bought, when

from Chicago on 'the first day of October I started for India'.

The Mackinnons, who had lived in India, had long badgered Moody. During a sea-loch trip in Scotland in August 1882 an Indian clergyman, who had come on board at Holy Loch, 'stood on the gangway holding Mr Moody's hand, pleading for a visit to India. Mr Moody said he did not want to say No, but that he could not promise.' The Student Volunteers convinced him. At the Second Conference, 1887, 'Forman and I,' Robert Wilder wrote, 'went to him and said, "God has blessed you greatly to the students in North America and Great Britain and we believe God wants you to go out to India and speak to the students there." He listened attentively but did not say much.' To Japanese students he remarked: 'I would like to see the whole world for which Christ died.' Later he sent for Wilder to Chicago, and 'asked me many questions as to where the universities were located, etc. He did not think he could stand the climate. However, he did show clearly how deeply he was moved by the call that had come to him from India.'

Mrs Moody, Emma and Paul travelled from Chicago on the afternoon of October 1st, 1888, as far as Turlington, Nebraska, home of the Harveys where 'Papa left us,' Mrs Moody told Will at Yale, 'and we felt pretty lonely. It was hard to let him go but I believe it will be all right.' Before he reached San Francisco prominent ministers boarded the train, reminded him that the year previous he had promised them a West Coast campaign 'and they say that they shall hold me to my word... so I am in duty bound to stay'. He needed little prompting to escape sea-sickness and heat (which brought on headaches), and wired his wife, whose relief was profound: 'It is such a comfort to me not to have Papa go so far from us... Aren't you glad that Papa is not going to India this winter?'

Moody sent instead George Pentecost, an able assistant who had not yet revealed his Achilles' heel, and moved up into Canada, with George Stebbins to sing. From Victoria, British Columbia, he wrote on October 13th: 'the weather is like May at Northfield, the Sound is full of all kinds of fish, splendid fishing smelts cod salmon herrings haddock etc just across the bay from here is the snow cap mountain of Washington territory it is the Rocky Mountain range they say they are grand & beautiful but of course they do not come up to dear old Northfield.' 'I am having,' he told Will a week later, 'a grand work here & all the ministers are much pleased with the work & all united & I think will do a good work after I am gone.' 'I get lonely at times,' he confessed from Portland, Oregon, early in December, '& if it was not for the work I would be wild for we do not see the Sun more than 4 to 5 days in a month.' At San Francisco the family except Will joined him for Christmas, catching colds across the Rockies. 'The people are kind and do all they can to make it pleasant for them. The work is good here & I am having a much better time than when out here in 81.'

Stories abound of that time. There was the young opium smuggler in British Columbia whom Moody told he must make restitution. 'He said "I have a young wife and a child, and all my furniture in my house I have bought with money I have got in this dishonest way. If I become a Christian, that furniture will have to go, and my wife will know it." "Better let your wife know it, and better let your home and furniture go." He said "Would you come up and see my wife? I don't know what she will say." I went up to see her, and when I told her the tears trickled down her cheeks and she said, "Mr Moody, I will gladly give up everything if my husband can become a true Christian."'

There was Judge Williams in Portland, who surprised an audience of three thousand of his fellow citizens: 'I'm seventy-three years old, have sat on the bench for forty-three years, have rendered many important decisions, but the greatest of all was rendered this morning when for the first time, in the presence of Brother Moody, I prayed on my knees in my home for forgiveness for my sins and joy came into my heart. Have posed as a Christian, belong to church - all form and sham. Friends, forgive me, didn't know any better, I know better now. I and my house, we'll serve the Lord.'

There was the Jewish professional photographer in San Francisco called George B Rieman who wanted to add Moody to his collection of actors, politicians, etc. Moody declined with thanks the offer of a free sitting, saying he had not come to San Francisco to have his photograph taken but to save Rieman's soul. 'The reply made Mr Rieman furious,' according to a man who knew him well and recounted the incident. Each day Rieman would read the newspaper accounts of the meetings 'and get madder and madder'. When he saw by glaring banner headlines that the final day had come he took his wife, both curious 'to see this man Moody... They listened to the sermon and were interested, but not deeply impressed. When the after-meeting was announced, Mr Rieman said to his wife: "Well, we have been to the circus, let us go into the sideshow also"... In there two earnest Christian workers met them and talked to them about Christ. They knelt and prayed...' Rieman became 'one of the most earnest Baptist preachers on the Pacific coast, greatly beloved'.

The Moodys moved south to Los Angeles early in March 1889. 'I am much encouraged with all the work so far and shall hope to close up in good shape on the 25 of this month and may go to the Yo Semite if we can get in by that time if not I think I shall leave my family to go in.' Heavy rains stopped them. Moody left the family in Colorado for Mrs Moody's catarrh and hastened to Chicago.

He would brook no further delay. The Bible Institute must be brought to birth.

The previous summer at Northfield Charles F Goss, the thirty-six-year-old pastor of Moody's Church in Chicago, had been riding with him in a buggy up a 'beautiful and quiet valley' when Moody began talking about his plans for the Institute. 'His eyes kindled and his face glowed. Suddenly he stopped the horse, took off his hat, and said, in tones that sent a positive thrill through me, "I am awfully concerned about this matter. Let us pray God to consecrate ourselves to it!" That prayer went to heaven if anything ever did! It was propelled by a spiritual force that would have carried it across infinity. It filled my mind with an indescribable awe.'

Moody had told the Chicago Evangelization Society to convene in April 1889 a short-term training school for ministers, laymen and women, 'something like the conference at Northfield', and this was 'a great success. We had over 500 ministers from all over the northwest.' In his first address Moody stated that 'Word and Work is the keynote of this convention', as it would be of the residential institute.

During the convention Moody threw himself into establishing the great enterprise that had eluded him three years. To Goss it was 'the most impressive mental and spiritual exhibition I had ever witnessed. The fervor, the intensity of feeling, the prodigious energy of will, the confident faith, were like the mighty forces of nature.' To Moody these April and May weeks were 'about the darkest 40 days and nights I have ever passed through'. He battered at rich men's purses, until he had $185,000. Mrs McCormick gave him a further $25,000 and, in a gesture that eased his path, a similar sum to Miss Dryer to enable her to carry on her own work in her own way apart from Moody.

He bought three houses next to the church to adapt for a women's dormitory. He bought the site which he had prayed for 'and am now putting up a building that will accommodate 200 young men... So we can take in 250: 50 ladies and 200 men.' And all the time he was speaking at the convention, joining its mission work in street and tenement, arranging for the CES to work three tent missions throughout the coming summer. The family, back from Colorado and staying at the Holdens, saw him briefly and unpredictably. He slept short hours there and took quick naps at odd breaks, ate enormously. 'Dashing into my house one evening,' Goss records, 'after a day of terrific effort, he exclaimed, "Have you got anything to eat?" A large dish of pork and beans (of which he was very fond) was placed before him. He sat down, murmured a silent prayer, and, without interrupting his repast by a word, emptied the entire dish as fast as he could carry the food to his mouth. And yet this was done with a certain indefinable grace! He often ate voraciously, but never like an animal nor ever like an epicure.'

By May 10th, when the convention ended, Moody knew that the Bible Institute would open in the autumn.

He had no doubt that it was needed. Urging Whittle, who was in Britain, to hurry to Glasgow and extract £1,000 from Campbell White, he wrote 'The hour is now come for us to lay hold of the ministers and get them stirred up but my plan is to raise up a class

of men and women that will go for the ¾ that do not go anywhere
to church, and I am inclined to think I am going to succeed and get
a lever under all the churches. I have never been so hopeful about
anything I have ever undertaken.' As he said to a newspaper reporter the following year, 'There is a class of people whom no man
can reach successfully except one of their own number... There is
far more demand for trained lay workers than is commonly appre-
hended... I am not seeking to make any short cut to the ministry. I
do not consider this work to be in conflict with the work of the
theological seminaries.'

The return to Northfield in mid-May was graced by a charming
incident.

Moody had ordered a pony for ten-year-old Paul. 'We got home
in time and Uncle Ed had Paul's pony and cart at the station. Paul
knew nothing of it until he got through the bridge and Emma's
horse stood there and the span, and back of the span stood Paul's
all on fire. I told him it was his. You should have seen the dear
fellow. He stood looking at it for a few seconds and then flew at me
and kissed me. I told him to get in and drive home. Sam [Walker]
went with him and he got home long before we did.' It was 'a black
pony,' Paul remembers, 'and while small in stature he was great of
heart and I learned to fall off his back with alacrity and enthusiasm. All summer long he was my inseparable companion. His name
was Toppy ...'

Northfield's summer of 1889 – the schools, the college conference and the General Workers' Conference – had the additional
thrill of constant reports from Chicago and letters back ('see if we
cannot stir up a fire that will spread all over the city') mounting to
the climax of Moody's return in time for a second short convention
to inaugurate the Bible Institute, beginning on September 26th.
The new building which would be the men's dormitory was unfin-
ished and the staff used part of the women's houses while the first
male boarders lodged near-by. For superintendent of the 'Bible Institute of the Chicago Evangelization Society' Moody had secured
Reuben Archer Torrey.

Torrey's record and abilities were as remarkable as his looks –

he was nearly as grey in hair and beard at thirty-four as Moody at fifty-two, and had the piercing eyes of a prophet. Unlike Moody he was a rich man's son, a college graduate, had sown wild oats in his youth and even attempted suicide before conversion. Torrey knew the slums: he was head of a city mission in Indianapolis when Moody called him to Chicago. Torrey was a man of intellect, wide reading, theological training – Yale, Leipzig and Erlangen – who read the New Testament in Greek each day and the Old Testament in Hebrew: Moody's choice for superintending simple men was no simpleton.

A further factor gave Torrey a special attraction for Moody: he had been a disciple of the higher critics: 'There was a time,' he once said, 'when I was so wise that I believed so much of the Bible as was wise enough to agree with me.' He went to Germany to learn from higher critics – and returned wholeheartedly to belief 'in the Bible, the whole Bible, as the Word of God: an altogether reliable revelation from God Himself, of His own character, His Will, His purposes; and of man, his nature, his possibilities, his duty, his destiny'.

The Institute, pioneer of its kind, owed much to Torrey and his able interpretation of Moody's distinctive plan: free tuition and boarding at low cost; the blend of systematic Bible teaching and practical ministry, 'daily study with daily practice'; the time given to music; the shaping of the curriculum so that a student could begin at any time.

'I have no trouble with Miss Dryer I think the storm is past & it is clear sailing just now. The meetings are good & all goes well.' 'I got a 1000 pds today from Peter Mackinnon,' Moody wrote to Will on November 9th, 1889; 'it did me good it is grand to have such good friends I think my dark days in Chicago are nearly over I am getting out all right I think but it has been a hard haul I am so thankful that it is behind me & not before me for I would not like to see another three years like this.'

The new building was dedicated on January 18th, 1890, and three weeks afterwards, starting a month's mission at Brooklyn,

Moody wrote to a fellow-trustee, 'I think now the old ship has got out on to the deep water let us get up all the steam we can and put up the sails and go ahead.'

By the end of that year, in all his schools, Moody had a total of over a thousand students. To the Mackinnons he wrote on December 31st: 'The dream of twenty years has at last been reached, and I will always look on 1890 as the year that I reached the top of the hill and you helped me to get there...'

Northfield, Mount Hermon, Chicago: 'My school work will not tell much until the century closes, but *when I am gone I shall leave some grand men & women behind.*'

29: A Dark Valley and the Sea

The Moody children never had any doubts that theirs was the best father in the world. 'He was so full of humour – the things done in this house...' There was hide and seek, Moody popping up and down stairs with a student lamp in his hand. There was the day when Emma, thirteen or fourteen, was with her friends in the playroom when Father went by the open window and suddenly a piglet was squirming and squealing among the shrieking girls.

In early days at the Homestead Moody spent much time and pride on coaxing his lawn to emulate that of an English country house. 'It was just coming up,' May Whittle, afterwards Will's wife, recalls, 'when some way or other Paul and Will got the horses loose from the barn and they came galloping all over that lawn. Well, Mr Moody just saw red! That's one time he had to go and ask forgiveness of all he had said to the boys. Oh yes, he had a quick temper, but my husband's and Paul's great memory of their father was when he had lost his temper with them, and after they had gone to bed they would hear those heavy footsteps and he'd come into their room and put a heavy hand on their head and say, "I want you to forgive me, that wasn't the way Christ taught." To them that was the greatest Christian evidence they had seen. Mr Sankey couldn't do that. He had three sons and I loved Mr Sankey but he was always right and they were always wrong.'

Moody's attitude to his children carried a double but hidden tension.

He wanted them to enjoy what he had lacked – education, travel, toys and hobbies – yet to learn the discipline of hardship and denial. This went little further than occasional fits of ordering Will, and later Paul, to do an hour or two of weeding a day during vacation, and attempting to persuade them that it should be done barefoot. The weeding usually lapsed early because Moody wanted them to share his fun with the hens and bees and swans and peacocks and pheasants and deer and all the other animals and things that somehow came to the Homestead and farm. To his sons Moody on vacation 'was a stout and bearded Peter Pan, a boy who never grew up'.

His heart was set also on his children being strong Christians, yet he wished, far in advance of his time, to protect them from an overdose. Thus, family prayers never preceded breakfast: 'no tantalizing a hungry family by the smell of coffee and bacon while devotions were going on, for Father!' – and if the young Moodys grew up in a home devoted to religion there was no constraint or self-conscious pious talk, and Moody did not subscribe to the current convention that children should be seen and not heard. Nevertheless to be the offspring of a world-famous religious leader and constantly among earnest godly adults who expected them to be little credits to Papa and Ma Ma, could not make for a normal childhood.

Moody's letters to Will as a boy were jovial and chatty and only occasionally, as on Will's fifteenth birthday, sending him from London much love and best wishes and a crisp five-pound note, did he add: 'may you live to take the place of your father in the blessed work of leading souls to Christ', or 'I long to have you out and out on the Lord's side'. Will's spirit progressed intermittently through an adolescence shadowed by frequent illness, until during the happy Northfield summer of 1886 he had seemed at last a true Christian.

The spark proved a feeble flicker and early in December, when nearly seventeen and three-quarters, Will wrote from Mount Hermon (which he had entered on its reorganization as a secondary school) a letter making plain that he rebelled from the religion of his parents.

Moody's reply from Binghamton, New York, on December 8th, 1886, throws a beam of light deep into his character, revealing not only the quality of his love and his sincerity, but also his vivid sense of Christ as an intimate, living Friend.

Moody wrote: 'Yours is at hand & I am glad you told me for I would far rather have you come to me with your faults than to hide them. Of course I am very sorry you were ever tempted to smoke. I was in hopes it would never be a temptation to you but the thing that hurts me worst is that you have no desire to know Christ. Sometimes my heart is so heavy & sad to think that you have such contempt for one that has done so much for your mother & father, all that we are or have has come from him & you have been saved from an early grave I think in answer to prayer & now when you have strength & health given you & are now in a position to do good you turn against the truest & best friend you will ever have. For the life of me I cannot see why you should have taken such a dislike to Christ.

'I sometimes think it is my fault, if I had lived more consistent you would not be so disgusted with what is so near my heart. Last Sept was the happiest month of my life when I thought you had really started for the kingdom of God but when I returned home & found you were more indifferent than ever my heart sank within me. I have not talked much with you for fear I would turn you more & more against him whom I love more than all the world & if I have ever said or done any thing unbecoming a Christian father I want you to forgive me & would rather die than to stand in your way.

'The thing that shames me is that I am preaching to others & my son does not believe in the gospel I preach. It was hard preaching last night after reading your letter, it seemed as if I could almost hear a voice saying look to home. I have always felt when a father & mother both were Christians & their children were not that there was something decidedly wrong with them & I still think so & last night I was speaking to parents & how my life condemned me – I have tried not to make religion offensive in my home & if I thought I had neglected to do all my duty towards my three children I think I would rather die than to live. I have tried to make your home life as pleasant as I can & have done all in my power to make you happy. I thought when I started the schools it would bring a good influence into the town for my own family & day & night my desire and prayer has been that we might all be united in Spirit but you seem to hate the things I love. The gulf seems to grow darker & deeper every day between us & I am afraid in 5 years there will be nothing in common between us. If you choose the world for your portion you will die some day a sad disappointed man I am sure. Dear Willie the world will deceive you but never satisfy you. You have not been happy for a year & your discontent has increased & it has hurt your father & mother far more than you will ever know until you become a father yourself.

'I hope there is no *sin* that is keeping you from Christ but times I am afraid there is something that I do not know in your life but I pray God to show it to you if there is & may God help you confess it & turn against it. I have never prayed for you as I do now. I think it is a crisis in your life & now dear Willie take this in the same spirit it is written – your Father D L Moody.'

Hardly had this letter gone than Moody heard that Will was sick again, and the Christmas holidays were shadowed by his illness and the depression that followed. When Moody went to Chicago for the founding of the CES he sent affectionate daily notes. 'I do wish I could be with you,' he wrote on January 7th, 1887, '& help cheer you up. You must not loose heart for it may be you will be far better after this is over.' Will regained health in the spring, and his father had to rebuke him for over-teasing Emma who, though twenty-three and about to tour Europe with her uncle, Fleming H Revell, was inclined to rise too easily. In October 1887 Will entered Yale.

On the way to Chicago Moody called at Yale, and being dismayed by thought of his son entering college not a Christian, was unhappy. 'I am afraid I spoilt my visit to you last night and this morning but I was so burdened that I could not keep cheerful. I have had a good day today it troubles me far more than you will ever know if I did not love you so much it would be different but the thought that you may be cut down unsaved troubles me I do hope you will take the gift of God.'

His adored father's unwonted gloom shocked Will into an immediate letter to his mother, who replied by return: 'About Papa. I don't think he is changed. I think and know he is anxious about you the same as I am. He does not worry over your going to Yale. He does not mention that to me, but I know that the thought of you being in any college without reliance on the help of Christ, it is to both of us an anxiety that we can only generally pray about. I have feared to "nag" at you as it might seem and yet it seems often that I cannot bear the thought of you being so unsafe... Papa I know is praying, and I am that God's Spirit may lead you to give up yourself to Christ entirely, not to please us but because it is "your reasonable service". You know what you ought to do, then do it, not halfway but out and out. I shall keep praying for you. It is not for dying alone but for right living you will need help stronger than your own.'

They were such a close-knit family. 'If you miss us as much as we miss you you will be quite lonely tonight,' runs a letter from Moody on Will's return to Yale in January 1888, and in another, during March when Mrs Moody left Northfield to join him on tour: 'I am thinking that you will all be lonely without Mother but what is your loss is my gain for I am getting lonely without any of you, after I have been away a few weeks it gets lonely enough.' This closeness, and the constant concern that sprinkled the correspondence with medical advice ('And now Willie be careful about getting sweaty and cooling off too soon') made Moody the more distressed and puzzled that Will, a charming well-mannered youth, full of zest and humour when not downcast by sickness, should lack love for the Christ so precious to his parents. If the longed-for Bible Institute showed no sign of coming to birth in the early months of 1888, neither did Will's soul; which could not be 'pushed for all we are worth' without certain abortion.

In the summer of 1888, when Will was nineteen, Moody saw the dark valley opening. Will began to 'take a stand for the Son of God', genuinely but diffidently. His faith matured slowly over the next four years. He relinquished voluntarily an ambition to be a doctor in order to prepare himself to help his father in the administration of the schools, but not until May Whittle, his childhood and boyhood friend, returned from Europe in 1893 (they became engaged, and were married in 1894) did Will enter fully on the steady, quiet and unashamed Christian discipleship that rejoiced his father's last years, a discipleship and faith all the deeper for the long years of uncertainty.

The postscript to that unhappy letter that Moody had written in 1886 is another on Will's twenty-fifth birthday in 1894: '... for 25 years I have prayed for you & I think the last year you have given me more real joy than any other year of your life. I have had one desire for you & that was you might be engaged in some Christian work & now the time has come & my prayer is answered & I can hardly [?] return it. And I think May will be a real help to you. You will never know unless you have a son & get your heart above him for some special thing & pray 25 years & see no answer & then have it come about & you will understand what joy you have given your Father in the year of 1893.'

It was Will who was with him when Moody was shipwrecked in the Atlantic.

In the summer of 1891 at the Northfield Conference Moody was presented with an illuminated scroll of invitation from Scotland, one hundred and fifty feet long carrying two thousand signatures from fifty places and all churches.

Moody made no promise, and when he arrived unexpectedly in London early in November with his entire family and Sankey, his intended destination was India. Doctors and British friends of Indian experience dissuaded him: 'they say it might cause me a stroke'.

He decided instead to tour Scotland, sending the family to the Continent. After hurried consultations among ministers in Edinburgh, Moody expressing his 'great desire to work in country places as well as in large towns', Sankey and he began in north-west Scotland on November 23rd.

The Scots found him after seven years' absence wondrously stouter: as somebody laughingly put it, 'he could lay his Bible on the book-rest which nature had provided him, which he carried with him wherever he went, between two buttons of his waistcoat'. His well trimmed beard showed grizzly to white, and at nearly fifty-four he looked an old man but his eye was not dim nor his natural force abated. 'I do hope the Lord will help me in England as He has here,' he wrote to his mother for her eighty-seventh birthday in February 1892. 'It is a privilege to live if I can be used as I have been of late.' And from Paisley to Peter Mackinnon, 'I am encouraged .. I am happy in the work... I wish you had as good health as I had & could have been with me all this winter I remember what grand times we had in Ireland England & Scotland 18 years ago I have now been in over 50 towns & found fruit in each one in nearly every place I find the ministers were converted at that time.'

The family had gone to Venice and Rome. 'Paul is much excited & thinks it all great fun. Emma studies up the guide book & helps us, & Will attends to paying bills & all the business & studies Italian.' They crossed in January to Egypt, then a great winter tourist resort with special attractions for weak chests and neuralgia sufferers, and Will went on to Palestine. Early in April Moody met them in Paris and decided after considerable dither to accept the Mackinnons' invitation to visit the Holy Land as their guest, all expenses paid. 'Emma did not want to go, Will had just been, so in the evening Paul and Mr Moody and I started for Rome,' Mrs Moody scribbled to her mother on April 8th. Moody greatly enjoyed Rome and the Holy Land, 'even though he hates the sea journey more and more' (at Jaffa on the return they had to climb on to the steamer from small boats '& as there was quite a heavy sea we had an exciting time. D L was too excited or frightened to get sea sick...'). He preached on Easter Day at a service arranged by the Church Missionary Society at the probable site of Calvary. 'I have preached for thirty years,' he began, 'but have never felt the awe of God as I do at this moment.'

Back in Britain for the summer Moody worked where he had never been, and after Mrs Moody left for America in August with the family except for Will, who studied in Germany, he took a ten day campaign in London in September at the Metropolitan Tabernacle,[1] lately bereft of Spurgeon, and went to Ireland, where from Dublin his nephew Ambert wrote home: 'The meetings have been grand and my! don't the people think a lot of Uncle D!' Will rejoined his father in London in November. Their passages were booked in the crack liner of the North German Lloyd, the *Spree*.

Before sailing Moody agreed to consult Sir Andrew Clark, the Harley Street heart specialist, who confirmed what a doctor had lately diagnosed: slight heart trouble. Clark asked how often Moody preached.

'Oh, I usually preach three times a day. On Sunday four or even five.'

'How many days a week?'

'Six, but during the last winter seven.'

'You're a fool, sir, you're a fool! You're killing yourself!'

'Well, doctor, usually I take Saturday to rest. This year has been an exception. But may I ask how many hours a day you work?'

'Oh, I work sixteen or seventeen.'

'How many days a week?'

'Every day, sir, every day.'

'Then you're a bigger fool than me! And you'll kill yourself first.' Which he did, dying almost exactly one year after the consultation.

Will and his father boarded the *Spree* on the following Wednesday, November 23rd, and immediately heard a hearty American voice, 'Why, Moody! The sight of you does me good!' It was the one-armed General Oliver Otis Howard who long ago before the Atlanta campaign had encouraged Moody to preach to his corps. The Moodys had 'a lovely cabin', wrote Lady Kinnaird, who had come to see them off. Moody was in 'great dread of sea sickness'

---

1. The future Queen Mary attended his services with her mother. Many years later her son (now the Duke of Windsor), introduced in Chile to a man connected with Mount Hermon, said: 'My mother thought Mr Moody quite a chap!'.

and she naughtily asked, quoting a popular Sankey hymn, if 'he felt like singing all the time... Will was indefatigable: he let his father have no trouble and seemed so happy in surrounding him with every comfort.'

During the first two days, prostrate on his bunk, Moody did some hard thinking, for despite jocularity he had taken the heart specialist's warning.

He reached the conclusion 'that I would not work quite so hard'. In particular he would revise his plans for mounting a five months' monster evangelistic campaign at Chicago to run beside the World's Fair or Columbian Exhibition scheduled for the coming summer of 'ninety-three. He had talked and prayed about it, had warned European evangelists to be ready to come over, had engaged a young Irish law-student, Percy Fitt, as his secretary, unaware what happiness this would introduce to the family, and had left Torrey and the Institute to enlarge their buildings in preparation. The World's Fair would be the 'opportunity of the century', millions from every American state and abroad flocking to a Chicago already filled with immigrants and, despite churches and ardent Christians, deserving its reputation for wickedness.

On the *Spree* Moody accepted that his World's Fair campaign must be muted.

During the third morning out, Saturday, the Moodys, both on their bunks because of bad weather, were 'startled by a terrible crash and shock'. Will rushed on deck, and returning said: 'The shaft is broken. The ship's sinking, Father.'

Moody dressed and went on deck. Passengers were shouting that water was flooding their cabins. Officers and crew kept perfect discipline and mustered everybody, first class, cabin class and terrified Central European immigrants from the steerage, into a main saloon. The drifting ship settled at the stern. She 'rolled from side to side, lurching fearfully' in the heavy sea, for the fractured ends of the shaft had broken the stern-tube and pumping failed to empty the three after-compartments beyond the promptly closed bulkheads.

Captain Willigerod at noon told the passengers the water was under control and that they could expect to drift in the track of a steamer by mid-afternoon. Night fell without a ship having been sighted. Alone on the open Atlantic before the days of radio; lights blazing, rockets firing to no avail; drifting steadily away from the sea lanes, 'that was an awful night, the darkest in all our lives – several hundred men, women and children waiting for the doom that seemed to be settling upon us... No one dared to sleep.' During the long hours Moody wrestled with his soul. He felt seasickness no longer – the accident cured him permanently – and his mind ran clear.

He heard as it were the voice of his Lord: 'Were you ready to let up, to go slow? Then I will take you to Myself. You are no use to Me unless you are out and out.'

'No one on earth,' Moody related, 'knows what I passed through as I thought that my work was finished, and that I should never again have the privilege of preaching the Gospel of the Son of God. And on that dark night, the first night of the accident, I made a vow that if God would spare my life and bring me back to America,' the World's Fair campaign should be undertaken with 'all the power that He would give me'. He would work till he dropped, a year, five years, seven. Let the weak heart look to itself.

Sunday dawned with seas high, sky overcast, ocean empty. Passengers were allowed to move more freely. Thirty years earlier the immature Moody would have shouted the announcement of a revivalist service. This Sunday, sensing that such talk might create a panic by suggesting the end, he did nothing until the evening. With the Captain's permission ('Certainly! I am that way myself') General Howard and Moody held a service in the dining-saloon, almost every passenger attending. 'With one arm clasping a pillar to steady myself on the reeling vessel,' and a German translating, Moody read the 91st Psalm, the words 'He shall give his angels charge over thee to keep thee in all thy ways,' coming with fresh vitality, 'like a voice of divine assurance.' Then he prayed.

Moody had no fear of death. 'There was no cloud between my soul and my Saviour. I knew my sins had been put away, and that if

I died it would only be to wake up in heaven.' But he had been thinking all day of his dear Emma, his two children in America, his schools, his friends, 'and as I realized that perhaps the next hour would separate me for ever from all these, so far as this world was concerned, it almost broke me down... I could not endure it. I must have relief, and relief came in prayer.'

Moody prayed in that lurching saloon and his prayer echoed the deepest thoughts of all present, that God would still the storm, bring them safe home, but above all would do His will. 'Thy will be done!'

Peace flowed across the room. Hearts were brave again. Peace filled Moody's heart: 'Northfield or heaven it made no difference now.' He went to bed and fell sound asleep.

About three in the morning Will shook him awake. 'Come on deck, Father!' and Will's voice was excitedly happy. They saw, far away, a light rising and falling, slowly drawing nearer.

The rescue ship was the Canadian Pacific freighter *Lake Huron* (Captain Frank Carey, bound from Montreal to Liverpool), which had seen the mast-head flares and closed on the *Spree*. 'Twice during the darkness,' relates a *Lake Huron* passenger, 'an effort was made to get a cable aboard, and each time we had almost gripped it when the force of the waves snapped the rope as if it had been cotton thread. Then the captain signalled: "I'll stand by until morning!" and for five hours we kept steaming around the helpless vessel.'

At dawn wind and seas dropped 'as though God spoke to the elements as He had done years ago on Galilee', and an officer of the *Spree* could board the *Lake Huron* to consult Carey, who said he would attempt a tow and if necessary try to transfer the *Spree's* passengers. 'The operation of getting the tow lines aboard and made fast was accomplished and about nine o'clock we again started on our journey to Liverpool with the great ship dragging after us. For six days we travelled on without a mishap, covering 130 miles a day. Steamers passing us in either direction showed by their appearance that they had experienced rough weather, yet the storms did not come near us.'

As they saw the hills of Ireland Will said to his father that he had always doubted if direct answers to prayer ever came, 'but I am no longer doubtful'.

30: The Incomparable Moody

The World's Fair campaign from May 28th to October 31st, 1893, drew a total attendance of 1,933,240 of every state and almost every nationality, according to the register made at the Bible Institute.

Architect, speaker at scores of the hundreds of meetings, soul and brain of the entire operation, Moody worked right through the heat of a Chicago summer as if his heart was as sound as an athlete's. Unlike any other campaign, Chicago 1893 was not sponsored or directed by a local committee but by himself through the Bible Institute. 'I think it would have been utterly impossible to have carried on this work without the Bible Institute,' he said at the close. It was headquarters and nerve-centre. Moody used the two hundred and twenty men and women students and the augmented staff as shock troops: 'if there was any part of the city where we needed to throw a detachment, we could sent fifty men over and placard and ticket the whole neighbourhood and fill a building.' The campaign steeled and cemented the infant Institute, stamped it with its President's personality and ideal.

The Chicago churches, dispirited by the concomitance of high summer and the dazzling counter-attraction of the Fair, were slow to assist until Moody's campaign gathered momentum. The city was evangelized systematically. Churches, theatres and halls were filled. Moody rented Forepaugh's Circus Tent the two Sundays it was in Chicago and was half amused, half annoyed when he saw its proprietor's placard: *'Ha! Ha! Ha! Three Big Shows. Moody in the Morning. Forepaugh in the Afternoon and Evening.'* Down near the stockyards he took Tattersalls, where were held the political conventions and Wild-West shows, saying, 'We have got something better than Buffalo Bill and we must get a bigger audience than he does.'

Moody certainly could claim at the close of the Fair: 'thousands have apparently been genuinely converted to Christ... Fires have been kindled in many parts of this land as a result of the summer campaign.'

1893 inaugurated six years of unceasing activity.

Moody seemed a juggler keeping in the air six or seven balls. J H Harwood, Chicago friend since early days, 'expected that I might at any time hear that he had died suddenly', but Moody did not care. No resting on fame or achievement, no self-satisfaction; Moody's attitude to himself and his enterprises was expressed in two favourite phrases: 'We must grow or go to the wall,' and 'Let us push out in all directions.' He gave the whole of himself to whatever occupied his mind. Bible Institute, Northfield Schools, evangelistic campaign committees, each found it hard to believe that *this* was not his prime interest. None of his colleagues or associates, not even Whittle, certainly not Sankey, saw the whole of him. He wanted Will to be his biographer after his death 'because so many friends will think they knew me better than anyone else and they don't'. Approachability, sympathy, his frankness and his bluntness drew scores of people to consult him in trouble or difficulty and count him intimate. George F Pentecost accused him searingly behind his back, and after his death, of betraying friends: 'the moment they ceased to be useful or were in his way he dropped them, and even flung them away', but Pentecost had been disloyal. Having reached considerable eminence through association with Moody, Pentecost allowed incipient pride and love of ease and an uncontrollable temper to turn him into an open embarrassment and hindrance at Northfield where he had his home. Moody did not drop close associates who drifted in outlook but remained true to Christ. Charles F Goss, the lovable but too socialist former pastor of Chicago Avenue, kept Moody's staunch friendship after they had ceased to work together, and Goss's brief biography came very near the real Moody. Yet it failed to show the whole of him.

Moody was like a gem of many facets, the light catching now one colour, now another.

Religious leaders down the centuries have been moulded generally in the pattern of St Peter, or St Paul, or St John. Moody was much of each. He had Peter's impulsiveness, full-bloodedness, quick temper, rough humanity; he had the single-mindedness, strategic skill in evangelism, strong church centredness, the hardihood of Paul, if without his scholarship; he had John's love and spiritual appetite and steady growth in devotion.

The years fell into a pattern. At some time in each twelve months Moody would descend on Chicago like a whirlwind. 'If I should speak on Friday night at the church I should want tickets got out and all the work done to get the people out... Get all the press to work at once & all the Institute men and women & let it be known it will be my only night in the city. All the houses within a mile of the church should be visited at once with tickets...'

He would stay at the Institute, interview officers and administrators, make lightning decisions. 'His perception of the right and wrong in things, the true and false, the thing to be done in any circumstance, were almost like inspiration,' Harwood thought. 'His intuitions were as quick as a flash and almost absolutely accurate.' 'All he seemed to require,' Charles F Goss wrote, 'was to have a given problem set before him in the clearest light possible, and he instantly saw the answer in all its bearings.'

No one could doubt what the Institute meant to its President. 'We must make the Institute a mighty power,' was a constant theme. On his travels he picked likely candidates and nearly drove the business staff to despair by insistence that 'we must take all that come, that is if they are worth taking... I do not want it ever to go out that we are full... I want to see 1,000 students and we must all work for that end.'

A F Gaylord, business manager since 1891, received a stream of brisk, brief letters in the familiar large scrawl filling a sheet of hotel paper or, more often, at the foot or on the back of the letter Gaylord had written to him. If Moody thought of a point he would dash off a note, perhaps several a day. Thus from Charleston and Savannah in March 1896 Gaylord had eight letters in six days.

Moody's mail, always forwarded, reached proportions enormous by the scale of the eighteen nineties. 'His pen was kept constantly busy,' wrote Percy Fitt, close to him as secretary and, from 1894, as Emma's husband. 'He always wrote his letters by hand. I never knew him to dictate to a stenographer.' He opened his own mail, dealt with it at once, handing many letters to Mrs Moody and the less important he would flip to a member of the family or a guest if at Northfield, or when on tour to a local friend or a secretary or his singer. If somebody asked what to say he would look over his glasses poised on the end of his nose and, Paul recalls, 'playfully snort, "I gave it to you to answer! I don't intend to hire a dog and do the barking."'

The letter answered, a decision made, it was finished. 'He never procrastinated,' says Fitt. 'His mind was not cluttered with held over matters,' and through disappointments, financial burdens, perplexities, 'he never lost his faith and nerve... One could not be downhearted or defeated in his presence. He could always pray if no open door presented itself.' Gaylord says Moody's *prayer life* was the one thing above everything else that made an impression upon my life'.

He always sought means of expansion. 'How would it do to send out a Gospel Wagon into the towns of the West (Small) and load them down with books and let them preach and sell books. Could they not go into towns where there is no book store and sell enough to keep them going. They could preach evenings and sell books from house to house day times.' This letter to Torrey from Baltimore, March 8th, 1893, was the germ of the Bible Institute Colportage Association, which grew to be the Moody Press.

Moody's discovery in the autumn of 1894 that the entire state of Wisconsin held one store that sold religious books turned idea into reality. He was told they were not in demand unless cheap, although the vast sale of his own collected sermons, authorized or pirated, would contradict this. Early in 1895 he launched with Revell's help an edition of 100,000 copies of *The Way to God,* Moody's equivalent of Billy Graham's *Peace with God,* and thereby founded the Colportage Library of popular religious authors, well-produced cheap paperbacks, and organized the Colportage Association to distribute them.

No sooner had Institute men with the books pushed out in Gospel Wagons through the Middle West than Moody learned that three-quarters of a million Americans were passing in and out of prison, or serving long sentences in rigorous, soul-decaying conditions, and that except in the great state penitentiaries libraries were almost non-existent. Moody had long been concerned for prisoners. He had preached in scores of jails; the most trusted deputy in the sheriff's office at St Louis in 1895, and a valued local preacher, was a one-time old lag called Valentine Burke who had spent half his life in prison until converted in 1880 by reading a newspaper report of Moody's sermon on the Philippian Jailer. Moody began to flood testaments and Colportage books into every cell of every county jail and state penitentiary. When the Spanish-American War broke out and Moody united with the YMCA for Christian activity at the military base in Florida, he ordered the Colportage Association to 'turn our forces now on to getting books for the army & let up on the prisoners a little... I am now going to push hard to get books into the camps.'

Moody books quickly became important. In the tooth-and-claw jungle that was American publishing of the 'nineties Moody insisted that Colportage practice be unimpeachable: 'I would rather close up the business than to have anyone be able to say we had not been *Honest*': and when an allegation of cruelty to the Gospel Wagon horses reached his ears he was grim: 'If the men were cruel they should be dealt with by Mr Torrey, it is shame that young men on a mission like that should do a thing of that kind...'

Moody never wrote a book. His Gospel sermons, Bible characters, devotional and doctrinal studies were all compiled from his spoken word, those after 1893 by Fitt: 'I came to know his vocabulary and mannerisms of language so well that I could do him justice and reproduce his true flavour'. Moody read every book and article before signing.

Moody had already circled the globe in print, as John R Mott soon found. In 1902 Mott could say he had not 'visited a country in

Europe, Asia or Africa where the words of Mr Moody are not bearing fruit. Next to the words of the Bible, and possibly those of Bunyan, his words have been translated into more tongues than those of any other man.'

'I am in hopes God will use the books to stir up the nation,' Moody wrote in 1896. If astronomical figures of distribution be any guide, God certainly did.

Every autumn, and again if he had spent Christmastide at Northfield, came Moody's time to 'turn my back on the most beautiful home on earth'.

'He went from end to end of this land,' as a Chicago Congregationalist said, 'calling multitudes away from mere earthliness of interest and the greed for wealth and prosperity to the problem of individual salvation and the concerns of everlasting life.' He travelled between 1893 and 1899 throughout North America from Canada to Mexico; no longer staying months at one city, though occasionally several weeks, as in New York and Boston the winter of 1896-7, but in most seasons moving through a wide area, two or three nights at each centre, until there was scarcely a city of importance that had not heard Moody.

In his travels 'he was such a good sport in regard to hardships, laughing at them', writes Paul. Moody liked to be comfortable but not luxurious, preferring small temperance hotels. He enjoyed scenery, always soaked up information on local background and personalities, pumped people about their families and work and interests. Occasionally the rush snapped his never very strong patience. 'I'm so ashamed of myself,' he confessed after losing his temper with porters. 'Some of these men may have known me, and if so I have dishonoured my Master.' Once in a train with the singer, D B Towner, a drunk having a badly bruised eye recognized Moody and started bawling hymns. 'Let's get out of here,' Moody said, but Towner knew the other cars were full. When the conductor came along Moody pointed out the drunk. The conductor quietly took the fellow, bathed and bandaged his eye and sent him back to the car, where he fell asleep.

'Towner,' said Moody after a while, 'that is an awful rebuke for me! I preached last night to that crowd against pharisaism and exhorted them to imitate the Good Samaritan, and now this morning God has given me an opportunity to practice what I preached and I find I have both feet in the shoes of the priest and Levite.' For the rest of that tour he told the story publicly against himself.

In the campaigns of the 'nineties Towner was often with him, or other singers, for Sankey's voice and physique no longer could keep abreast.

None equalled Sankey. Sankey in his prime had lasted entire campaigns with few breaks but now Moody would wear out two or three singers on a tour. Moreover none had that extraordinary, indefinable quality which could still cause a hearer to exclaim: 'I would rather Sankey with his worn out voice than the greatest prima donna in the world'. Sankey tried all the harder and became, Paul says, 'a little heavy and pompous, and mannerisms grew upon him at which some of the thoughtless used to laugh, and this never failed to hurt my father... There was never any lessening of affection.' Sankey survived Moody some six years and went totally blind: the legend that he lost his faith at the end has no basis in contemporary sources.

Moody's voice had lost nothing with the years: 'Thank God, when the Almighty created me,' he once chaffed, 'He set my head so close to my body that He hardly gave me any neck, and what little there was He macadamized!' Nor had lessened his power to sway audiences. The 'chronic crush' of his collar had gone, for on tour he now dressed carefully, in black or dark blue, well cut to offset his girth and unadorned by watch chain or gold cuff-links: 'he wanted nothing about him to distract in any way the attention of his hearers,' Will said. Eye and tongue retained their astonishing power to command; in the eighteen nineties, rising sixty, he was at his zenith.

A massed audience packed shoulder to shoulder and well prepared by song lay in the hollow of his hand. 'From the first moment to the last,' wrote Charles Goss who knew him well at this period, 'the fact that he meant *business* and not fireworks, oratory, or theatricals was apparent. He was there to convince and persuade men, and for nothing else whatever. Nothing could be more impressive than his determination to secure the results he aimed at. The evidences of a supreme and terrible resolution were manifest in every move.' Occasionally he reached a real height of unintended oratory. Goss heard, in Detroit, his sermon on Elijah 'when it appeared to me that supernatural things were actually occurring in the room... In the final outburst we actually beheld the chariot swoop down from heaven, the old man ascend, the blazing car borne through the still air; and when the impassioned orator uttered that piercing cry "My father, my father, the chariot of Israel and the horsemen thereof!" the excitement was almost unendurable.' Those close to him on the platform thrilled to the contagion of Moody's expectancy, his joy of victory. 'Was he not about to see avaricious men abandon their love of gold, defaulters restore their ill-gotten gains, adulterers abandon their lust, drunkards dash down their cups, the captives loosed, the bowed down lifted up? As the words poured in torrents from his lips he knew that those eternal deeds were being done. He pierced the mask of those faces and saw the operations of the souls. He beheld Christ moving among them.'

Moody's expectancy, his belief that no person present was too foul or too hard to be beyond the reach of God's love, had not dimmed but increased with the years, and it was therefore small surprise that men and women, as a Hermonite saw, 'rose so easily and went forward to confess Christ'. Once more Moody would hurry to the inquiry room. In the quiet, broken only by murmur of converse between 'personal workers' and 'anxious souls', Moody was like some doctor after a battle or a mine disaster. A woman journalist seized the opportunity of a brief pause as he mopped his brow, to accost him on his future plans. Moody, in its proper place always courteous to the press, 'turned on me like a wounded lion, and said, "I have no time to talk about myself. I have to deal with these souls," and dashed back to his work.'

'People gathered round him like moths around a candle,' said Goss of Moody on campaign. 'They made absurd excuses to approach him.' His influence seemed hypnotic, but when Goss asked if he thought he had mesmeric gifts Moody dismissed the idea with a toss of the head: 'Not if I know myself! If I thought my influence was owing to that I would quit preaching to-morrow. Any power I have comes from the Spirit of God.'

As ever, the campaigns were deliberate expressions of Christian unity.

'I am more and more convinced of the importance of sustaining and working with the Church,' Moody wrote in a private letter at this time. 'Every effort is going to be put forth to arouse the churches to greater activity', he said before starting his 1897 campaign in Boston, where he urged every minister to co-operate 'by conducting gospel meetings in his own church'. 'If the Church was built up it would reach the world', was a constant theme. He wanted the churches to work together and deplored the multiplicity of sects falling over each other when wide tracts of America were barely churched, but any divisive tendencies among his supporters he suppressed rigidly: Hartzler and Pierson in his absence set up a Northfield Emergency Missionary Fund which would operate independently of denominational boards. It lasted exactly as long as it took Moody to return to Northfield.

His willingness to co-operate went far beyond the imagination of his friends, who were shocked that he subscribed towards the building of St Patrick's Roman Catholic Church for Northfield's Irish colony, and horrified when he accepted an invitation from a friend who had turned Roman to meet Archbishop Corrigan of New York, to whom he said he 'wanted to see New York shaken for Christ and wouldn't it be a grand thing if all the churches swung into a simultaneous effort... The Archbishop had the power to do it for the Roman Catholic churches, and the other churches would follow the lead.'

The 'nineties were a decade of increasing bitterness between religious groups, but not when Moody was around; of increasing scepticism, but not where Moody went. 'I have not seen so much religious interest in this country for twenty years. I think there will be more than 400,000 come into the churches this year,' he wrote in 1894, and in 1897: 'Never has America been so aroused over religious matters.' He believed that revival could spread everywhere if Churches co-operated and ministers were loyal: 'What the people want is to be fed, and then they will go to work... If you want a good church feed it on the Word of God.'

He would not pronounce on public questions. He was profoundly interested in political and international affairs, being 'a great reader of the daily papers. He wanted,' his last secretary, H W Pope, said, 'to know what was going on in the world. He wanted to have a hand in it.' He had his opinions, but said he lacked time to study up enough to make public comment, and criticized – sometimes a little glibly – ministers who spent pulpit time 'discussing topics which are treated far abler in the newspapers and magazines'.

His instinct was right. America in the 'nineties, an age of industrial strife, was a melting-pot of economic and political theories. To have pronounced on them would have made Moody partisan. He was a child of his age in economic outlook, with an inevitable lean towards the captains of industry, many of whom he knew, and a 'veiled admiration', in Paul's words, 'for men who came to the top in almost any line of activity'. But he loved the common man and rigidly opposed oppression when he recognized it.

His gospel was a social gospel because it made men whole. 'Mr Moody in preaching the Christian religion preaches... the brotherhood of men,' *Harpers Weekly* affirmed in 1896. 'He preaches against anarchy, against greed, against extortion and hate. He is the enemy of sectionalism and all hostility of class to class. His mission is to arouse the conscience and awaken the spiritual side of men.

Moody's impact on the social history of America – as of Great Britain – was enormous. His young missionary friend Robert E Speer was right when he said (in 1931): 'Every community where he worked felt the effect in a better and friendlier community life, in more just and humane economic relationship, in more solicitude for the unfortunate and needy. The Kingdom of God had come nigh.'

31: Northfield

Moody's return to Northfield was always a time for rejoicing. In winter each Seminary girl would put her oil-lamp in her window 'so that all the buildings were brilliantly lighted up', in summer they would gather woodland flowers and decorate the Homestead and garland the Moody porch. Hermonites crossed the river and the combined choirs sang a welcome.

At Northfield and at Mount Hermon stony fields and woods were now well-laid campuses that merged in the hillsides of the Connecticut Valley. Moody avoided interference in professional affairs but kept in daily touch with his Principals, Miss Hall and Henry Franklin Cutler, whom he had appointed headmaster in 1890 at the age of twenty-eight: a man of deep faith and breadth of understanding, who continued in office until 1932, and was the chief moulder of Mount Hermon into an institute of first-class education.

'I think dear Hermon is much nearer my heart now than ever before,' Moody wrote to Cutler in 1892, '& I am determined if I live, to do all I can to make it still stronger & a greater power for good I am convinced that what the world wants is true men & women not great but true honest & upright persons God can use.' When at Northfield he would visit frequently: 'his appearance on a rainy day was much like Santa Claus, with his hoary beard, wrinkled, ruddy, kindly, smiling face, rubber boots and corduroy coat', one Hermonite remembers. At the start of every school year Moody would 'make a direct appeal to the boys to give themselves to God. Very few indeed could resist his appeal... Every boy felt that Mr Moody was personally interested in his fortunes and success,' and should a boy be expelled for mischief Moody would often intercede: 'Give him another chance'; but if the complaint was 'He is lazy', he would dismiss the matter with his characteristic half-grunt, half-snort. 'Let him go. We have no room here for boys who won't work.' Hermonites never forgot Moody's proverb, 'The school is not going to spend a hundred dollars on a ten cent boy.'

Paul Moody believed that the Seminary meant even more to him. 'His boys were five miles away, and added to this Miss Hall was longer in his service than anyone else and certainly more trusted.' 'He took such an interest in the girls' lives,' says Moody's daughter-in-law, who as May Whittle entered at fifteen in 1885, 'and they would love to tell him all their troubles. He broke up a number of engagements of the girls in school if he didn't think the man was worthy. He would investigate. And he was always right.' 'We all realized that we had in him not only a spiritual adviser, but one with interest akin to that of an earthly father,' another girl wrote.

The staff probably would have sometimes dubbed it 'grandfatherly' rather, especially when he indulged his boyish delight in suspending all studies once or twice a summer term by calling for a 'Mountain Day' as it was known at both schools, when every one went up Northfield Mountain for picnic and fun.

In the 'eighties Moody would join the romps and games, literally crushing the opposition and playing pranks such as tying his end of a tug-of-war rope to a tree or a stake. In his last years he pranked by proxy: Dan Sutherland, who worked when young as a hired man on the Moody place, tells how one Mountain Day he had driven Moody up to join the girls under the great chestnuts and old apple trees on the mountain top, and waited a little below with 'the horse and old wagon. He hollered "Come up", well, I went up. "Do you think you can shinny up that tree?" "Sure." I shinnied up the tree to shake the branches so the nuts would fall down, and when he had got me up the tree he called at the girls, "Here, go for him!" Well, all the girls started picking up the apples and they did paste me! I beat a hasty retreat. But it tickled Mr Moody.'

The schools would have died in infancy had not Moody thrown enormous energy and acumen into raising funds, for hymn-book money could not cover the expense of expansion, and whenever the trustees advocated higher fees Moody would toss his head: 'Not in my lifetime!'

Millionaires gave to Moody because, they said, 'he's one of us'. 'In the course of a life-long commercial experience I have never met a man with more business capacity and sheer executive ability than D L Moody,' Peter Mackinnon said to Henry Drummond. It was a time of great fortunes fast made, often by men with no sense of responsibility or idea of how to spend aright, a time of swift transitions from cabin to mansion, of absurd extravagances and ostentation. Moody believed implicitly in his right to direct this wealth into service. 'When a man makes money by jumps I go by jumps,' he told one protesting plutocrat; Moody regretted that 'sanctified wealth is a very rare commodity in America' as contrasted with Britain where many families had been born and bred in riches and knew how to use them.

Moody had a slight suspicion of an enterprise run on 'faith' without open appeal. He did not understand the circumstances that gave Hudson Taylor his conviction that the China Inland Mission must not ask for money, though the affection between the two men deepened with each meeting. And Moody, who had never asked money for himself from the day he left business, claimed that he did indeed run his schools on faith. 'I always have and I always expect to. I believe I show my faith when I go to men and state to them the needs of the Lord's work and ask them to give to it.'

'Now make some room for faith,' he would tell the trustees if they wondered where money was coming from. The story was sprinkled with incidents of donors suddenly remembering Moody, who would receive an unexpected cheque at a critical moment. In 1897, during an evangelistic series at Chicago's Auditorium, he prayed alone in his room at the Bible Institute: 'Oh Lord, you know I have been so busy preaching that I haven't had time to go out after money. I need $3,000 to pay the bills and must leave it to you to send in.' During the afternoon meeting an envelope was thrust into his hand, which he opened later to find $3,000 from Mrs McCormick. She told him when he called to thank her that it had occurred to her he would need money for the rent of the Auditorium, that she wrote a cheque for $2,000 but immediately felt strongly that she should increase it.

Although Moody liked big gifts with which to put up school buildings, for the day-by-day expenses he preferred a large number of small amounts in order to widen and sustain interest. 'And a good part of the time when not otherwise occupied,' Paul says, 'he would be signing, literally by the thousand, typed begging letters.' He would not have his signature rubber-stamped and disliked blotting paper. 'He wanted the ink to dry, and the room, floor and furniture would be covered by these myriad letters.'

Northfield proudly gave Moody honour in his own country. Town and family alike benefited from its attraction to a widening world as a centre of education and conference in surroundings of natural beauty. In 1894 he built the Auditorium seating two thousand. F B Meyer thought it too large. 'Do you think you can fill it?' he asked.

'God is marching on,' Moody replied, 'and I must keep pace with Him.'

Moody at conference time put a bushel basket of apples at the bottom of his drive, free for all. 'The capacity for apples among attendants at the conferences was amazing,' records Paul who in boyhood had to keep the basket full; he was also expected to devote hours laboriously preparing ice-cream 'for the hordes who would be invited in after the evening service'. Once he got his own back in true Moody manner by freezing it so hard that at serving time he had 'my father looking more and more baffled'.

At Northfield, Drummond wrote, Moody 'gathers round him the best men he can find... but when one comes away it is always Mr Moody one remembers', yet he never sought to dominate. 'What a time we had year after year in getting him to consent to speak,' John R Mott writes of the college conferences. At the General Workers' conference Moody would leave the platform after introducing a speaker, and sit at his feet, 'always with his Bible open', Charles Blanchard noticed, 'always with a pen or pencil in his hand, and if anything was said which was particularly good he noted it and used it without hesitation'. He was no longer a great reader and the conferences were his pumping stations. If a man had something to give, Moody wanted it. 'On any other subject he did not care a button for my opinion,' the aged President Weston of Crozier Theological Seminary wrote to Will. 'But when I opened to him the Bible which was so precious to him, the tears would come to his eyes and he would say, "Say that again, Doctor."'

'The central idea of the Northfield conference is Christian unity...
but it is understood that along with the idea of Christian unity goes
the Bible as it stands.'

Moody's theological views were, in Speer's words, 'the simple
central convictions of the evangelical tradition, the Wesleyan evangelistic warmth appealing to human freedom, and the sinews of
the Calvinistic reverence for God and His will which Moody felt
and knew as a will of love' – a Biblical theology. As put by Dr
James M Gray of the Bible Institute, Torrey's future successor, 'The
brain of his theology was the grip he had on the authority and integrity of the Bible as the Word of God.' Sankey gave as one of the
reasons for Moody's phenomenal success 'that he believed absolutely, implicitly in the message he gave to men... No doubts ever
dimmed his faith in the Word of God. To him it was the truth, and
the whole truth.' 'To the Bible he went continually with the spirit
of a little child,' Dr Weston wrote. When he preached he held his
Bible in his hand through much of the sermon, 'often adjusting his
glasses to read in a manner that made every hearer feel "these are
the oracles of the living God".'

Moody was already established when the superbly confident
stream of higher criticism broke out of the confines of German
theological schools. 'The storm of literary criticism began to beat
upon the Bible and many people were frightened, but Mr Moody
was not frightened,' said C I Scofield, the Southern ex-lawyer whom
Moody brought to Northfield as pastor, later to be eminent as editor of the *Scofield Reference Bible*. Higher criticism in its extreme
literary stage busily dissected the Bible into a haphazard collection
of documents expressing human aspirations in ancient times; its
opponents retorted by piecemeal defence of each position. Moody
saw that the battle had been won already on a different part of the
front.

He had depended upon promises, obeyed commands, proved
the Bible God's Word in his own life and by its influence upon
others beyond any force of critical theories to detract. He could
trust the Bible as he could trust a man without needing to know
exactly how the man had come to be what he was, biologically or

in development of mind or character. Moody had seen the power of the Bible. And therefore, as Speer said, 'he believed in the living Book, the living message to men, as complex and varied as all the problems of life'.

'If you ask,' Moody put in one of his books, 'do I understand what is revealed in Scripture, I say no, but my faith bows down before the inspired Word, and I unhesitatingly believe the great things of God even when reason is blinded and the intellect confused. Now what we want is to be so sure of the Word that the Spirit coming upon us shall bring to mind – bring to our remembrance – the words of the Lord Jesus.' Moody knew and trusted the Christ of the Bible. 'I am sure Christ believed it,' he wrote to Will about a controverted point, '& shall the servant be above the master? I hope you will have the courage to stand up against any man that does not preach all the truth I have little sympathy with any man that would attempt to undermine any man in the Bible.'

Moody stressed the positive power of truth. Certain that criticism could not shake the Gospel – lesser men feared that it would, feared it vindicated contemporary confidence in man's upward march, his moral evolution which left redemption redundant – Moody held that critical problems were less important than soul-winning and the increase of Churches. He may not have appreciated the strength of intellectual pressures, but he knew that the way to fight error was to emphasize truth, for which the common man hungered. 'The masses are sick and tired of speculative theology in the pulpit,' he said in 1897. 'That is why our Churches are half empty and also why millions never darken a Church door. People are not fed. They are hungering and thirsting for the pure Gospel and they get pulpit essays and discussions of questions. They go away empty and disgusted and then they stay away.' Time proved Moody right. Had clergy been in less of a hurry to trot out the latest undigested critical theory, the churches of America and Britain would not have sunk into the trough of the 'twenties and 'thirties.

Moody refused to indulge in personalities. 'The critics raise questions which do not help the spiritual life, their opponents retort with bad temper and personal recriminations,' he said, and after

Torrey had been ungracious to George Adam Smith at Northfield Moody exclaimed to Will and Percy Fitt: 'Awful! Awful! They often put us to shame by their more Christian attitude.' He found it hard to understand how an evangelical of deep personal loyalty to Christ could absorb himself in the literary origins of the Bible when a world needed saving – 'Why talk of two Isaiahs when most people don't know of one?' he asked G A Smith – or in attempting, like the later Henry Drummond, to reconcile Darwinism with the Bible view of life; but if a man's fundamental loyalty was to Christ and the Gospel Moody heard him gladly. He stood by Drummond while deploring 'the unscriptural things he is now teaching'.

On hearing of Drummond's untimely death at forty-five in 1897, Moody at Goss's house in Cincinnati 'cried like a child. "He was the most Christlike man I ever met. I never saw a fault in him," he said over and over again through his sobs.'

Moody was his own best testimony to the Bible's power.

Gamaliel Bradford, the agnostic who attempted a biography, sympathetic but puzzled, in the late nineteen twenties, wrote that Moody had 'reduced the population of hell by a million souls'. Moody would not have put it negatively (and would have puffed away the numeral), but that God had used him to bring them to the joy of life in Christ here and in eternity, so that Christ had not died in vain for them. And no man in the nineteenth century put more of his fellow-beings to service for God and humanity, an inspiration that continues through his foundations.

Drummond called him 'the biggest human I ever met'. And again: 'I had no idea of the moral size of the man, and I think very few know what he really is.' An early Hermonite, George L Cady, looking back after thirty years, described him in an article, perhaps with a pinch of hyperbole, as 'human in the sense that one can hardly tell where the human leaves off and the divine begins, when God really has a chance to do His Will with one'. An Englishman, T Farmer Hall, wrote of him in 1899 as 'the only friend I utterly believed in... I never heard him without feeling the strongest desire to love and know Christ... He was that rarest man in the world, an absolutely (in my opinion) consistent Christian. The same, wherever he was, with only one thought in his life, how to bring glory to Christ by loving and working for those whom Christ loves and died to save.'

Woodrow Wilson, when President of Princeton, was at a barber's when another customer entered and 'sat in the next chair to me. Every word that he uttered, though it was not in the least didactic, showed a personal and vital interest in the man who was serving him; and before I got through with what was being done to me, I was aware that I had attended an evangelistic service, because Mr Moody was in the next chair. I purposely lingered in the room after he left, and noted the singular effect his visit had upon the barbers in that shop. They talked in undertones. They did not know his name, but they knew that something had elevated their thought. And I felt that I left that place as I should have left a place of worship.'

32: The Grandchildren

The Homestead at Northfield never was sweeter to Moody than in his brief vacations.

At summer dawn he put on his outrageous 'Bumble Bee' suit of yellow Donegal tweed trousers and waistcoat and brown velveteen coat, 'an old pair of rubber boots and an utterly disreputable hat', and went out, sometimes to sit and study his Bible, sometimes to drive around. He did not spend long hours on his knees. At mention of Luther praying all night Moody said he had tried it once, 'and woke up a very stiff Moody'. Young Paul, sharing an hotel room, was quite shocked by the extreme brevity of his father's devotions. Moody prayed anywhere 'all the time', Mrs W R Moody says, 'everything that came up, he'd say a dozen words perhaps, I never heard him make a long prayer'. Christ was so close. 'How dark this world would be without Jesus Christ!' he exclaimed to a friend as they walked out into one of Northfield's most beautiful mornings.

Spanking round – or over – his own small farm and the school estates, he would first visit his pampered, overfed hens. 'Father loved them, not individually but in the mass... he held endless wordless communication with them... It may have been that after a winter of crowded meetings their very unresponsiveness made an appeal to him.' He kept acres of vegetables, for he liked to watch things grow. He had cows – including a few Jerseys for their milk – pigs, bees, and he tried sheep unsuccessfully. Dan Sutherland, who was expected to leave a cow half milked so that family prayers should start on the dot, thought Moody as a farmer 'amateurish, very much of an amateur', but he grew for fun and gave quantities of fruit and vegetables away, racing around to the backyards of relatives and neighbours 'in the most uncomfortable of express wagons'. 'Many a time,' George's daughter Mary said, 'has my uncle driven into our yard and would call out "Come here, I have something for you". And it would be three or four baskets of home-grown strawberries.'

Farming was a hobby and he thought up others: 'You never knew where he would break out next... He shamefacedly did things he knew he would be lovingly scolded for doing,' Paul writes. 'But he had a perfectly wonderful time both doing them and defending himself afterwards. And he actually seemed to enjoy the remonstrances of the family and particularly those of my mother, who was, before everything else, practical and orderly.' Moody had fits of mild megalomania, such as ordering barrel-loads of china when he thought the house short, and Paul swears that his father impatient at finding himself out of a pair of braces ('suspenders'), bought a gross, one hundred and forty-four pairs, large size, all white.

His impulsiveness once nearly ruined him. To save a quarrel over a barn he offered $10,000 for a farm he did not want that was worth only $2,500, the option to run until the following Wednesday. 'The words were hardly out of Father's mouth before cold fear assailed him.' The Yankee neighbour figured that if D L offered $10,000 he must want the place enough to give a few thousand more, and realized his mistake only when the option expired. 'Father gave gigantic sighs of relief.' Paul watched the neighbour on the sofa in the library desperately bringing his price lower and lower 'and Father sitting at his desk pretending to read his mail and refusing every offer'.

Every day Moody called on his aged mother in the cottage until her death in February 1896 at the age of ninety-one. Since her conversion from Unitarianism old Betsey Moody kept an intense interest in her son's work and remained a cynosure of pilgrimage for the good and great who visited Northfield. The younger generation found her forbidding. No cookie jar or sweets, 'she seemed to be afraid of spoiling us... remarkably undemonstrative... suffered our filial kisses with a sort of grim resignation', wrote Paul, and May recalls accompanying her father-in-law: 'I sat there and watched them, they may have said good evening and good night but if they did, that was all they said. They just sat, never spoke, and he came home saying he had had a lovely call on his mother. It seemed strange to me, but that's the way they were, very close, they could just sit together and not have to talk at all.'

Back at the Homestead Moody hurried over supper to be in time for the sunset. He would sit on the front porch and drink in the superb view of the Great River bending in a sweep of an S, and watch the sun sink slowly behind the wooded hills beyond.

The only person in all the world who really knew D. L. Moody was his wife.

'Aunt Emma and Uncle Dwight were so perfectly *one*,' his niece Mary said, 'that no one could possibly tell which was *the* one.' 'I have never seen anything more idyllic,' Paul wrote towards the end of his life, 'nor do I believe two people, young or old, were ever more completely wrapped up in each other.' White-haired, calm and self-effacing, efficient, touchy about nothing except detraction of her husband, humorous without Moody's boisterousness but with an occasional gentle sarcasm 'which we both enjoyed and feared', she was the 'balance-wheel'. Dan Sutherland said he was 'more sold on Mrs Moody than I was on Mr Moody, to be strictly honest', and Paul found her easier to confide in. Moody never took her for granted. He looked up to her until the day of his death, and for her and no other would he drive quietly and not career off the road across a field.

She had seen him in the raw, had polished and brushed him until, for all his abrupt directness, he had courtesy and social grace. 'Only the closest and oldest of his associates know the extent to which he leaned upon her. She did not intend they should.'

Arthur Percy Fitt was 'a good Irishman, blunt and forceful, always came straight to the point, very popular in Town', a Northfield resident described him.

Moody's pleasure at Percy Fitt's engagement to Emma is prettily reflected in a joke-letter written from a Providence, Rhode Island, hotel. Moody had called Emma out to see a cousin and found she had paper ready to write to her fiancé. Moody did it for her: 'My dearly beloved Piercey, I cannot tell you with pen how very much *I love you* you will never know in this world how very much *I do love you.* Your last letter lifted me up into the clouds but I expect the dentist will pull me down again...'

Emma and Percy were married in May 1894, Will and May Whittle in August. The W R Moodys went to live in a little house at Mount Hermon where Will assisted in the administration.

Early on a beautiful morning of August 1895 a horseman crossed the ferry and pounded up Northfield main street on the old white mare, Ouida, having already called at Major Whittle's house. Moody heard 'me coming and stuck his head out of the upper window. Says he, "Is it good news?" "Yes."' Moody had the buggy out and was away. 'D'you hear I have a granddaughter?' he called to any neighbour he passed. 'I'm taking her a present.' 'What is it?' 'Doughnuts!' He bought her a Bible: 'for the last forty years the dearest thing on earth to me'.

The birth in December 1895 of Emma Moody Fitt made Moody a doting double grandfather. He sent nonsense letters: 'I have just heard that the milk you get at your house doesn't agree with you,' he wrote from Georgia to three-months-old Emma, '...It must be your parents' fault... You slip down to Miss Johnson or Florrie and they will give you some hot doughnuts and icecream that will agree with you if bottle milk does not.' And to Irene: 'When summer comes I am going to have Emma and yourself at our house and I will show you some little pigs chickens ducks turkies and lots of things... I want you to keep things lively till I get back, do not let them bother you about sleeping after daylight, keep good natured but laugh crow and make the rattle go hard so all the house will be stirred up.'

Moody seldom drove in good weather without one or both grandchildren. The arrival on November 7th, 1897, of Dwight Lyman Moody, Jr, added to the fun. Nobody guessed that grandchildren would precipitate the final crisis in Moody's life.

In 1898, aged sixty-one, Moody rode the crest of the wave in campaigns, institutions, home. He warned Gaylord, who had been ill, 'you cannot be too careful of life. When a man gets into a position to do what you are doing you should aim to live as long as you can for one year now is worth ten years before you got started,' but Moody did not abide by his own doctrine. Far from placating his weak heart, 'I asked the Lord to give me a hard field' for the winter of 1898-9.

He went to the wicked West with Mrs Moody, and D B Towner to sing, through Colorado, New Mexico, Arizona, and up the length of California. At Denver, Colorado, a welcoming committee could not find Moody; he 'had escaped unnoticed to the rear of the train and now appeared with a suitcase in his hand, and a slender consumptive young man by his side', with whom he had got acquainted on the train; the welcome committee was ignored until he had put the man in a cab for the sanatorium. Denver crowded to hear Moody, but of Arizona Towner wrote, 'We were in the midst of iniquity such as I never read of in a civilized land. I was real surprised that Mr Moody at his advanced age should think of working there with as little prospect as there was.' At the mining town of Tucson, with six thousand inhabitants, thirty-six saloons and four churches, Moody and Towner had to distribute the tickets themselves.

On November 30th Moody received a tragic telegram: baby Dwight had died, after being unwell for some months. Moody was desolate. 'How I wish I could be with you and comfort you,' he wrote to May, 'but the Lord will comfort you, my heart aches for you and Will more than I can tell.'

He invited them to bring three-year-old Irene to the West, and in the Los Angeles area Will acted as associate evangelist. Stebbins replaced Towner, and Moody ventured to use a lady singer, a Miss Boole whom the *Los Angeles Times* called 'exceedingly pretty' and 'a treasure, for the lady not only has a powerful voice, but she can throw more "tears" into it than any other sacred singer who has ever appeared on the Coast'.

While in Los Angeles Moody received an invitation to Australia and New Zealand. He was obliged to decline, but the 15,831 signatures on the petition were a happy assurance.

After three days in Pasadena the Moodys began to work northwards. At Santa Barbara on March 1st Irene caught pneumonia. Moody was miserable, and at Stockton and Sacramento waited impatiently for the daily telegram he insisted Will should send. 'I got a wire today saying she was better,' he wrote to Torrey on March 11th, 'but the danger is not past, I wish you would pray for them, if they lose her it will be a terrible blow & my heart aches for them.' 'If I do not get better news soon,' he wrote on March 14th from Santa Rosa, 'I shall close up the M [issio] n and go down there... if they lose Irene I do not know what will become of them they are so fond of children.'

The fever broke, the mission was completed with six days at San Francisco. The tug of love and uncertainty had been hard on Moody's heart.

33: Heaven Opens

On the way cast in April 1899 Moody addressed his own church in Chicago, where a reporter could see 'no sign of added years; no evidence of faltering strength; no trace of failing vigour'.

The sermon made a veritable tract for the times. 'I'd like to-day to speak about the book of Acts. People nowadays seem to think they should get as far away from the Bible as possible - it is my opinion that the closer we can keep to the apostolic times the better... Human nature has not changed in the last nineteen hundred years. Preach a different gospel from that which was successful in apostolic days? Oh, bosh!' He talked of deep clouds darkening the horizon, foresaw riots and revolutions all over the world – 1914 lay only fifteen years ahead. 'What can save the life of the nation? Only the strength of a quickened church, and the church can only be quickened by a visitation of power such as the old apostles knew!' He said, laughingly, that he had been criticized for not bringing his preaching into line with modern beliefs. 'If my theology wasn't the same now as I preached thirty years ago I would bundle it up, drop it into the Mississippi and let it drift down to the Gulf of Mexico!'

He reached Northfield, after a day campaign at Detroit, 'all tired out but had to go out & stir things up to keep things goin'. The Colportage and Prison Fund needed support, school benefactors must be met, next winter's campaigns discussed. Phrases such as 'the load is heavy at times' crept into his letters.

He seemed his brisk self to all Northfield that summer. At the college conference his stories by the camp fire were the best. But Irene was wasting away with tuberculosis. Moody brought Will, May and Irene under his roof. The August Conference started. Few present detected that his thoughts strayed continually to Irene, and at Chicago Gaylord and Norton wondered why letters remained unanswered. Every day he deserted the company of important speakers to give Irene a little air, driving her and her mother unwontedly gently, 'and he'd stop his horse and he'd make a prayer and he'd drive on'. Once he came back with Irene asleep in his arms and would not dismount until she woke, but took a nap himself.

A day or two later Dan Sutherland milked in the barn, 'and Mr Moody was in the grain room praying and I heard him distinctly say, "the Lord's will, the Lord's will"'. When showing F B Meyer Irene's pet lamb he broke down. He 'poured out his heart in prayer as a number of us knelt in the drawing room in definite entreaty that her life be spared if it was God's will'.

Irene died on August 22nd. 'He was with us in the room and he said to my husband, "Will, there is a lot of work to do. Come on," and got him out and put him to work.' At the open-air funeral Moody rose unexpectedly and spoke of Elijah 'waiting in the Valley of Jordan so many years ago, for the chariot of God to take him home. Again the chariot of God came down to the Connecticut Valley yesterday morning, about half-past six and took our little Irene home.' On the Auditorium platform for the remainder of the Conference, beside Torrey and Meyer and Wilbur Chapman and young Campbell Morgan 'he looked so weary and troubled', a Northfield girl thought. And to Gaylord from Philadelphia on September 11th Moody wrote: 'I am sorry I got behind but my dear little grandchild has taken up nearly all my thoughts for months.'

The visit to Philadelphia was in itself a strain, for John Wanamaker had plans for a winter campaign like that of twenty-three years ago, and John Wanamaker, Moody's dear friend, for the past year or two had been committing adultery in secret with another man's wife. There was no open scandal. Wanamaker's position as a leading Christian remained, with his enthusiasm for the Gospel. Moody had discovered the facts, had brought Wanamaker and the woman to talk the matter over in the Murray Hill Hotel in New York. Wanamaker refused to give her up. 'That's where your grandfather broke his heart,' Emma Fitt said to her daughter in the hotel many years after. Moody had not seen much of Wanamaker since, but what should be the right course when Philadelphia wished to follow their honoured citizen's lead and have Moody in January 1900?

Moody's body seemed to weigh more than its seventeen or eighteen stone as he pushed on to Chicago for the autumn convention at the end of September. 'I do not want to speak next Sabbath afternoon,' Gaylord read to his surprise, and on the Monday or Tuesday Moody handed the preaching to Gray at the last minute. 'I'm not feeling well.'

Back in the East he threw off a heavy cold, spoke at Boston, travelled back and forth in New England and had two days in New York, speaking with force, foxing even Mrs Moody into the belief that he was again well and strong, until the day came in the second week of November to leave Northfield for Kansas City, Missouri, where three Hermonites had enthused the city to book the enormous Convention Hall for an eight-day campaign.

On the Sunday before he left for the West he preached at Mount Hermon in the chapel that had been given him as a sixtieth birthday present, and on the day he travelled, shortly before Dan Sutherland drove him to the train, Moody addressed the four hundred Seminary girls on a favourite text: 'Search me, O God, and know my heart: try me and know my thoughts.'

He walked slowly out, the girls singing softly the Northfield benediction, 'The Lord bless thee and keep thee'. Outside he stood at the foot of the steps, tears trickling down his cheeks, until the last note died away.

Wanamaker walked with Moody down a Philadelphia street towards the depot. 'I coaxed him very hard to defer his journey as I thought he wasn't very well, and to go home with me; but he resolutely set his face to carry out his program.' Moody uttered a deep sigh: 'My great longing has been to get a good hold upon one of the cities on the Atlantic coast. If I could just get under New York or Philadelphia, and lift them to God, I believe I could sweep the country to the Pacific.'

He travelled West alone, because Mrs Moody was needed at Northfield where May would be having a baby within a few days, but he took comfort in the thought of the three Mount Hermon boys in Kansas: Charley Vining, doing very well in the Union National Bank, Syd Bishop, head of the city YMCA, and English-born David Baines-Griffiths, a pastor. Moody stopped over at Chicago for one train, checked up on administration and addressed his beloved Bible Institute: 'he stood before us in the lecture room, and as he closed, resting one hand on the desk and using the other in slight gestures, the tears running down his cheeks, he said: "I need power! Pray for me that I may have the power of the Holy Spirit. Power is what I need."'

Kansas reporters meeting Moody's train on Saturday, November 11th, 1899, thought he looked well, 'and says he feels equal to the campaign', but when Charley Vining went to the Coates House hotel 'he excused himself from rising, when I shook hands with him, saying he was tired. That afternoon he, Baines-Griffiths and myself, went driving through the City; while he seemed in good spirits, and joked some, I noticed that he was not himself.' Vining told the other Hermonites that they must keep people from Moody. 'The boys thought that I had better accompany him to the hall.'

Convention Hall, a huge building used for horse-shows and grand opera and balls and the Megaphone Minstrels, twice drew, on the Sunday, its capacity of about fifteen thousand, 'the great arena like a valley filled with upturned faces, and the balconies thronged like receding hillsides covered with a countless multitude'. Moody 'preached with his old fire and spirit', his voice sounding 'as though he was talking confidentially to a man in the eighth or tenth row, and without effort it carried to every part of the building'. At both services he took 'my old text', 'Whatsoever a man soweth, that shall he also reap'. Afterwards he said happily it was like the great days at Philadelphia in the 'seventies.

In his hotel room that night, a little lonely, he slipped into reminiscence and drawing a sheet of hotel paper wrote to Jane Mackinnon: 'I am off here all alone thinking of the past & you & your good husband have come into my mind & I just long to see you both once more it would do my eyes good to see you all & ride down that western coast once more I wonder if I should like your new house as well as the old one.

'I cannot tell you how much I miss dear Drummond it does not seem possible I shall not see him again on earth what a good time we shall have when we get to heaven only think what a lot have gone home since 1873 when we first met I get homesick for them sometimes & yet I would not be off until the work that the Lord has given me to do is finished the work is sweeter now than ever & I think I have some streams started that will flow on forever what a joy to be in the harvest field & have a hand in God's work.'

On Monday he told Charley Vining that he had not slept well 'but I must not let it get out, as he did not wish the papers to know it'. There was no falter on the platform that day, the pain in his chest (he had said nothing of it to his wife lest she should stop him going to Kansas) lifted as he preached, until he returned to his room, where he was grateful for the services of a masseur engaged by Vining last thing at night. The man failed. Moody tried sitting up in a chair. 'I had a dreadful night.'

His singer, C C Case, at breakfast 'saw he looked pale and he didn't eat much... Of course I knew if he could not lie down he was a sick man,' and at length Moody allowed him to telephone for Dr Schaufler, whose mustard plaster on the chest relieved some of the pain. 'After that he preached six times but I could see being with him all the time that he was all the time growing weaker.' A telegram was thrust into his hands. Mary Whittle Moody had been born. 'Thankful for good news,' Moody wired back. 'Dear little child,' he wrote on Tuesday to Will, 'I already feel my heart going out towards her... Thank God for another grandchild.' Soon he was busily scribbling to his other grandchild about how they would all play together. Vining sat with him Tuesday and Wednesday nights and Moody slept rather more, and when awake chatted to Charley about the school and Will and the grandchildren. He now had to have a carriage for the two-block ride to the Hall.

The campaign was reaching the heights: Moody told Case he was enjoying it 'as much as any I have ever had'. The deep interest assured him he would be used yet, once he had thrown off this weakness and pain. 'Look at the other world!' he cried to the massed thousands, his arm pointing heavenward in the old familiar gesture. 'No death, no pain, no sorrow, no old age, no sickness, no bending forms, no dimmed eyes, no tears. But joy, peace, love, happiness. No grey hairs. People all young. Think of it! Life! Life! Life without end! And yet so many men choose this life on earth instead of life in heaven. Don't close your heart against eternal life. Only take the gift, only take it. Will you do it?'

After Thursday night's sermon he was 'in a dripping sweat... I had never seen him so exhausted,' Vining wrote, and Moody had to rest and lean on the gate the short way over to the after-meeting, in which he took no part. In the carriage he said to Baines-Griffiths, 'David, I'm finished,' and on reaching his room sat in his chair two hours without moving. He was a little delirious in the night, but next morning kept assuring Vining that he would pull through.

Not until Friday afternoon would he let them telegraph Northfield, arrange to take him home, and send for Torrey to complete the campaign.

A Chapel car, *Messenger of Peace,* was placed at Moody's disposal by Dr and Mrs S M Neil, field secretaries of Railway Evangelism, who accompanied him as far as St Louis. Moody left Kansas at 9.45 p.m. on Friday, Vining and the doctor looking after him the whole journey of two nights and a day.

He improved immediately. Hopeful telegrams kept the family abreast of his progress. The train on Saturday evening reached Detroit late owing to engine trouble, and Vining feared the next connection would be missed. When the engineer who was to take N. 4 the next stage heard that Moody, sick, was on the train he sent a message: 'Tell him I was converted under him fifteen years ago and owe everything to him. Tell Mr Moody one of his friends is at the throttle, and just hold your breath!' They covered the stretch from Detroit through Canada to St Thomas, including stops, at a mile a minute.[1]

Mrs Moody and Will had gone West to meet Moody, but missed him. Paul, hastily back from Yale, went to Greenfield early on the Sunday afternoon 'and felt greatly reassured when in his old manner he chided me for having brought the slower horses... and laughed at my old fogeyness at being cautious'. At the Homestead Moody rested at the bottom of the stairs, then mounted them at his usual speed to prepare for tea, but decided to go to bed.

Letters and telegrams poured into Northfield. On Sunday prayers were offered all over the nation. 'Even up in the Adirondacks,' one friend wrote, 'the rough men in that region are deeply interested in your condition. It is a joy to know that God has given you the hearts of the people as He has.' America and the world hailed the news that Moody's illness 'is not as serious as we feared at first'. Perfect

---

1. This fascinating incident is verified by the reply from the Superintendent, Wabash Railway Company, Peru, Indiana, to W R Moody, November 24th 1899, acknowledging his letter of appreciation.

strangers wrote to him. 'I might not agree with you in all your views,' runs a letter from a woman of Granby, Massachusetts, 'but I believe in *you* with all my heart. Your genuineness, honesty, sincerity have helped me more than you will ever know. There isn't an atom of sham in you.'

Moody hated being bedridden, impatiently counting the days until he would return to work, if at less pace. In his chair much of the time facing the favourite view over the Valley, he chatted with whichever of the family kept him company, asked news of boys and girls, played with baby Emma a little each day and planned with her for Christmas, tried to get a laugh or at least a smile out of the heart specialist's 'doleful but efficient' nurse. Paul returned to college and at the start of the vacation 'we were still hopeful'.

To Moody the past sixty-two years were merely a prologue.

'Some day you will read in the papers that Moody is dead,' he had said at New York on a hot Sunday in August 1899. 'Don't you believe a word of it. At that moment I shall be more alive than I am now... I was born of the flesh in 1837, I was born of the Spirit in 1855. "That which is born of the flesh may die. That which is born of the Spirit shall live for ever." ' It would not be eternity merely, but eternity with Christ. The thin veil would drop. On the evening of December 21st, lying on his bed at Northfield, Moody wrote in pencil in his usual bold hand, barely palsied by weakness: 'To see his star is good but to see his face is better.'

As the next winter dawn broke, Friday, December 22nd, 1899, Moody stirred from an hour's deep sleep that had ended a fitful night of increasing weakness.

Suddenly Will heard 'in slow and measured words: "Earth recedes, heaven opens before me!" ' Will hurried across.

'No, this is no dream, Will. It is beautiful. It is like a trance. If this is death it is sweet. God is calling me and I must go. Don't call me back!'

At that moment Mrs Moody entered.

'Here is Mother, Father!'

Moody said 'rather faintly but clearly', 'Mama, you have been a good dear wife,' and began to slip into unconsciousness, murmuring 'No pain, no valley, it's bliss.'

Dr Wood, who had stayed overnight, came in and gave him an injection. Emma and Percy, Paul, George Moody gathered round the bed as the room brightened with growing daylight reflected from the snow outside. Moody revived, and wondered why they were there. In Mrs Moody's record, made the same day: 'Then he said "What does it all mean? I must have had a trance. I went to the gate of heaven. Why, it is so wonderful, and I saw the children!"

'Will said, "Oh, Father did you see them?"'

'And he said "Yes, I saw Irene and Dwight," and then when Will cried, he said: "You must not cry, Will, you have work to do."'

'Will said with anguish, "Oh, if I could only go."'

'But he said, "No, Will, your work is before you." '

He had another spell of unconsciousness, and when he came round, divided the oversight of his institutions among the children. When Emma asked which their mother should look after, a flash of the old wit brought the instant riposte: 'Why, Mother, she's like Eve, the mother of us all!'

'Don't leave us, Father,' young Emma cried.

'I'm not going to throw my life away. I'll stay as long as I can but if my time is come I'm ready.' Then he said: 'I think I'll get up! Perhaps I may not die. If God wished he could work a miracle. I'll get up. Doctor, I can die in a chair just as well as in bed can't I?'

The fussy nurse busily applying warm cloths he waved away. Once again wit flashed like summer lightning: 'The first thing I suppose we should do would be to discharge the doctor!'

He rose, crossed to his chair almost unaided, and sat a few moments. His head swam and he allowed them to lead him back to bed.

He had received his signal for eternity. Nothing need keep him. The chariot was in the room.

PRINCIPAL SOURCES

Manuscripts, etc.

THE MOODY PAPERS

At Chicago:

(a) Washburne Collection. Early letters of Moody, etc., collected by his youngest sister, Mrs Franklin Bryant Washburne, whose daughter left them to Moody Bible Institute.

(b) Bible Institute Correspondence. Principally letters between Moody and R A Torrey and A F Gaylord.

(c) Colportage Correspondence. Principally letters between Moody and William Norton.

(d) Miscellaneous, including many MSS and typescripts of Moody's early Chicago friends, and photostats of McCormick correspondence.

At Northfield:

(a) Mrs W R Moody Collection. Principally early family letters, letters of Moody and his wife to W R Moody, letters from American and British friends, especially on Moody's death and in connection with the biography of 1900.

(b) Mrs E M Powell Collection. Principally family and other letters to and from Moody, collected by his daughter and enlarged by Mrs Powell, including correspondence between the Moodys and the Mackinnons, the MS of Mrs Mackinnon's *Recollections,* and Mrs Moody's diary of 1873-5.

(c) Schools Correspondence. Letters of Moody and others in the archives of Northfield and Mount Hermon Schools.

(d) Diaries of D. W. Whittle, 1875-6, 1883-4, MSS. in possession of Mrs W R Moody.

(e) Recollections of May Whittle Moody (Mrs W R Moody), tape-recorded by author.

(f) Recollections of Mr and Mrs Daniel F Sutherland, tape-recorded by author.

Other Unprinted Sources

The Diary of the 7th Earl of Shaftesbury (MSS in Broadlands archives).
Memoirs of John Barton and his wife (loaned by the late Miss Jesse Barton
of Cambridge).
Higginbotham, Sam. *Recollections of D L Moody* (paper read at Landour,
N. India, 1929). Mt. Hermon archives.
Holton, W T *D. L. Moody as I Knew Him.* T/S, Mt. Hermon archives.
Powell, Elmer W. *Moody of Northfield: A Revelation.* T/S, 269 pp., with
annotations by author. 1940. (Crozier.)
A number of unpublished theses on D. L. Moody have been consulted.

Printed Sources

(This is *not* a bibliography, which space excludes, nor does it list every
work consulted.)
L=London. NY=NewYork. C=Chicago.

BIBLIOGRAPHY

Smith, Wilbur M *An Annotated Bibliography of D L Moody.* C 1948 (with
some omissions, very full up to 1948; also printing some unpublished
documents *verbatim).*

SHORT LIST OF SERMONS, ETC, BY MOODY

Addresses by D L Moody. L 1875 (anonymously ed by Henry Drummond).
D .L. Moody's Addresses. Revised by himself. L and C 1876.
New Sermons, Addresses and Prayers by Dwight Lyman Moody. (Unau-
thorized, ed Henry G Goodspeed.) C 1877.
*The Gospel Awakening: Sermons and Addresses of the Great Revival
Meetings conducted by Moody and Sankey.* (Unauthorized. Copyright L.T.
Palmer, 1877. 3rd ed Scammell, St Louis. 1878.)
Moody's Talks on Temperance. Ed J B Dunn. NY. 1877.
Notes From My Bible. By D L Moody. NY 1895.
Daily Gems: The D L Moody Year Book. Selected by Emma Moody Fitt.
C. nd
Echoes from Pulpit and Platform. Ed C F Goss. Hartford, Conn. 1900.
(For extensive list of shorter works of Moody, including variously revised
editions of *The Way To God, Heaven,* etc., see Wilbur M Smith, above.
Many are still in print from Moody Press, and Fleming H Revell.)

BIOGRAPHIES OF MOODY
(In chronological order. Not a complete list, nor indicating relative reliability.)

1875   Daniels, W. H. *D L Moody and His Work.* L and NY
      Clark, R. W. *The Work of God in Great Britain.* NY
1876   Goodspeed, E. J. *The Wonderful Career of Moody and Sankey in Great Britain and America.* NY
1877   Boyd, R. *The Life and Labors of Moody and Sankey.* Toronto.
      Daniels, W H. *Moody, His Words, Works and Workers.* NY
      Nason, E. *Lives of Moody, Sankey and Bliss.* Boston.
1900   Moody, W. R. *The Life of Dwight L Moody.* NY and L
      Chapman, J Wilbur. *The Life and Work of Dwight L Moody.* Philadelphia and C.
      Davis, G T B. *Dwight L Moody: The Man and His Mission.* C
      Drummond, Henry. *Dwight L Moody: Impressions and Facts.* (Articles of 1894/5 ed, with a Personal Tribute by George Adam Smith.) NY
      Fitt, A P. *The Shorter Life of D L Moody.* C. (Original ed gave Paul Moody's name as co-author.)
      Goss, C F. *Echoes From Pulpit and Platform.* Hartford, Conn. (with biographical sketch).
1905   J M[ackinnon]. *Recollections of D L Moody.* Priv Edinburgh.
1907   Farwell, J. V. *Early Recollections of D L Moody.* C.
1915   McDowell, John. *Dwight L Moody, Discoverer of Men and Maker of Movements.* NY
1923   Torrey, R A. *Why God Used D L Moody.* C.
1927   Bradford, Gamaliel. *D L Moody: A Worker in Souls.* NY.
1928   Erdman, C R *D L Moody: His Message for To-Day.* NY.
1930   Moody, W R. *D L Moody.* NY.
1931   Speer, Robert E. *D L Moody: Founder's Day Address.* Northfield.
1936   Day, Richard Ellsworth. *Bush Aglow.* Philadelphia.
1937   Fitt, A P. *Moody Still Lives.* NY
      McDowell, John (ed) *What D L Moody Means to Me.* Northfield.
1938   Moody, Paul. *My Father.* Boston.
1943   Powell, Emma Moody. *Heavenly Destiny: The Life Story of Mrs D L Moody.* C.
1962   Curtis, Richard K. *They Called Him Mr Moody.* N.Y.

PERIODICALS
Periodicals of Moody foundations

The Hermonite, 1887-
Moody Monthly (formerly Institute Tie, 1891, 1900-1910.
    Christian Worker's Magazine, 1910-1920
     Moody Bible Institute Monthly, 1920-38.)
*Mount Hermon Alumni Quarterly,*1902-
Northfield Schools Bulletin, 1912-
Northfield Echoes, 1894-
Record of Christian Work, 1881-
A large number of general newspapers and periodicals, American and British, have also been examined either in files or in collections of cuttings. Special mention should be made of *Advance* (Chicago, 1876-), the *Christian* (London), and the special Moody number of the *Congregationalist and Christian World* (Boston) November 12th, 1914. Newspapers and periodicals in 1937, Moody's centenary year, are a specially rich source.

PAMPHLETS
Chicago Young Men's Christian Association Ninth Annual Report. C. 1867.
'I. A. M. Cumming.' *Tabernacle Sketches.* Boston. 1877.
Dale, R. W. *Mr Moody and Mr Sankey.* L. 1875. *The Day of Salvation: A Reply to the Letter of the Archbishop of Canterbury.* L. 1875.
Kennedy, J. *Hyper-Evangelism, 'Another Gospel' though A Mighty Power.* Dingwall. 7th ed. 1875.
Manual of the Illinois Street Independent Church. C. 1867.
Moody, W R. *The Story of the Northfield Schools.* [Northfield 1930.]
Popham, J. K. *Moody and Sankey's Errors Versus the Scriptures of Truth.* L. 1875.
Varley, Henry. *Souvenir Account of Conversation with Mr D L Moody in 1872.* Boston. 1902

BOOKS
Aberdeen and Temair, Lord and Lady. *We Twa.* L. 1925.
Anon. *Harriet Ford Cutler.* Northfield, n.d.
Benson, A C. *The House of Quiet.* L. 1910.
Blanchard, F C. *Charles Albert Blanchard.* NY. 1932.
Braithwaite, R. *Life and Letters of Rev William Pennefather.* L. 1878.
Brown, W A. *Morris Ketchum Jessup.* NY. 1910.

Cook, Fredk Francis. *Bygone Days in Chicago.* C. 1910.

Cooke, Sarah A. *Wayside Sketches.* Grand Rapids. n.d.

Coyle, Thomas. *The Story of Mount Hermon.* Mt Hermon. 1906.

Cuyler, Theodore L. *Recollections of A Long Life.* NY. 1902.

Dale, A W W. *R W Dale.* L. 1899.

Davidson, David. *Memories of A Long Life.* Edinburgh. 1890.

Davidson, R T and Benham, W. *Archibald Campbell Tait.* L. 1891.

Day, R W. *A New England Schoolmaster.* Bristol, Conn. 1950.

DeRemer, Bernard R. *Moody Bible Institute: A Pictorial History.* C. 1960.

Dodge, D. S. *Memorials of William E Dodge.* NY. n.d.

Farwell, Abby. *Reminiscences of John V Farwell.* C. 1928.

Gammic, A. *John McNeill.* L. n.d.

Gibbon, H A. *John Wanamaker.,* NY. 1926.

Gronfell, Wilfred. *A Labrador Doctor.* L. 1919.

Grubb, Norman. *C T Studd.* L. 1933.

Hartzler, H B. *Moody in Chicago.* C. 1894.

Hogg, E M. *Quintin Hogg.* L. 1904.

Howard, O O. *Autobiography.* NY. 1907.

Hutchinson, W T. *Cyrus Hall McCormick: Harvest.* NY. 1935.

MacEwan, A R. *Life and Letters of John Cairns.* L. 1895.

McLoughlin, W G. *Modern Revivalism.* NY. 1959.

Macpherson, J. *Henry Moorhouse.* L. nd.

Mears, D. O. *Edward Norris Kirk.* Boston. 1877.

Morgan, G E. *A Veteran in Revival.* L. 1909.

Morsc, Richard C. *History of North American YMCA.* N.Y. 1913. *My Life with Young Men.* N.Y. 1918.

Moss, L. *Annals of the US Christian Commission.* Philadelphia. 1868.

Needham, G. *Recollections of Henry Moorhouse.* C. 1881.

Parsons, Herbert C. *A Puritan Outpost.* NY. 1937.

Phelps, William Lyon. *Autobiography with Letters.* NY. 1939.

Pierce, Bessie Louise. *A History of Chicago.* Vol II. NY. 1940.

Pierson, D L. *Arthur T Pierson.* NY. 1912.

Pollock, J C. *A Cambridge Movement.* L. 1953. *The Cambridge Seven.* L. 1955.

Runyan, W M. *Dr Gray at Moody Bible Institute.* NY. 1935.

Sankey, Ira D. *My Life and the Story of* the *Gospel Hymns.* NY.1906.

Shanks, T J. *Gems from Northfield.* C. [1881]. *D L Moody at Home.* NY. 1886.

Silverthorne, M E and Moody, P D. *Life Story of Evelyn Hall.* NY. 1914.

Simpson, P Carnegie. *Life of Principal Rainy*. L. n.d.

Smith, G A. *Henry Drummond*. L. 1899.

Stebbins, George C. *Reminiscences and Gospel Hymn Stories*. NY. 1924.

Stuart, George H. *Life, written by Himself*. Philadelphia. 1890.

Trumbull, C G. *Life Story of C I Scofield*. NY. 1920.

Varley, H. *Henry Varley's Life Story*. L. n.d.

Weisberger, Bernard A. *They Gathered At The River*. Boston. 1958.

Wells, J. *James Hood Wilson*. L. 1904.

Whittle, D W. *Memoirs of Philip P Bliss*. NY. 1877.

Wilder, Robert P. *The Great Commission*. L. 1936.

Willard, Frances E. *Glimpses of Fifty Years*. C. 1899.

Acknowledgements

The author is most grateful for permission to quote from copyright material as follows:

Her Majesty the Queen: Letter from Queen Victoria to the Countess of Gainsborough.

The late Earl Mountbatten of Burma, KG: the Diaries of the 7th Earl of Shaftesbury.

The late Mrs W. R. Moody: Moody Papers, Northfield.

The President, Moody Bible Institute: Moody Papers, Chicago.

The Moody Press: *Heavenly Destiny* by Emma Moody Powell: material from *Moody Monthly*.

John Murray: *The House of Quiet* by A. C. Benson.

Fleming H. Revell & Co. Inc.: *Moody Still Lives* by A. P. Fitt; *My Life and Gospel Hymns* by Ira D. Sankey.